P9-CQM-644

Gestalt Therapy Verbatim

Frederick S. Perls, M.D., Ph.D.

Compiled and edited by John O. Stevens

Copyright © 1969
Real People Press
Box F
Moab, Utah 84532

Standard Book Number   *911226-02-8 clothbound $5.00*
                          911226-03-6 paperbound $3.50

Library of Congress Catalog Card Number 79-80835

Cover photograph by Hugh Wilkerson, Big Sur, California.

Other useful books from Real People Press:

PERSON TO PERSON, by *Carl Rogers and Barry Stevens.* Professional papers by Rogers and others—about therapy, experiencing and learning—are set in a matrix of personal response and the use that Barry Stevens has made of these papers in arriving at better understanding of herself, and her view of the problem of being human as she has encountered it in her life. 276 pp. 1967 Cloth $4.50 Paper $3.00

AWARENESS, by *John O. Stevens.* Detailed instructions lead you through more than a hundred experiments in exploring your awareness of yourself, your surroundings, and your interaction with others. These experiments—based on Gestalt Therapy and developed in the classroom and in groups—give you actual experience with methods that you can use further, either as teacher, group leader, or on your own, to work through difficulties and get more in touch with your own flow of experiencing. 275 pp. 1971. Cloth $7.00 Paper $3.50

IN AND OUT THE GARBAGE PAIL, by *Frederick S. Perls.* A novel autobiography in which he applies his theory of focusing on awareness, and writes "whatever wants to be written." Partly in poetic form, often playful, sometimes theoretical, the book is a many-faceted mosaic of memories and reflections on his life—in the past and at the moment—and on the origins and continuing development of Gestalt Therapy. Illustrated. 280 pp. 1969 Cloth $7.00 Paper $4.00

DON'T PUSH THE RIVER, by *Barry Stevens.* A first-person account of the author's use of Gestalt Therapy and the ways of Zen, Krishnamurti and the American Indian to deepen and expand personal experience and work through difficulties. "We have to turn ourselves upside down and reverse our approach to life." This autobiographical episode shows the author doing this during a three-month period in association with Fritz Perls at the Gestalt Institute of Canada in 1969. 280 pp. 1970 Cloth $7.00 Paper $3.50

NOTES TO MYSELF, by *Hugh Prather.* Cogent and incisive short paragraphs, personal yet general, about living: feelings and experiences, behavior and relationships. These serve both as beginnings for the reader's exploration of his own experiences, and as thoughtful and insightful reminders about them. 150 pp. 1970 Cloth $4.00 Paper $2.00

The name *Real People Press* indicates our purpose: to publish ideas and ways that a person can use independently to become more *real*—to further his own growth as a human being and to develop his relationships and communication with others.

9   10   printing   75   74   73   72

To suffer one's death
and to be reborn
is not easy

Fritz

Contents

Intensive Workshop

Acknowledgement

Almost all of the material in this book, except for the last section, *Intensive Workshop*, is selected and edited from audiotapes made at week-end dreamwork seminars conducted by Fritz Perls at Esalen Institute, Big Sur, California, from 1966 through 1968.

The transcripts of Gestalt Therapy sessions presented here are essentially verbatim. Small changes have been made to clarify meaning, and some of Perls' explanatory comments have been inserted. *All* names have been changed, except for those individuals in the *Intensive Workshop* who explicitly gave permission to use their real names.

Copies of the original tape recordings quoted from in this book are available, and are recommended for serious study of the methods of Gestalt Therapy. There is much to be gained from hearing the voices, the inflections, the silences, the timing, and the nuances that cannot be adequately reproduced in print. Address inquiry to: *Gestalt Training Tapes, Big Sur Recordings, P. O. Box 6633, Carmel, California 93921.*

Excellent and moving 16 mm. films of Gestalt Therapy sessions are also available. Address inquiry to: *Sessions in Gestalt Therapy, The Mediasync Corporation, P. O. Box 486, Del Mar, California 92014.*

There is also a series of eight very beautiful 30-minute color films of Fritz Perls teaching and demonstrating Gestalt Therapy. These were made in the spring of 1969 by Aquarian Productions of Vancouver, and are distributed by Films Incorporated, 38 West 32nd St. New York, NY 10001.

Fritz Perls died on March 14, 1970, after a brief illness at the age of 76. No acknowledgement can begin to express how full his life was and how much he gave to so many of us.

Introduction

I want to talk about the present development of humanistic psychology. It took us a long time to debunk the whole Freudian crap, and now we are entering a new and more dangerous phase. We are entering the phase of the turner-onners: turn on to instant cure, instant joy, instant sensory-awareness. We are entering the phase of the quacks and the con-men, who think if you get some break-through, you are cured—disregarding any growth requirements, disregarding any of the real potential, the inborn genius in all of you. If this is becoming a faddism, it is as dangerous to psychology as the year-decade-century-long lying on the couch. At least the damage we suffered under psychoanalysis does little to the patient except for making him deader and deader. This is not as obnoxious as this quick-quick-quick thing. The psychoanalysts at least bring good will with them. I must say I am *very* concerned with what's going on right now.

One of the objections I have against anyone calling himself a Gestalt Therapist is that he uses technique. A technique is a gimmick. A gimmick should be used only in the extreme case. We've got enough people running around collecting gimmicks, more gimmicks, and abusing them. These techniques, these tools, are quite useful in some seminar on sensory awareness or joy, just to give you some idea that you are still alive, that the myth that the American is a corpse is not true, that he *can* be alive. But the sad fact is that this jazzing-up more often becomes a dangerous substitute activity, another phony therapy that *prevents* growth.

Now the problem is not so much with the turner-onners but with the whole American culture. We have made a 180-degree turn from puritanism and moralism to hedonism. Suddenly everything has to be fun, pleasure, and any sincere involvement, any really *being here*, is discouraged.

> A thousand plastic flowers
> Don't make a desert bloom
> A thousand empty faces
> Don't fill an empty room

In Gestalt Therapy, we are working for something else. We are here to promote the growth process and develop the human potential. We do not talk of instant joy, instant sensory awareness, instant cure. The growth process is a process that takes time. We can't just snap our fingers and say, "Come on, let's be gay! Let's do this!" You can turn on if you want to with LSD, and jazz it up, but that has nothing to do with the sincere work of that approach to psychiatry which I call Gestalt Therapy. In therapy, we have not only to get through the role-playing. We also have to fill in the holes in the personality to make the person whole and complete again. And again, as before, this can't be done by the turner-onners. In Gestalt Therapy we have a better way, but it is no magic short-cut. You don't have to be on a couch or in a Zendo for twenty or thirty years, but you have to invest yourself, and it takes time to grow.

The conditioners also start out with a false assumption. Their basic premise that behavior is "law" is a lot of crap. That is: we learn to breathe, to eat, we learn to walk. "Life is nothing but whatever conditions into which it has been born." *If*, in the behaviorist reorganization of our behavior, we get a modification towards better self-support, and throw away all the artificial social roles we have learned, then I am on the side of the behaviorists. The stopping block seems to be anxiety. Always anxiety. Of course you are anxious if you have to learn a new way of behavior, and the psychiatrists usually are afraid of anxiety. They don't know what anxiety *is*. Anxiety is the excitement, the *élan vital* which we carry with us, and which becomes stagnated if we are unsure about the role we have to play. If we don't know if we will get applause or tomatoes, we hesitate, so the heart begins to race and all the excitement can't flow into activity, and we have stage fright. So the formula of anxiety is very simple: anxiety is the gap between the *now* and the *then*. If you are in the now, you can't be anxious, because the excitement flows immediately into ongoing spontaneous activity. If you are in the now, you are creative, you are inventive. If you have your senses ready, if you have your eyes and ears open, like every small child, you find a solution.

A release to spontaneity, to the support of our total personality—yes, yes, yes. The pseudo-spontaneity of the turner-onners as they become hedonistic—just, let's do something, let's take LSD, let's have instant joy, instant sensory-awareness—*No*. So between the Scylla of conditioning, and the Charybdis of turning on, there is something—a person that is real, a person who takes a stand.

As you know, there is a rebellion on in the United States. We discover that producing things, and living for things, and the exchange of things, is not the ultimate meaning of life. We discover that the meaning of life is that it is to be lived, and it is not to be traded and conceptualized and squeezed into a pattern of systems. We realize that manipulation and control are not the ultimate joy of life.

But we must also realize that so far we only have a rebellion. We don't have a revolution yet. There is still much of substance missing. There is a race on between fascism and humanism. At this moment it seems to me that the race is about lost to the fascists. And the wild hedonistic, unrealistic, jazz-it-up, turner-onners have nothing to do with humanism. It is protest, it's a rebelliousness, which is fine as such, but it's not an end. I've got plenty of contact with the youngsters of our generation who are in despair. They see all the militarism and the atomic bomb in the background. They want to get something out of life. They want to become real and exist. If there is any chance of interrupting the rise and fall of the United States, it's up to our youth and it's up to you in supporting this youth. To be able to do this, there is only one way through: to become real, to learn to take a stand, to develop one's center, to understand the basis of existentialism: a rose is a rose is a rose. I am what I am, and at this moment I cannot possibly be different from what I am. That is what this book is about. I give you the Gestalt prayer, maybe as a direction. The prayer in Gestalt Therapy is:

> I do my thing, and you do your thing.
> I am not in this world to live up to your expectations
> And you are not in this world to live up to mine.
> You are you and I am I,
> And if by chance we find each other, it's beautiful.
> If not, it can't be helped.

Fritz Perls.

I

I would like to start out with very simple ideas which, as always, are difficult to grasp because they are so simple. I would like to start out with the question of control. There are two kinds of control: One is the control that comes from outside—I am being controlled by others, by orders, by the environment, and so on—and the other is the control that is built in, in every organism—my own nature.

What is an organism? We call an organism any living being, any living being that has organs, has an organization, that is self-regulating within itself. An organism is not independent from its environment. Every organism needs an environment to exchange essential substances, and so on. We need the physical environment to exchange air, food, etc.; we need the social environment to exchange friendship, love, anger. But within the organism there is a system of unbelievable subtlety—every cell of the millions of cells which we *are*, has built-in messages that it sends to the total organism, and the total organism then takes care of the needs of the cells and whatever must be done for different parts of the organism.

Now what is first to be considered is that the organism always works as a whole. We *have* not a liver or a heart. We *are* liver and heart and brain and so on, and even this is wrong. We are not a summation of parts, but a *coordination*—a very subtle coordination of all these different bits that go into the making of the organism. The old philosophy always thought that the world consisted of the sum of particles. You know yourself it's not true. We consist originally out of one cell. This cell differentiates into several cells, and they differentiate into other organs that have special functions which are diversified and yet needed for each other.

So, we come to the definition of health. Health is an appropriate balance of the coordination of all of what we *are*. You notice that I emphasized a few times the word *are*, because the very moment we say we *have* an organism or we *have* the body, we introduce a split— as if there's an *I* that is in possession of the body or the organism. We *are* a body, we *are* somebody—"I *am* somebody," "I *am* nobody." So it's the question of *being* rather than *having*. This is why we call our approach the existential approach: We exist *as* an organism—as an organism like a clam, like an animal, and so on, and we relate to the external world just like any other organism of nature. Kurt Goldstein first introduced the concept of the *organism as a whole*, and broke with the tradition in medicine that we *have* a liver, that we have a this/that, that all these organs can be studied separately. He got pretty close to the actuality, but the actuality is what is called the ecological aspect. You cannot even separate the organism and the environment. A plant taken out of its environment can't survive, and neither can a human being if you take him out of his environment, deprive him of oxygen and food, and so on. So we have to consider always the segment of the world in which we live as part of ourselves. Wherever we go, we take a kind of world with us.

Now if this is so, then we begin slowly to understand that people and organisms *can* communicate with each other, and we call it the *Mitwelt*—the common world which you have and the other person has. You speak a certain language, you have certain attitudes, certain behavior, and the two worlds somewhere overlap. And in this overlapping area, communication is possible. You notice if people meet, they begin the gambit of meeting—one says, "How are you?" "It's nice weather." and the other answers something else. So they go into the search for the common interest, or the common world, where they have a possible interest, communication, and togetherness, where we get suddenly from the *I* and *You* to the *We*. So there is a new phenomenon coming, the *We* which is different from the I and You. The *We* doesn't exist, but consists out of I *and* You, is an everchanging boundary where two people meet. And when we meet there, then I change and you change, through the process of encountering each other, except—and we have to talk a lot about this—

except if the two people have *character*. Once you have a *character*, you have developed a rigid system. Your behavior becomes petrified, predictable, and you lose your ability to cope freely with the world with all your resources. You are predetermined just to cope with events in one way, namely, as your character prescribes it to be. So it seems a paradox when I say that the richest person, the most productive, creative person, is a person who has *no* character. In our society, we *demand* a person to have a character, and especially a *good* character, because then you are predictable, and you can be pigeonholed, and so on.

Now, let's talk a bit more about the relationship of the organism to its environment, and here we introduce the notion of the *ego boundary*. A boundary defines a thing. Now a thing has its boundaries, is defined by its boundaries in relation to the environment. In itself a thing occupies a certain amount of space. Maybe not much. Maybe it wants to be bigger, or wants to be smaller—maybe it's not satisfied with its size. We introduce now a new concept again, the wish to change based upon the phenomenon of dissatisfaction. Every time you want to change yourself, or you want to change the environment, the basis always is *dis*satisfaction.

The boundary between organism and environment is more or less experienced by us as what is inside the skin and what is outside the skin, but this is very very loosely defined. For instance, the very moment we breathe, is the air that comes in still part of the outside world, or is it already our own? If we eat food, we ingest it, but can still vomit it up, so where is the place where the self begins, and the otherness of the environment ends? So the ego boundary is not a *fixed* thing. If it is fixed, then it again becomes character, or an armor, like in the turtle. The turtle has a very fixed boundary in this respect. Our skin is somewhat less fixed, and breathes, touches, and so on. The ego boundary is of great, great importance. The phenomenon of the ego boundary is very peculiar. Basically, we call the ego boundary the differentiation between the self and the otherness, and in Gestalt Therapy we write the self with a lower case s. I know that many psychologists like to write the self with a capital S, as if the self would be something precious, something extraordinarily valuable. They go at the discovery of the self like a treasure-digging. The self means nothing but this thing as it is defined by *otherness*. "I do it myself " means that nobody else is doing it, it is this organism that does it.

Now the two phenomena of the ego boundary are *identification* and *alienation*. I identify with my movement: I say that *I* move my arm. When I see *you* sit there in a certain posture, I don't say, "*I* sit there," I say, "*You* sit there." I differentiate between the experience here and the experience there, and this identification experience has several aspects. The *I* seems to be more precious than the otherness. If I identify with, let's say, my profession, then this identification may become so strong that if my profession is then taken away, I feel I don't exist any more, so I might just as well commit suicide. In 1929, you remember how many people committed suicide because they were so identified with their money that life wasn't worth living any more when they lost it.

We are easily identified with our families. If a member of our family is slighted, then we feel the same is done to us. You identify with your friends. The members of the 146th infantry regiment feel themselves to be better than the members of the 147th regiment, and the members of the 147th regiment feel themselves superior to the members of the 146th. So, inside the ego boundary, there is generally cohesion, love, cooperation; outside the ego boundary there is suspicion, strangeness, unfamiliarity.

Now this boundary can be very fluid, like nowadays in battles— the boundary stretches as far, let's say, as your air power goes. This is how far the security, familiarity, wholeness, extends. And there is the strangeness, the enemy who is outside the boundary, and whenever there is a boundary question, there is a conflict going on. If we take likeness for granted, then we wouldn't be aware of the existence of the boundary. If we take the unlikeness very much for granted, then we come to the problem of hostility, of rejection—pushing away. "Keep out of my boundaries," "Keep out of my house," "Keep out of my family," "Keep out of my thoughts." So you see already the polarity of attraction and rejection—of appetite and disgust. There is always a polarity going on, and inside the boundary we have the feeling of familiarity, of right; outside is strangeness, and wrong. Inside is good, outside is bad. The own God is the right God. The other God is the strange God. My political conviction is sacred, is mine; the other political conviction is bad. If a state is at war, its own soldiers are angels, and the enemy are all devils. Our own soldiers take care of the poor families; the enemy rapes them. So the whole idea of good and bad, right and wrong, is always a matter of boundary, of which side of the fence I am on.

So I want to give you a couple of minutes now for time to digest, and to make comments, and see how far we have come. You have to let me in a bit into your private world, or you have to come out of your private world into that environment which includes this platform.

Q: When a person's in love, his own boundary expands to include the you, or the other, that was previously outside himself.

F: Yah. The ego boundary becomes an *us* boundary: I and you are separate against the whole world and, in a moment of ecstasy of love, the world disappears.

Q: If two people are in love, do they accept—would they accept each other so completely that their ego boundaries would expand to include other persons completely, or would it just include the person they had contact with?

F: Well, this is a very interesting, relevant question. And the misunderstanding of this leads to many tragedies and catastrophes. We don't usually love a *person*. That's very, very rare. We love a certain *property* in that person, which is either identical with our behavior or supplementing our behavior, usually something that is a supplement to us. We think we are in love with the total person, and actually we are disgusted with other aspects of this person. So when the other contacts come up, when this person behaves in a way that creates disgust in us, then again we don't say, "*This* of you is disgusting, though this other part is lovable." We say, "*You* are disgusting—get out of my life."

Q: But Fritz, doesn't this apply to an individual also? Do we include all of ourselves in our ego boundaries? Aren't there things in us that we refuse to include in our ego boundaries?

F: Well, we are going to talk about that when we come to the *inner split*, the fragmentation of the personality. The very moment you say, "*I* accept something in myself," you split yourself up into *I* and *myself*. Right now, I am talking about more or less the total encounter of an organism, and I am not talking about pathology. Basically there are very few among us that are whole persons.

Q: How about the reverse situation, hate or intense anger? Does that then have a tendency to shrink ego boundaries so that a person's hate toward another person can absorb their whole life?

F: No. Hate is a function of kicking somebody out of the boundary for something. The term we use in existential psychiatry is *alienation*, disowning. We disown a person, and if this person's existence constitutes a threat to us, we want to annihilate this person. But it is definitely an *ex*clusion from our boundary, from ourselves.

Q: Well, I understand that. What I'm trying to understand is what that kind of intense situation—intense involvement in that kind of situation—does in terms of ego boundaries. Does it tend to make them smaller, or make them more rigid?

F: Well, definitely, it does make them more rigid. Let me postpone these questions until we come to talk about projections. This is a special case in pathology, the fact that in the last instance we only love ourselves and hate ourselves. Whether we find this loved or hated thing in ourselves or outside has to do with breaks in the boundary.

Q: Fritz, you mentioned the polarity of attraction and disgust, yet it's possible to feel both of these things toward the same person which, as far as I can understand it, creates a conflict.

F: This is exactly what I am talking about. You are not attracted to a person; you are not disgusted with a person. If you look closer, you are attracted to a certain behavior or part of that person, and disgusted with a certain other behavior or part of that person, and if you find, by chance, both the beloved and the hated thing—we call it a thing, of course—in the same person, you're in a quandary. It is much easier to be disgusted with one person and to love another. At one time you find you hate this person and another time you love the person, but if both love and hate come together, then you get confused. This has a lot to do with the basic law that the gestalt is always so formed that only one figure, one item, can become fore-ground—that we can think, basically, of only one thing at a time, and as soon as two opposites or two different figures want to take charge òf this organism, we get confused, we get split and fragmented.

I can already see where the whole trend of the question goes. You are already coming to the point where you begin to understand what happens in pathology. If some of our thoughts, feelings, are unacceptable to us, we want to disown them. *Me* wanting to kill you? So we disown the killing thought and say, "That's not me—that's a *compulsion*," or we remove the killing, or we repress and become blind to that. There are many of these kinds of ways to remain intact, but always only at the cost of disowning many, many valuable parts of ourselves. The fact that we live only on such a small percentage of our potential is due to the fact that we're not willing—or society or whatever you want to call it is not willing—to accept myself, yourself, as the organism which you are by birth, constitu-tion, and so on. You do not allow yourself—or you are not allowed—to be totally yourself. So your ego boundary shrinks more and more. Your power, your energy, becomes smaller and smaller. Your ability to cope with the world becomes less and less—and more and more rigid, more and more allowed only to cope as your character, as your preconceived pattern, prescribes it.

Q: Is there some kind of a fluctuation in this ego boundary that might be determined by a cyclic rhythm? The way that a flower will open and close—open—close—

F: Yah. *Very* much.

Q: Does the word "uptight" mean shrink?

F: No. This means *compression*.

Q: What about the opposite in the drug experience, where the ego boundary—/F: Where you lose your ego boundary./ Would this be an explosion in terms of your theory?

F: Expansion, not explosion. Explosion is quite different. The ego boundary is a completely natural phenomenon. Now I give you some examples about the ego boundary, something we are more or less all concerned with. This boundary, this identification/alienation boundary, which I rather call the ego boundary, applies to every situation in life. Now let's assume you are in favor of the freedom movement, of acceptance of the Negro as a human being like your-self. So you identify with him. So where is the boundary? The boundary disappears between you and the Negro. But immediately a new boundary is created—now the enemy is not the Negro, but the non-freedom fighter; *they* are the bastards, the bad guys.

So you create a new boundary, and I believe there is no chance of ever living without a boundary—there is always, "I am on the right side of the fence, and you are on the wrong side," or *we* are, if you have the clique formation. You notice any society or any community will quickly form its own boundaries, cliques—the Millers are always better than the Meyers, and the Meyers are better than the Millers. And the closer the boundary defenses, the greater the chance of wars or hostility. You find wars always start on the boundary—boundary clashes. The Indians and the Chinese have a much greater chance of fighting each other than the Indians and the Finns. Because there is no boundary between the Indians and the Finns, except if now a new kind of boundary is created—let's say an ideological boundary. We are all Communists, we are right. We are all Free Enterprisers, we are right. So you are the bad guys—no, *you* are the bad guys. So we seldom look for the common denominator, what we have in com-mon, but we look for where we are different, so that we can hate and kill each other.

Q: Do you think that it is possible to become so integrated that a person could become objective, and not become involved in any-thing?

F: I personally believe that objectivity does not exist. The objec-tivity of science is also just a matter of mutual agreement. A certain number of persons observe the same phenomena and they speak about an objective criterion. Yet it was from the scientific side where the first proof of subjectivity came. This was from Einstein. Einstein realized that all the phenomena in the universe cannot possibly be objective, because the observer and the speed within its nervous system has to be included in the calculation of that phenomenon outside. If you have perspective, and can see a larger outlook, you seem to be more fair, objective, balanced. But even there, it's you as the subject who sees it. We have not much idea what the universe looks like. We have only a certain amount of organs—eyes, ears, touch, and the elongation of these organs—the telescope and electrical computers. But what do we know about other organisms, what kind of organs they have, what kind of world they have? We take for granted the elegance of the human being, that our world—how *we* see the universe—is the only right one.

Q: Fritz, let me go back to the ego boundary again because when you're experiencing yourself, when you're experiencing an expanded state, then the feeling of separation seems to disintegrate or melt. And at that point it seems that you are totally absorbed in the process of what's going on. At that point, it seems there are no ego boundaries at all, except a reflection of the process of what's going on. Now I don't understand that in relation to your concept of ego boundary.

F: Yah. This is more or less the next theme I wanted to come to. There is a kind of integration—I know that's not quite correctly formulated—of the subjective and the objective. That is the word *awareness*. Awareness is always the subjective experience. I cannot possibly be aware of what you are aware of. The Zen idea of absolute awareness, in my opinion is nonsense. Absolute awareness cannot possibly exist because as far as *I* know, awareness always has content. One is always aware of *something*. If I say I feel nothing, I'm at least aware of the *nothingness*, which if you examine it still further has a very positive character like numbness, or coldness, or a gap, and when you speak about the psychedelic experience, there is an awareness, but there is also the awareness of *something*.

So, let's now go a step further and look at the relationship of the world and the self. What makes us interested in the world? What is our need to realize that there is a world? How come I cannot function, cannot live just as a kind of autistic organism, completely self-contained? Now, a thing, like this ashtray, is not a type of relating organism. This ashtray needs very little to exist. First, temperature. If you put this ashtray in a temperature of 4,000°, this is not an environment in which it will retain its identity. It needs a certain amount of gravity. If it would be subjected to a pressure of, let's say, 40,000 pounds, it would break into pieces. But we can, for practical purposes, say that this thing is self-contained. It doesn't need any exchange with the environment. It exists to be used by us as a receptacle of cigarettes, to be cleaned, to be sold, to be thrown away, to be used as a missile if you want to hurt somebody, and so on. But in itself it is not a living organism.

A living organism is an organism which consists of thousands and thousands of processes that require interchange with other media outside the boundary of the organism. There are processes here in the ashtray, too. There are electronic processes, atomic processes, but for our purpose, these processes are not visible, not relevant to its existence for us here. But in a living organism, the ego boundary has to be negotiated by us because there is something outside that is needed. There is food outside: I want this food; I want to make it mine, *like me*. So, I have to like this food. If I don't like it, if it is un-like me, I wouldn't touch it, I leave it outside the boundary. So something has to happen to get through the boundary and this is what we call *contact*. We touch, we get in contact, we stretch our boundary out to the thing in question. If we are rigid and can't move, then it remains there. When we live, we spend energies, we need energies to maintain this machine. This process of exchange is called the metabolism. Both the metabolism of the exchange of our organism with the environment, and the metabolism within our organism, is going on continually, day and night.

Now what are the laws of this metabolism? They are very strict laws. Let's assume that I walk through the desert, and it's very hot. I lose, let's say, eight ounces of fluid. Now how do I know that I lost this? First, through self-awareness of the phenomenon, in this case called "thirst." Second, suddenly in this undifferentiated general world something emerges as a gestalt, as a foreground, namely, let's say, a well with water, or a pump—or anything that would have plus eight ounces. This minus eight ounces of our organism and the plus eight ounces in the world can balance each other. The very moment this eight ounces goes into the system, we get a plus/minus water which brings balance. We come to rest as the situation is finished, the gestalt is closed. The urge that drives us to do something, to walk so and so many miles to get to that place, has fulfilled its purpose.

This situation is now closed and the next unfinished situation can take its place, which means our life is basically practically nothing but an infinite number of unfinished situations—incomplete gestalts. No sooner have we finished one situation than another comes up.

I have often been called the founder of Gestalt Therapy. That's crap. If you call me the finder or re-finder of Gestalt Therapy, okeh. Gestalt is as ancient and old as the world itself. The world, and especially every organism, maintains itself, and the only law which is constant is the forming of gestalts—wholes, completeness. A gestalt is an organic function. A gestalt is an ultimate experiential unit. As soon as you break up a gestalt, it is not a gestalt any more. Take an example from chemistry. You know that water has a certain property. It consists of H_2O. So if you disturb the gestalt of water, split it up into two H's and one O, it's not water any more. It is oxygen and hydrogen, and if you are thirsty you can breathe as much hydrogen and as much oxygen as you want, it won't quench your thirst. So the gestalt is the experienced phenomenon. If you analyze, if you cut it further up, it becomes something else. You might call it a unit, like, say, volts in electricity, or ergs in mechanics and so on.

Gestalt Therapy is one of the—I think right now it is one of three types of existential therapy: Frankl's Logotherapy, the Daseins Therapy of Binswanger, and Gestalt Therapy. What is important is that Gestalt Therapy is the first existential philosophy that stands on its own feet. I distinguish three types of philosophy. One is the "aboutism." We talk about it and talk about it, and nothing is accomplished. In scientific explanation, you usually go around and around and never touch the heart of the matter. The second philosophy I would call the "shouldism." Moralism. You should be this, you should change yourself, you should not do this—a hundred thousand commands, but no consideration is given to what degree the person who "should" do this can actually comply. And furthermore, most people expect that the magic formula, just to use the sounds, "You should do this," might have an actual effect upon reality.

The third philosophy I call existentialism. Existentialism wants to do away with concepts, and to work on the awareness principle, on phenomenology. The setback with the present existentialist philosophies is that they need their support from somewhere else. If you look at the existentialists, they say that they are non-conceptual, but if you look at the people, they all borrow concepts from other sources. Buber from Judaism, Tillich from Protestantism, Sartre from Socialism, Heidegger from language, Binswanger from psycho-analysis, and so on. Gestalt Therapy is a philosophy that tries to be in harmony, in alignment with everything else, with medicine, with science, with the universe, with what *is*. Gestalt Therapy has its support in its own formation because the gestalt formation, the emergence of the needs, is a primary biological phenomenon.

So we are doing away with the whole instinct theory and simply consider the organism as a system that is in balance and that has to function properly. Any imbalance is experienced as a need to correct this imbalance. Now, practically, we have hundreds of unfinished situations in us. How come that we are not completely confused and want to go out in all directions? And that's another law which I have discovered, that from the survival point of view, the most urgent situation becomes the controller, the director, and takes over. The most urgent situation emerges, and in any case of emergency, you realize that this has to take precedent over any other activity. If there would be suddenly a fire here, the fire would be more impor-tant than our talks. If you rush and rush, and run from the fire, suddenly you will be out of breath, your oxygen supply is more important than the fire. You stop and take a breath because this is now the most important thing.

So, we come now to the most important, interesting phenome-non in all pathology: self-regulation versus external regulation. The anarchy which is usually feared by the controllers is not an anarchy which is without meaning. On the contrary, it means the organism is left alone to take care of itself, without being meddled with from outside. And I believe that this is the great thing to understand: *that awareness per se—by and of itself—can be curative*. Because with full awareness you become aware of this organismic self-regulation, you can let the organism take over without interfering, without interrupting; we can rely on the wisdom of the organism. And the contrast to this is the whole pathology of self-manipulation, environmental control, and so on, that interferes with this subtle organismic self-control.

Our manipulation of ourselves is usually dignified by the word "conscience." In ancient times, conscience was thought to be a God-made institution. Even Immanuel Kant thought that the conscience was equivalent to the eternal star, as one of the two absolutes. Then Freud came and he showed that the conscience is nothing but a fantasy, an introjection, a continuation of what he believed was the parents. I believe it's a projection *onto* the parents, but never mind. Some think it is an introjection, an institution called the superego, that wants to take over control. Now if this were so, then how come the analysis of the superego is not successful? How come that when we tell ourselves to be good or to do this or that, we are *not* successful? How come that this program does not work? "The road to hell is paved with good intentions" is verified again and again. Any intention toward change will achieve the opposite. You all know this. The New Year's resolutions, the desperation of trying to be different, the attempt to control yourself. All this always comes to nought, or in extreme cases the person is apparently successful, up to the point where the nervous breakdown occurs. The final way out.

Now if we are willing to stay in the center of our world, and not have the center either in our computer or somewhere else, but really in the center, then we are ambidextrous—then we see the two poles of every event. We see that light cannot exist without non-light. If there is sameness, you can't be aware any more. If there is always light, you don't experience light any more. You have to have the rhythm of light and darkness. Right doesn't exist without left. If I lose my right arm, my center shifts to the left. If there is a *super*ego, there must also be an *infra*ego. Again, Freud did half the job. He saw the topdog, the superego, but he left out the underdog which is just as much a personality as the topdog. And if we go one step farther and examine the two clowns, as I call them, that perform the self-torture game on the stage of our fantasy, then we usually find the two characters like this:

The topdog usually is righteous and authoritarian; he knows best. He is sometimes right, but always righteous. The topdog is a bully, and works with "You should" and "You should not." The topdog manipulates with demands and threats of catastrophe, such as, "If you don't, then—you won't be loved, you won't get to heaven, you will die," and so on.

The underdog manipulates with being defensive, apologetic, wheedling, playing the cry-baby, and such. The underdog has no power. The underdog is the Mickey Mouse. The topdog is the Super Mouse. And the underdog works like this: "Mañana." "I try my best." "Look, I try again and again; I can't help it if I fail." "I can't help it if I forgot your birthday." "I have such good intentions." So you see the underdog is cunning, and usually gets the better of the topdog because the underdog is not as primitive as the topdog. So the topdog and underdog strive for control. Like every parent and child, they strive with each other for control. The person is fragmented into controller and controlled. This inner conflict, the struggle between the topdog and the underdog, is never complete, because topdog as well as underdog fight for their lives.

This is the basis for the famous self-torture game. We usually take for granted that the topdog is right, and in many cases the topdog makes impossible perfectionistic demands. So if you are cursed with perfectionisn, then you are absolutely sunk. This ideal is a yardstick which always gives you the opportunity to browbeat yourself, to berate yourself and others. Since this ideal is an impossibility, you can never live up to it. The perfectionist is not in love with his wife. He is in love with his ideal, and he demands from his wife that she should fit in this Procrustes bed of his expectations, and he blames her if she does not fit. What this ideal exactly is, he would not reveal. Now and then there might be some stated characteristics, but the essence of the ideal is that it is impossible, unobtainable, just a good opportunity to control, to swing the whip. The other day I had a talk with a friend of mine and I told her, "Please get this into your nut: mistakes are no sins," and she wasn't half as relieved as I thought she would be. Then I realized, if mistakes are not a sin any more, how can she castigate others who make mistakes? So it always works both ways; if you carry this ideal, this perfectionistic ideal around with yourself, you have a wonderful tool to play the beloved game of the neurotic, the self-torture game. There is no end to the self-torture, to the self-nagging, self-castigating. It hides under the mask of "self-improvement." It never works.

If the person tries to meet the topdog's demands of perfectionism, the result is a "nervous breakdown," or flight into insanity. This is one of the tools of the underdog. Once we recognize the structure of our behavior, which in the case of self-improvement is the split between the topdog and the underdog, and if we understand how, by listening, we can bring about a reconciliation of these two fighting clowns, then we realize that *we cannot deliberately bring about changes in ourselves or in others.* This is a very decisive point: Many people dedicate their lives to actualize a concept of what they *should* be like, rather than to actualize *themselves.* This difference between *self*-actualizing and self-*image* actualizing is *very* important. Most people only live for their image. Where some people have a self, most people have a void, because they are so busy projecting themselves as this or that. This is again the curse of the ideal. The curse that you should not be what you are.

Every external control, even *internalized* external control—"you should"—interferes with the healthy working of the organism. There is only one thing that should control: the *situation.* If you understand the situation which you are in, and let the situation which you are in control your actions, then you learn how to cope with life. Now you know this from certain situations, like driving a car. You don't drive a car according to a program, like, "I want to drive 65 miles per hour." You drive according to the situation. You drive a different speed at night, you drive a different speed when there is traffic there, you drive differently when you are tired. You listen to the situation. The less confident we are in ourselves, the less we are in touch with ourselves and the world, the more we want to control.

Q: I've been wondering about Joe Kamiya's brain-wave test and the question of self-control. If he puts himself in a calm state when he experiences irritation, would this be avoidance?

F: Avoidance of what?

Q: The cause of the irritation, that he is leaving by putting himself in a calm state of mind. I suppose it depends on what causes the irritation that is alleviated.

F: Well, I partly don't follow you, partly don't know if your report is correct, and I don't know enough of it from the little I have understood. It seems that the alpha waves are identical with organismic self-regulation, the organism taking over and acting spontaneously instead of acting on control. I think he describes that as long as he tries to control something, the alpha waves are not there. But I don't like to talk about it because I have no experiences with this set-up yet. I hope to get to see it. I think it is for once a gadget that seems to be very interesting and possibly productive.

Q: I can see how, on the level of organismic functions, such a thing as this water loss and the need to fill this loss—this process of allowing the organism to function by itself will work. But then when you get to the level of relationships, what happens? Then it seems as if there is necessity for discrimination in what's foreground and what's not.

F: Can you give us an example?

Q: Say I'm in a situation in which there are four or five emergencies occurring, what I consider to be emergencies, in which I should be taking some part and doing something. Then comes what I call discrimination, in that one or the other of these is more important than the rest of them. And it's just that it's not as easy for me to see how the organism makes a decision like that, as how it makes a decision that it needs water.

F: Yah. The organism does not *make decisions*. Decision is a man-made institution. The organism works always on the basis of *preference*.

Q: I thought you said it was the feeling of need.

F: Well, the need is the primary thing. If you had no needs, you wouldn't do a thing. If you had no need for oxygen, you wouldn't breathe.

Q: Well, I guess I—what I mean is, the most pressing need is the one that you go to.

F: Yah. The most pressing need. And if you talk about five

emergencies, I would say none of them are emergencies, because if one was really an emergency, it would *emerge*, and there would be no decision or computing done. This emergency would take over. Our relationship to this emergency, to the world, is the same as, for instance, in painting. You've got a white figure. Then you make certain blots on this canvas, and then suddenly comes a moment of re-centering. Suddenly the *canvas* makes demands, and you become the servant. It is as if you said, "What does this thing want?" "Where does it want to have some red?" "Where does it want to be balanced?" Except you don't ask questions, you just respond.

Now the next thing that I want to talk about is the differentiation between *end-gain* and *means-whereby*. The end-gain is always fixed by a need. The free choice is in the means-whereby. Let's say that I have to send a message to New York. That is the thing that is fixed, the *end-gain*. The *means-whereby* to send the message, the medium, is of secondary importance—whether you send it by wire, by mouth, by letter, by telepathy if you believe in it. So in spite of McLuhan's thesis "The medium is the message," I still say that the end-gain is the primary thing. Now, for instance, in sex, the end-gain is the orgasm. The means-whereby can be a hundred different possibilities and as a matter of fact, the recognition of this by Medard Boss, the Swiss psychiatrist, is how he cured homosexuality. By having the patient *fully* accept homosexuality as one of the means to get to the organismic satisfaction, the end-gain, in this case the orgasm, he then had the possibility of changing the means-whereby. All perversions are variations of the means-whereby, and the same applies to any of the basic needs. If you want to eat, the end-gain is to get enough calories into your system. The means-whereby differ from very primitive eating some popcorn or whatever, to the discriminating experience of the gourmet. The more you realize this, the more you begin to select the means, come to select all the social needs, which are the means to the organismic ends.

This type of organismic self-regulation is very important in therapy, because the emergent, unfinished situations will come to the surface. We don't have to dig: it's all there. And you might look upon this like this: that from within, some figure emerges, comes to the surface, and then goes into the outside world, reaches out for what we want, and comes back, assimilates and receives. Something else comes out, and again the same process repeats itself.

The most peculiar things happen. Let's say, you suddenly see a woman licking calcium from the wall—licking the plaster from the wall. It's a crazy thing. Then it turns out that she is pregnant and needs calcium for the bones of her baby, but she doesn't know that. Or she sleeps through the noises of the Beatles, and then her child just whimpers a little bit and suddenly she wakes up, because this is the emergency. This is what she is geared for. So she can withdraw from the loudest noise, because this is not gestalt-motivated. But the whimper is there, so the whimper emerges and becomes the attraction. This is again the wisdom of the organism. The organism knows all. We know very little.

Q: You said the organism knows all, and we know very little. How is it possible to get the two together? I guess there aren't two of them.

F: They are often split up. They can be together. If you have these two together, you would be at least a genius, because then you might have perspective, sensitivity, and the ability to fit things together at the same time.

Q: Would you then class experiences that are sometimes called "instinctive" or "intuitive" as integrated experiences?

F: Yah. Intuition is the intelligence of the organism. Intelligence is the whole, and intellect is the whore of intelligence—the computer, the fitting game: If this is so, then this is so—all this figuring out by which many people replace *seeing and hearing what's going on.* Because if you are busy with your computer, your energy goes into your thinking, and you don't see and hear any more.

Q: This is a contradictory question because I am asking you to use words. Could you explain the difference between words and experiences? (Fritz leaves podium, goes to the woman who asked the question, puts his hands on her shoulders, kisses her. Laughter) O.K.! That'll do it!

F: I experience a dismissing pat from you. (Fritz pats himself lightly on the shoulder as he returns to the podium)

Q: You were talking about self-control or inner control, versus external control. I'm not sure that I understood you. I feel sometimes that external control is fantasy—that you are actually doing it yourself.

F: Yah, that's true. That's what I call self-manipulation or self-torture. Now this organismic self-regulation I am talking about is not a matter of fantasy, except if the object in question is not there. Then you have a fantasy, which so to say guides you until the real object appears, and then the fantasy of the object and the real object melt together. Then you don't need the fantasy any more.

I am not yet talking about the fantasy life as such, as rehearsal and so on. This is quite a different story. I am talking about the ability of the organism to take care of itself without external interference—without momma telling us, "It's good for your health," "I know what's best for you," and all that.

Q: I have a question. You talked about control. If what you said is so, that the organism can take care of itself once the integration is complete and self-regulation is available for the total organism, then control no longer becomes a factor—externally or internally; it's something that *is*, and is in operation.

F: That's right, and then the essence of control is that you begin to control the means-whereby to get satisfaction. The usual procedure is that you don't get satisfaction, you merely get exhaustion.

Q: I can recognize that what you say is true, that if I keep on computing, I'll stop seeing and hearing. And yet the problem comes with me all the time how, when I have many many things to accomplish in the day—

F: Wait a moment. We have to distinguish—do you have to accomplish them as an organismic need or as part of the social role you play?

Q: As part of the social role.

F: That's a different story. I am talking about the organism *per se*. I am not talking about ourselves as social beings. I don't talk about the *pseudo*-existence, but of the basic natural existence, the foundation of our being. What you are talking about is the role-playing which might be a *means-whereby* to earn a living, which is a *means-whereby* to get your basic needs satisfied—give you food, etc.

Q: And yet—I know there's something sick about this—at the beginning of each day, computing, thinking, planning, scheduling my day, planning that at this hour I'm going to do this and at another hour, that. And I do this all during the day. And I know that it cuts out just seeing and hearing, and yet if I go around just staying with the seeing and the hearing, then certain other things don't get done and I get completely confused.

F: That's right. This is the experience that comes out of the clash between our social existence and our biological existence—confusion.

Q: Well, you're leaving me in that confusion, then.

F: Yah. That's what I'm talking about. *Awareness per se.* If you become aware each time that you are entering a state of confusion, this is the therapeutic thing. And again, nature takes over. If you understand this, and stay with confusion, *confusion will sort itself out by itself.* If you *try* to sort it out, *compute* how to do it, if you ask me for a *prescription* how to do it, you only add more confusion to your productions.

II

I want to talk now about maturation. And in order to understand maturation, we have to talk about learning. To me, learning is *discovery*. I learn something from this experience. There is another idea of learning which is the drill, the routine, the repetition, which is an artifact produced in the person which makes a person an automaton—until he discovers the *meaning* of the drill. For instance, you learn to play the piano. First you start with the drill. And then comes a closure, then comes the discovery: Ahah! I got it! This is it! Then you have to learn how to use this technique.

There is another kind of learning which is the feeding information into your computer, so you accumulate knowledge, and as you know, knowledge begets more knowledge until you want to fly to the moon. This knowledge, this secondary information, might be useful whenever you have lost your senses. As long as you have your senses, as long as you can see and hear, and realize what's going on, then you *understand*. If you learn concepts, if you work for information, then you don't understand. You only *explain*. And it is not easy to understand the difference between explanatoriness and understanding, just as often it is not easy to understand the difference between the heart and the brain, between feeling and thinking.

Most people take explaining as being identical with understanding. There is a great difference. Like now, I can explain a lot to you. I can give you a lot of sentences that help you to build an intellectual model of *how* we function. Maybe some of you feel the coincidence of these sentences and explanations with your real life, and this would mean understanding.

Right now I can only hypnotize you, persuade you, make you

believe that I'm right. You don't know. I'm just preaching something. You wouldn't learn from my words. Learning is discovery.
There is no other means of effective learning. You can tell the child a
thousand times, "The stove is hot." It doesn't help. The child has to
discover it for himself. And I hope I can assist you in learning, in
discovering something about yourself.

Now what are you supposed to learn here? We have a very
specific aim in Gestalt Therapy, and this is the same aim that exists
at least *verbally* in other forms of therapy, in other forms of discovering life. The aim is to mature, to grow up. I would like some
audience participation already about maturation. What is your
opinion? What is a mature person? How would you define a mature
person? Can we start here?

A: I know the answer already, Fritz.

F: Yah. You know the printed answer, according to the gospel
of St. Gestalt. What is *your* definition of the mature person?

A: Well, I have had some introduction to Gestalt and maybe this
influences me, but I think the mature person is the person who is—

F: Well, if you want to give *my* formulation, I don't want it,
because this would be again only information, and not understanding.

A: I was going to say the integrated person is the person who is
aware of his various component parts and has put them together into
a unified functional whole.

F: And this would be a mature person?

A: He has a minimum of parts of himself of which he is completely unconscious or unaware. There is always a residual—we never
get completely aware, or completely conscious.

F: In other words, for you the mature person is the *complete*
person.

A: Yes.

F: (to another person) Could I have *your* definition, please?

B: I was thinking of a person who knows himself and accepts
himself—all the things he likes about himself and the things he
doesn't like about himself—who is aware of his many potentialities
and seeks to develop them as much as possible—knows what he
wants.

F: You certainly have described some important characteristics of the mature person, but this might also apply to a child, wouldn't you say?

B: To me—sometimes children in my opinion are often more mature than adults.

F: Thank you! Often children are more mature than adults. You notice here we have a different equation, or rather a different formulation. We have not the equation: adult equals a mature person. As a matter of fact, the adult is very seldom a mature person. An adult is in my opinion a person who plays a *role* of an adult, and the more he plays the role, the more immature he often is. (to another person) What would be *your* formulation?

C: The first thought that came to me was that the mature person is someone who wonders from time to time what a mature person is, and who every once in a while has an experience which makes him feel: "Oh! So *this* could be part of maturity! I never realized that before."

F: What would be *your* formulation?

D: A person who is aware of himself and others, and also aware that he is incomplete and has some—an awareness of where he is incomplete.

F: Well, I would rather formulate this as the matur*ing* person. He is aware of his incompleteness. So: so far we would say, from these remarks, that what we want to do is to facilitate the completion of our personality. Is this acceptable to everybody?

Q: What do you mean by completion?—or incomplete?

F: Yah. These terms were brought out here. Could you answer this, please? What do you mean by complete or incomplete?

A: I used it to begin with, and I feel this is a goal to strive for that is never achieved. No one ever achieves it. It is always a becoming, a growing. But, relatively, the complete person is the one who is most aware of his component parts, most accepting of them, and has achieved an integration—a continuing integrating process.

F: Now the idea of the incomplete person was first brought about by Nietsche, and very soon afterwards by Freud. Freud's formulation is a little bit different. He says a certain part of one's personality is repressed, is in the unconscious. But when he speaks about the unconscious, he just means that not all of our potential is available. His idea is that there is a barrier between the person and the unconscious, the unavailable potential, and if we lift the barrier we can again be totally ourselves. The idea is basically correct, and every type of psychotherapy is more or less interested in enriching the personality, in liberating what is usually called the repressed and inhibited parts of the personality.

E: Fritz, I have the thought that "maturity" in Spanish is *maduro* which means "ripe." I wanted to make this contribution.

F: Thank you. This is exactly what I also want to completely agree with. In any plant, any animal, ripening and maturing are identical. You don't find any animal—except the domesticated animal who is already infected by mankind—no natural animal and no plant exists that will prevent its own growing. So the question is, how do we prevent ourselves from maturing? What prevents us from ripening? The word "neurosis" is very bad. I use it, too, but actually it should be called *growth disorder*. So in other words, the whole neurosis question shifts more and more from the medical to the educational field. I see more and more the so-called "neurosis" as a disturbance in development. Freud assumed there is such a thing as "maturity," which means a state from which you don't develop any further, you can only regress. We ask the question, what prevents—or how do you prevent yourself from growing, from going further ahead?

So let's look upon maturing once more. My formulation is that *maturing is the transcendence from environmental support to self-support*. Look upon the unborn baby. It gets all its support from the mother—oxygen, food, warmth, everything. As soon as the baby is born, it has already to do its own breathing. And then we find often the first symptom of what plays a very decisive part in Gestalt Therapy. We find the *impasse*. Please note the word. The *impasse* is the crucial point in therapy, the crucial point in growth. The impasse is called by the Russians "the sick point," a point which the Russians never managed to lick and which other types of psychotherapy so far have not succeeded in licking. The impasse is the position where environmental support or obsolete inner support is not forthcoming any more, and authentic self-support has not yet been achieved. The baby cannot breathe by itself. It doesn't get the oxygen supply through the placenta any more. We can't say that the baby has a choice, because there is no deliberate attempt of thinking out what to do, but the baby either has to die or to learn to breathe. There might be some environmental support forthcoming—being slapped, or oxygen might be supplied. The "blue baby" is the prototype of the impasse which we find in every neurosis.

Now, the baby begins to grow up. It still has to be carried. After awhile it learns to give some kind of communication—first crying, then it learns to speak, learns to crawl, to walk, and so, step by step, it mobilizes more and more of its potential, its inner resources. He discovers—or learns—more and more to make use of his muscles, his senses, his wits, and so on. So, from this I make the definition that the process of maturation is the transformation from environmental support to self-support, and the aim of therapy is to make the patient *not* depend upon others, but to make the patient discover from the very first moment that he can do many things, *much* more than he thinks he can do.

The average person of our time, believe it or not, lives only 5% to 15% of his potential at the highest. A person who has even 25% of his potential available is already considered to be a genius. So 85% to 95% of our potential is lost, is unused, is not at our disposal. Sounds tragic, doesn't it? And the reason for this is very simple: we live in clichès. We live in patterned behavior. We are playing the same roles over and over again. So if you find out how you prevent yourself from growing, from using your potential, you have a way of increasing this, making life richer, making you more and more capable of mobilizing yourself. And our potential is based upon a very peculiar attitude: to live and review every second afresh.

The "trouble" with people who are capable of reviewing every second what the situation is like, is that we are not predictable. The role of the good citizen requires that he be predictable, because our hankering for security, for not taking risks, our fear to be authentic, our fear to stand on our own feet, especially on our own intelligence—this fear is just horrifying. So what do we do? We *adjust*, and in most kinds of therapy you find that adjustment to society is the high goal. If you don't adjust, you are either a criminal, or psychopath, or loony, or beatnik or something like that. Anyhow, you are undesirable and have to be thrown out of the boundary of that society.

Most other therapies try to adjust the person to society. This was maybe not too bad in previous years, when society was relatively stable, but now with the rapid changes going on, it is getting more and more difficult to adjust to society. Also, more and more people are not willing to adjust to society—they think that this society stinks, or have other objections. I consider that the basic personality in our time is a neurotic personality. This is a preconceived idea of mine, because I believe we are living in an insane society and that you only have the choice either to participate in this collective psychosis or to take risks and become healthy and perhaps also crucified.

If you are centered in yourself, then you don't adjust any more—then, whatever happens becomes a passing parade and you assimilate, you understand, you are related to whatever happens. In this happening, the symptom of anxiety is very very important, because the more the society changes, the more it produces anxiety. Now the psychiatrist is very afraid of anxiety. I am not. My definition of anxiety is the gap between the now and the later. Whenever you leave the sure basis of the now and become preoccupied with the future, you experience anxiety. And if the future represents a performance, then this anxiety is nothing but stage fright. You are full of catastrophic expectations of the bad things that will happen, or anastrophic expectations about the wonderful things that will happen. And we fill this gap between the now and the later—with insurance policies, planning, fixed jobs, and so on. In other words, we are not willing to see the fertile void, the possibility of the future—we have no future if we fill this void, we only have sameness.

But how can you have sameness in this rapid-changing world? So of course anybody who wants to hold onto the status quo will get more and more panicky and afraid. Usually, the anxiety is not so deeply existential. It is just concerned with the role we want to play, it's just stage fright. "Will my role come off?" "Will I be called a good boy?" "Will I get my approval?" "Will I get applause, or will I get rotten eggs?" So that's not an existential choice, just a choice of inconvenience. But to *realize* that it's just an inconvenience, that it's not a catastrophe, but just an unpleasantness, is part of coming into your own, part of waking up.

So we come to our basic conflict and the basic conflict is this: Every individual, every plant, every animal has only one inborn goal—to actualize itself as it is. A rose is a rose is a rose. A rose is not intent to actualize itself as a kangaroo. An elephant is not intent to actualize itself as a bird. In nature—except for the human being— constitution, and healthiness, potential, growth, is all one unified *something*.

The same applies to the multi-organism, or society, which consists of many people. A state, a society, consists of many thousands of cells which have to be organized either by external control or inner control, and each society tends to actualize itself as this or that specific society. The Russian society actualizes itself as what it is, the American society, the German society, the Congo tribes—they all actualize themselves, they change. And there is always a law in history: Any society that has outstretched itself and has lost its ability to survive, disappears. Cultures come—and go. And when a society is in clash with the universe, once a society transgresses the laws of nature, it loses its survival value, too. So, as soon as we leave the basis of nature—the universe and *its* laws—and become artifacts either as individuals or as society, then we lose our *raison d'etre*. We lose the possibility of existence.

So where do we find ourselves? We find ourselves on the one hand as individuals who want to actualize themselves; we find ourselves also embedded in a society, in our case the progressive American society, and this society might make demands different from the individual demands. So there is the basic clash. Now this individual society is represented in our development by our parents, nurses, teachers, and so forth. Rather than to facilitate the development of authentic growth, they often intrude into the natural development.

They work with two tools to falsify our existence. One tool is the stick, which then is encountered again in therapy as the *cata-strophic expectation*. The catastrophic expectation sounds like this: "If I take the risk, I will not be loved any more. I will be lonely. I'll die." That's the stick. And then there is the hypnosis. Right now, I am hypnotizing you. I am hypnotizing you into believing what I say. I don't give you the chance to digest, to assimilate, to taste what I say. You hear from my voice that I try to cast a spell on you, to slip my "wisdom" into your guts until you either assimilate it or puke, or feed it into your computer and say: "That's an interesting concept." Normally, as you know if you are students, you are only allowed to puke on the examination paper. You swallow all the information and you puke it up and you are free again and you have got a degree. Sometimes, though, I must say, in the process you might have learned something, either discovered something of value, or some experience about your teachers, or about your friends, but the basic dead information is not easy to assimilate.

Now let's go back to the maturation process. In the process of growing up, there are two choices. The child either grows up and learns to overcome frustration, or it is spoiled. It might be spoiled by the parents answering all the questions, rightly or wrongly. It might be spoiled so that as soon as it wants something, it gets it—because the child "should have everything because papa never had it," or because the parents don't know how to frustrate children—don't know how to use frustration. You will probably be amazed that I am using the word frustration so positively. Without frustration there is no need, no reason to mobilize your resources, to discover that you might be able to do something on your own, and in order not to be frustrated, which is a pretty painful experience, the child learns to manipulate the environment.

Now, any time the child, in his development, is prevented from growth by the adult world, any time the child is being spoiled by not being given enough frustration, the child is stuck. So instead of using his potential to grow, he now uses his potential to control the adults, to control the world. Instead of mobilizing his own resources, he creates dependencies. He invests his energy in manipulating the environment for support. He controls the adults by starting to manipulate them, by discerning their weak spots. As the child begins to develop the means of manipulation, he acquires what is called character. The more character a person has, the less potential he has. That sounds paradoxical, but a character is a person that is predictable, that has only a number of fixed responses, or as T. S. Eliot said in *The Cocktail Party*, "You are nothing but a set of obsolete responses."

Now what are the character features which the child develops? How does he control the world? How does he manipulate his environment? He demands directional support. "What shall I do?" "Mommy, I don't know what to do." He plays the role of cry-baby, if he doesn't get what he wants. For instance, there is a little girl here, about three years old. She always puts on the same performance with me. She always cries when I look at her. So today I was very careful *not* to look at her, and she stopped crying and then she started to look for me. Only three years, and already she is such a good ham. She knows how to torture her mother. Or, the child butters up the other person's self-esteem, so that the other will feel good and he will give him something in return. For instance, one of the worst diagnoses is if I encounter a "good boy." There is always a spiteful brat there, in the good boy. But by pretending to comply, at least on the surface, he bribes the adult. Or he plays stupid and demands intellectual support—asks questions, for instance, which is the typical symptom of stupidity. As Albert Einstein once said to me: "Two things are infinite: the universe and the human stupidity." But what is much more widespread than the *actual* stupidity is the *playing* stupid, turning off your ear, not listening, not seeing. Also very important is playing helpless. "I can't help myself. Poor me. You have to help me. You are so wise, you have so many resources, I'm sure you can help me." Each time you play helpless you create a dependency, you play a dependency game. In other words, we make ourselves slaves. Especially, if this dependency is a dependency of our self-esteem. If you need encouragement, praise, pats on the back from everybody, then you make everybody your judge.

If you don't have your loving at your disposal, and project the love, then you want to *be* loved, you do all kinds of things to make yourself lovable. If you disown yourself, you always become the target, you become dependent. What a dependency if you want everybody to love you! A person doesn't mean a thing and yet suddenly you set out and want to make a good impression on this person, want them to love you. It's always the image; you want to play the concept that you are lovable. If you feel comfortable in yourself, you don't love yourself and you don't hate yourself, you just live. I must admit, especially in the United States, loving for many people entails a risk. Many people look upon a person who loves as a sucker. They want to make people love *them*, so that they can exploit them.

If you look a bit into your existence, you will realize that the gratification of the needs of purely biological being—hunger, sex, survival, shelter, breathing—plays only a minor part in our preoccupations, especially in a country like this where we are so spoiled. We don't know what it means to be hungry, and anyone who wants to have sex can have sex plentifully, anyone who wants to breathe can breathe—the air is tax free. For the rest, we play games. We play games quite extensively, openly, and to a much greater extent, privately. When we think, we mostly talk to others in fantasy. We plan for the roles we want to play. We have to organize *in order to* do what we want to do, for the means-whereby.

Now it might sound a bit peculiar that I disesteem thinking, making it just a part of role-playing. Sometimes, we might communicate when we talk, but most times we hypnotize. We hypnotize each other; we hypnotize ourselves that we are right. We play "Madison Avenue" to convince other people or ourselves of our value. And this takes up so much of our energy that sometimes if you are unsure about the role you are playing, you wouldn't dare say a word, a sentence, without having rehearsed it again and again until it fits the occasion. Now if you are not sure of the role you want to play, and you are called away from your private stage to the public stage, then like every good actor, you experience stage fright. Your excitement is already mounting, you want to play a role, but you don't quite dare, so you hold back, and restrict your breathing, so the heart pumps up more blood because the higher metabolism has to be satisfied. And then, once you are on stage and play the role, the excitement flows into your performance. If not, your performance would be rigid and dead.

It is the repetition of this activity which then becomes a habit, the same action that grows easier and easier—a character, a fixed role. So you understand now, I hope, that playing a role, and manipulating the environment, are identical. This is the way we falsify, and very often you read in literature about the mask we are wearing, and about the transparent self that should be there.

This manipulation of the environment by playing certain roles is the characteristic of the neurotic—is the characteristic of our remaining immature. So you must already get an idea how much of our energy goes into manipulating the world instead of using this energy creatively for our own development. And especially, this applies to asking questions. You know the proverb, "One fool can ask more questions than a thousand wise men can answer." All the answers are given. Most questions are simply inventions to torture ourselves and other people. The way to develop our own intelligence is by changing every question into a statement. If you change your question into a statement, the background out of which the question arose opens up, and the possibilities are found by the questioner himself.

You see I am already running dry. Lecturing is a drag, I tell you that. Well, most professors take the way out by using a very somniferous, broken voice, so you fall asleep and don't listen, and so you don't ask embarrassing questions.

Q: I have a question. Could you give me some examples of how to turn questions into statements?

F: You have just asked me a question. Can you turn this question into a statement?

Q: It would be nice to hear some examples of how to turn a question into a statement.

F: "It would be nice." But I'm *not* nice. Actually, what's behind all this is the only means of true communication, which is the imperative. What you really want to say is, "Fritz, *tell me* how one does this"—make a demand on me. And the questionmark is the hook of a demand. Every time you refuse to answer a question, you help the other person to develop his own resources. Learning is nothing but discovery that something is possible. To teach means to show a person that something is possible.

What we are after is the maturation of the person, removing the blocks that prevent a person from standing on his own feet. We try to help him make the transition from environmental support to self-support. And basically we do it by finding the impasse. The impasse occurs originally when a child cannot get the support from the environment, but cannot yet provide its own support. At that moment of impasse, the child starts to mobilize the environment by playing phony roles, playing stupid, playing helpless, playing weak, flattering, and all the roles that we use in order to manipulate our environment.

Now any therapist who wants to be *helpful* is doomed right from the beginning. The patient will do anything to make the therapist feel inadequate, because he has to have his compensation for needing him. So the patient asks the therapist for more and more help, he drives the therapist more and more into the corner, until he either succeeds in driving the therapist crazy—which is another means of manipulation—or if the therapist doesn't oblige, at least to make him feel inadequate. He will suck the therapist more and more into his neurosis, and there will be no end to therapy.

So how do we proceed in Gestalt Therapy? We have a very simple means to get the patient to find out what his own missing potential is. Namely, the patient uses me, the therapist, as a projection screen, and he expects of me exactly what he can't mobilize in himself. And in this process, we make the peculiar discovery that no one of us is complete, that every one of us has holes in his personality. Wilson Van Dusen discovered this first in the schizophrenic, but I believe that every one of us has holes. Where something should be, there is nothing. Many people have no soul. Others have no genitals. Some have no heart; all their energy goes into computing, thinking. Others have no legs to stand on. Many people have no eyes. They project the eyes, and the eyes are to quite an extent in the outside world and they always live as if they are being looked at. A person feels that the eyes of the world are upon him. He becomes a mirror-person who always wants to know how he looks to others. He gives up his eyes and asks the world to do his seeing for him. Instead of being critical, he projects the criticism and feels criticized and feels on stage. Self-consciousness is the mildest form of paranoia. Most of us have no ears. People expect the ears to be outside and they talk and expect someone to listen. But who listens? If people would listen, we would have peace.

Now the most important missing part is a center. Without a center, everything goes on in the periphery and there is no place from which to work, from which to cope with the world. Without a center, you are not alert. I don't know how many of you have seen the film *The Seven Samurai*—a Japanese film, in which one of the warriors is so alert that anyone approaching him, or doing anything even at a distance, he is already sensing it. He is so much centered that anything that happens is immediately registered. This achieving the center, being grounded in one's self, is about the highest state a human being can achieve.

Now these missing holes are always visible. They are always there *in the patient's projection onto the therapist*—that the therapist is supposed to have all the properties which are missing in this person. So, first the therapist provides the person with the opportunity to discover what he needs—the missing parts that he has alienated and given up to the world. Then the therapist must provide the opportunity, the situation in which the person can grow. And the means is that we frustrate the patient in such a way that he is forced to develop his own potential. We apply enough skillful frustration so that the patient is forced to find his own way, discover his own possibilities, his own potential, and discover that *what he expects from the therapist, he can do just as well himself.*

Everything the person disowns can be recovered, and the means of this recovery is understanding, playing, becoming these disowned parts. And by letting him play and discover that he already has all this (which he thinks only others can give him) we increase his potential. We more and more put him on his own feet, give him more and more power in himself, more and more ability to experience, until he is capable of really being himself and coping with the world. He cannot learn this through teaching, conditioning, getting information or making up programs or plans. He has to discover that all this energy that goes into manipulation can be resolved and used, and that he can learn to actualize himself, his potential—instead of trying to actualize a concept, an image of what he wants to be, thereby suppressing a lot of his potential and adding, on the other side. another piece of phony living, pretending to be something he is not. We grow up completely out of balance if the support that we get from our constitution is missing. But the person has to discover this by seeing for himself, by listening for himself, by uncovering what is there, by grasping for himself, by becoming ambidextrous instead of closed, and so on. And the main thing is the listening. To listen, to understand, to be open, is one and the same. Some of you might know Herman Hesse's book, *Siddartha*, where the hero finds the final solution to his life by becoming a ferryman on a river, and he learns to listen. His ears tell him so much more than the Buddha or any of the great wise men can ever teach him.

So what we are trying to do in therapy is step-by-step to *re-own* the disowned parts of the personality until the person becomes strong enough to facilitate his own growth, to learn to understand where are the holes, what are the symptoms of the holes. And the symptoms of the holes are always indicated by one word: *avoidance*. We become phobic, we run away. We might change therapists, we might change marriage partners, but the ability to stay with what we are avoiding is not easy, and for this you need somebody else to become aware of what you are avoiding, because you are not aware, and as a matter of fact, a very interesting phenomenon occurs here. When you get close to the impasse, to the point where you just cannot believe that you might be able to survive, then the whirl starts. You get desperate, confused. Suddenly, you don't understand *any*thing any more, and here the symptom of the neurotic becomes very clear. The neurotic is a person who does not see the obvious. You see this always in the group. Something is obvious to everybody else, but the person in question doesn't see the obvious; he doesn't see the pimples on his nose. And this is what we are again and again trying to do, to frustrate the person until he is face to face with his blocks, with his inhibitions, with his way of avoiding having eyes, having ears, having muscles, having authority, having security in himself.

So we are always trying to get to the impasse, and find the point where you believe you have no chance of survival because you don't find the means in yourself. When we find the place where the person is stuck, we come to the surprising discovery that this impasse is mostly merely a matter of fantasy. It doesn't exist in reality. A person only *believes* he has not his resources at his disposal. He only prevents himself from using his resources by conjuring up a lot of catastrophic expectations. He expects something bad in the future. "People won't like me." "I might do something foolish." "If I would do this, I wouldn't be loved any more, I would die," and so on. We have all these catastrophic fantasies by which we prevent ourselves from living, from *being*. We are continually projecting threatening fantasies onto the world, and these fantasies prevent us from taking the reasonable risks which are part and parcel of growing and living.

Nobody really wants to get through the impasse that will grant this development. We'd rather maintain the status quo: rather keep in the status quo of a mediocre marriage, mediocre mentality, mediocre aliveness, than to go through that impasse. Very few people go into therapy to be cured, but rather to improve their neurosis. We'd rather manipulate others for support than learn to stand on our own feet and to wipe our own ass. And in order to manipulate the others we become control-mad, power-mad—using all kinds of tricks. I gave you a few examples already—playing helpless, playing stupid, playing the tough guy, and so on. And the most interesting thing about the control-mad people is that they always end up *being controlled*. They build up, for instance, a time schedule that then takes over control, and they have to be at every place at a specific time from then on. So the control-mad person is the first one to lose his freedom. Instead of being in control, he has to strain and push all the time.

Because of this control-madness, no bad marriage can be cured because the people do not want to get through the impasse, they do not want to realize how they are stuck. I could give you an idea how they are stuck. In the bad marriage, husband and wife are not in love with their spouse. They are in love with an image, a fantasy, with an ideal of what the spouse should be like. And then, rather than taking responsibility for their own expectations, all they do is play the blaming game. "You should be different from what you are. You don't fill the bill." So the bill is always right, but the real person is wrong. The same applies to the inner conflict, and to the relationship of therapist and patient: you change spouses, you change therapists, you change the content of your inner conflicts, but you usually maintain the status quo.

Now if we understand the impasse correctly, we wake up, we have a satori. I can't give you a prescription because everybody tries to get out of the impasse without going through it; everybody tries to tear their chains, and this is never successful. It's the awareness, the full experience, the awareness of *how* you are stuck, that makes you recover, and realize the whole thing is just a nightmare, not a real thing, not reality. The satori comes when you realize, for instance, that you are in love with a fantasy and you realize that you are not in communication with your spouse.

The insanity is that we take the fantasy for real. In the impasse, you have always a piece of insanity. In the impasse, nobody can convince you that what you are expecting is a fantasy. You take for real what is merely an ideal, a fantasy. The crazy person says, "I am Abraham Lincoln," and the neurotic says, "I wish I were Abraham Lincoln," and the healthy person says, "I am I, and you are you."

III

Now let me tell you of a dilemma which is not easy to understand. It's like a *koan*—those Zen questions which seem to be insoluble. The *koan* is: *Nothing exists except the here and now.* The *now* is the present, is the phenomenon, is what you are aware of, is that moment in which you carry your so-called memories and your so-called anticipations with you. Whether you remember or anticipate, you do it *now*. The past is no more. The future is not yet. When I say, "I was," that's not now, that's the past. When I say, "I want to," that's the future, it's not yet. Nothing can possibly exist except the now. Some people then make a program out of this. They make a demand, "You *should* live in the here and now." And I say it's *not possible* to live in the here and now, and yet, nothing exists except the here and now.

How do we resolve this dilemma? What is buried in the word *now*? How come it takes years and years to understand a simple word like the word *now*? If I play a phonograph record, the sound of the record appears when the record and the needle touch each other, where they make contact. There is no sound of the before, there is no sound of the afterwards. If I stop the phonograph record, then the needle is still in contact with the record, but there is no music, because there is the *absolute* now. If you would blot out the past, or the anticipation of themes three minutes from now, you could not understand listening to that record you are now playing. But if you blot out the now, nothing will come through. So again, whether we remember or whether we anticipate, we do it *here and now*.

Maybe if I say the *now* is not the scale but the point of suspense, it's a zero point, it is a nothingness, and that is the *now*. The very moment I feel that I experience something and I talk about it, I pay attention to it, that moment is already gone. So what's the use of talking about the *now*? It has many uses, very many uses.

Let's talk first about the past. *Now*, I am pulling memories out of my drawer and possibly believe that these memories are identical with my history. That's never true, because a memory is an abstraction. Right now, you experience something. You experience me, you experience your thoughts, you experience your posture perhaps, but you can't experience *everything*. You always abstract the relevant gestalt from the total context. Now if you take these abstractions and file them away, then you call them memories. If these memories are unpleasant, especially if they are unpleasant to our self-esteem, we change them. As Nietsche said: "Memory and Pride were fighting. Memory said, 'It was like this' and Pride said, 'It couldn't have been like this'—and Memory gives in." You all know how much you are lying. You all know how much you are deceiving yourselves, how many of your memories are exaggerations and projections, how many of your memories are patched up and distorted.

The past is past. And yet—in the now, in our being, we carry much of the past with us. But we carry much of the past with us only as far as we have unfinished situations. What happened in the past is either assimilated and has become a part of us, or we carry around an unfinished situation, an incomplete gestalt. Let me give you as an example, the most famous of the unfinished situations is the fact that we have not forgiven our parents. As you know, parents are never right. They are either too large or too small, too smart or too dumb. If they are stern, they should be soft, and so on. But when do you find parents who are all right? You can always blame the parents if you want to play the blaming game, and make the parents responsible for all your problems. Until you are willing to let go of your parents, you continue to conceive of yourself as a child. But to get closure and let go of the parents and say, "I am a big girl, now," is a different story. This is part of therapy—to let go of parents, and especially to forgive one's parents, which is the hardest thing for most people to do.

The great error of psychoanalysis is in assuming that the memory is reality. All the so-called *traumata*, which are supposed to be the root of the neurosis, are an invention of the patient to save his self-esteem. None of these traumata has ever been proved to exist. I haven't seen a single case of infantile trauma that wasn't a falsification. They are all lies to be hung onto in order to justify one's unwillingness to grow. To mature means to take responsibility for your life, to be on your own. Psychoanalysis fosters the infantile state by considering that the past is responsible for the illness. The patient isn't responsible—no, the trauma is responsible, or the Oedipus complex is responsible, and so on. I suggest that you read a beautiful little pocketbook called *I Never Promised You a Rose Garden*, by Hannah Green. There you see a typical example, how that girl invented this childhood trauma, to have her *raison d'etre*, her basis to fight the world, her justification for her craziness, her illness. We have got such an idea about the importance of this invented memory, where the whole illness is supposed to be based on this memory. No wonder that all the wild goose chase of the psychoanalyst to find out *why* I am now like this can never come to an end, can never prove a real opening up of the person himself.

Freud devoted his whole life to prove to himself and to others that sex is not bad, and he had to prove this scientifically. In his time, the scientific approach was that of causality, that the trouble was *caused* by something in the past, like a billiard cue pushing a billiard ball, and the cue then is the cause of the rolling of the ball. In the meantime, our scientific attitude has changed. We don't look to the world any more in terms of cause and effect: We look upon the world as a continuous ongoing process. We are back to Heraclitus, to the pre-Socratic idea that everything is in a flux. We never step into the same river twice. In other words, we have made—in science, but unfortunately not yet in psychiatry—the transition from linear causality to thinking of process, from the *why* to the *how*.

If you ask *how*, you look at the structure, you see what's going on now, a deeper understanding of the process. The *how* is all we need to understand how we or the world functions. The *how* gives us perspective, orientation. The *how* shows that one of the basic laws, the identity of structure and function, is valid. If we change the structure, the function changes. If we change the function, the structure changes.

I know you want to ask *why*, like every child, like every immature person asks *why*, to get rationalization or explanation. But the *why* at best leads to clever explanation, but never to an understanding. *Why* and *because* are dirty words in Gestalt Therapy. They lead only to rationalization, and belong to the second class of verbiage production. I distinguish three classes of verbiage production: chickenshit—this is "good morning," "how are you," and so on; bullshit—this is "because," rationalization, excuses; and elephantshit— this is when you talk about philosophy, existential Gestalt Therapy, etc.—what I am doing now. The *why* gives only unending inquiries into the cause of the cause of the cause of the cause of the cause of the cause. And as Freud has already observed, every event is *over*determined, has *many* causes; all kinds of things come together in order to create the specific moment that is the *now*. Many factors come together to create this specific unique person which is *I*. Nobody can at any given moment be different from what he is at this moment, including all the wishes and prayers that he should be different. We are what we are.

These are the two legs upon which Gestalt Therapy walks: *now* and *how*. The essence of the theory of Gestalt Therapy is in the understanding of these two words. *Now* covers all that exists. The past is no more, the future is not yet. *Now* includes the balance of being here, is experiencing, involvement, phenomenon, awareness. *How* covers everything that is structure, behavior, all that is actually going on—the ongoing process. All the rest is irrelevant—computing, apprehending, and so on.

Everything is grounded in *awareness*. *Awareness* is the only basis of knowledge, communication, and so on. In communication, you have to understand that you want to make the other person *aware of something*: aware of yourself, aware of what's to be noticed in the other person, etc. And in order to communicate, we have to make sure that we are *senders*, which means that the message which we send can be understood; and also to make sure that we are *receivers*—that we are willing to listen to the message from the other person. It is very rare that people can talk *and* listen. Very few people can listen without talking. Most people can talk without listening. And if you're busy talking you have no time to listen. The integration of talking and listening is a really rare thing. Most people don't listen and give an honest response, but just put the other person off with a question. Instead of listening and answering, immediately comes a counter-attack, a question or something that diverts, deflects, dodges. We are going to talk a lot about blocks in sending messages, in giving yourself, in making others aware of yourself, and in the same way, of being willing to be open to the other person—to be receivers. Without communication, there cannot be contact. There will be only isolation and boredom.

So I would like to reinforce what I just said, and I would like you to pair up, and to talk to each other for five minutes about your actual present awareness of yourself now and your awareness of the other. Always underline the *how*—*how* do you behave *now, how* do you sit, *how* do you talk, all the details of what goes on *now. How* does he sit, *how* does he look. . .

So how about the future? We don't know anything about the future. If we all had crystal balls, even then we wouldn't experience the future. We would experience a *vision* of the future. And all this is taking place here and now. We imagine, we anticipate the future because we don't want to have a future. So the most important existential saying is, we don't want to have a future, we are afraid of the future. We fill in the gap where there should be a future with insurance policies, status quo, sameness, *anything* so as not to experience the possibility of openness towards the future.

We also cannot stand the nothingness, the openness, of the past. We are not willing to have the idea of eternity—"It has always been"—so we have to fill it in with the story of creation. Time has started somehow. People ask, "When did time begin?" The same applies to the future. It seems incredible that we could live without goals, without worrying about the future, that we could be open and ready for what might come. No; we have to make sure that we have no future, that the status quo should remain, even be a little bit better. But we mustn't take risks, we mustn't be open to the future.

Something could happen that would be new and exciting, and contributing to our growth. It's too dangerous to take the growth risk. We would rather walk this earth as half-corpses than live dangerously, and realize that this living dangerously is much safer than this insurance-life of safety and not taking risks, which most of us decide to do.

What is this funny thing, risk-taking? Has anybody a definition for risk-taking? What's involved in risk-taking?

A: Getting hurt.

B: Taking a dare.

C: Going too far.

D: A hazardous attempt.

E: Inviting danger.

Now you notice you all see the catastrophic expectation, the negative side. You don't see the possible gain. If there was only the negative side, you just would avoid it, wouldn't you? Risk-taking is a suspense between catastrophic and anastrophic expectations. You have to see *both* sides of the picture. You might gain, and you might lose.

One of the most important moments in my life was after I had escaped Germany and there was a position as a training analyst available in South Africa, and Ernest Jones wanted to know who wanted to go. There were four of us: three wanted guarantees. I said I take a risk. All the other three were caught by the Nazis. I took a risk and I'm still alive.

An absolutely healthy person is completely in touch with himself and with reality. The crazy person, the psychotic, is more or less completely *out* of touch with both, but mostly with *either* himself *or* the world. We are in between being psychotic and being healthy, and this is based upon the fact that we have *two* levels of existence. One is reality, the actual, realistic level, that we are in touch with whatever goes on now, in touch with our feelings, in touch with our senses. Reality is awareness of ongoing experience, actual touching, seeing, moving, doing. The other level we don't have a good word for, so I choose the Indian word *maya*. *Maya* means something like illusion, or fantasy, or philosophically speaking, the *as if* of

Vaihinger. *Maya* is a kind of dream, a kind of trance. Very often this fantasy, this *maya*, is called the mind, but if you look a bit closer, what you call "mind" is fantasy. It's the rehearsal stage. Freud once said: *"Denken ist prober arbeit"*—thinking is rehearsing, trying out. Unfortunately, Freud never followed up this discovery because it would be inconsistent with his genetic approach. If he had accepted this statement of his, "Thinking is rehearsing," he would have realized how our fantasy activity is turned toward the future, because we rehearse for the future.

We live on two levels—the public level which is our *doing*, which is observable, verifiable; and the private stage, the thinking stage, the rehearsing stage, on which we prepare for the future roles we want to play. Thinking is a private stage, where you try out. You talk to some person unknown, you talk to yourself, you prepare for an important event, you talk to the beloved before your appointment or disappointment, whatever you expect it to be. For instance, if I were to ask, "Who wants to come up here to work?" you probably would quickly start to rehearse. "What shall I do there?" and so on. And of course probably you will get stage fright, because you leave the secure reality of the now and jump into the future. Psychiatry makes a big fuss out of the symptom *anxiety*, and we live in an age of anxiety, but anxiety is nothing but the tension from the *now* to the *then*. There are few people who can stand this tension, so they have to fill the gap with rehearsing, planning, "making sure," making sure that they don't have a future. They try to hold onto the sameness, and this of course will prevent any possibility of growth or spontaneity.

Q: Of course the past sets up anxiety too, doesn't it?

F: No. The past sets up—or let's say is still present with unfinished situations, regrets and things like this. If you feel anxiety about what you have done, it's not anxiety about what you have done, but anxiety about what will be the punishment to come in the future.

Freud once said the person who is free from anxiety and guilt is healthy. I spoke about anxiety already. I didn't speak about guilt. Now, in the Freudian system, the guilt is very complicated. In

Gestalt Therapy, the guilt thing is much simpler. We see guilt as projected *resentment*. Whenever you feel guilty, find out what you resent, and the guilt will vanish and you will try to make the other person feel guilty.

Anything unexpressed which wants to be expressed can make you feel uncomfortable. And one of the most common unexpressed experiences is the resentment. This is the unfinished situation *par excellence*. If you are resentful, you're stuck; you neither can move forward and have it out, express your anger, change the world so that you'll get satisfaction, nor can you let go and forget whatever disturbs you. Resentment is the psychological equivalent of the hanging-on bite—the tight jaw. The hanging-on bite can neither let go, nor bite through and chew up—whichever is required. In resentment you can neither let go and forget, and let this incident or person recede in the background, nor can you actively tackle it. The expression of resentment is one of the most important ways to help you to make your life a little bit more easy. Now I want you all to do the following collective experiment:

I want each one of you to do this. First you evoke a person like father or husband, call the person by name—whoever it is—and just say briefly, "Clara, I resent—" Try to get the person to hear you, as if there was really communication and you felt this. So try to speak to the person, and establish in these communications that this person should listen to you. Just become aware of how difficult it is to mobilize your fantasy. Express your resentment—kind of present it right into his or her face. Try to realize at the same time that you don't dare, really, to express your anger, nor would you be generous enough to let go, to be forgiving. Okeh, go ahead. . .

There is another great advantage to using resentment in therapy, in growth. Behind every resentment there are demands. So now I want all of you to talk directly to the same person as before, and express the demands behind the resentments. The demand is the only real form of communication. Get your demands into the open. Do this also as self-expression: formulate your demands in the form of an imperative, a command. I guess you know enough of English grammar to know what an imperative is. The imperative is like "Shut up!" "Go to hell!" "Do this!"...

Now go back to the resentments you expressed toward the person. Remember *exactly* what you resented. Scratch out the word *resent* and say *appreciate*. Appreciate what you resented before. Then go on to tell this person what else you appreciate in them. Again try to get the feeling that you actually communicate with them...

You see, if there were no appreciations, you wouldn't be stuck with this person and you could just forget him. There is always the other side. For instance, my appreciation of Hitler: If Hitler had not come to power, I probably would have been dead by now as a good psychoanalyst who lives on eight patients for the rest of his life.

If you have any difficulties in communication with somebody, look for your resentments. Resentments are among the worst possible unfinished situations—unfinished gestalts. If you resent, you can neither let go nor have it out. Resentment is an emotion of central importance. The resentment is the most important expression of an impasse—of being stuck. If you feel resentment, be able to express your resentment. A resentment unexpressed often is experienced as, or changes into, feelings of guilt. Whenever you feel guilty, find out what you are resenting and express it and make your demands explicit. This alone will help a lot.

Awareness covers, so to speak, three layers or three zones: awareness of the *self*, awareness of the *world*, and awareness of what's between—the intermediate zone of fantasy that prevents a person from being in touch with either himself or the world. This is Freud's great discovery—that there is something between you and the world. There are so many processes going on in one's fantasies. A complex is what he calls it, or a prejudice. If you have prejudices, then your relationship to the world is very much disturbed and destroyed. If you want to approach a person with a prejudice, you can't get to the person. You always will contact only the prejudice, the fixed idea. So Freud's idea that the intermediate zone, the DMZ, this no-man's land between you and the world should be eliminated, emptied out, brainwashed or whatever you want to call it, was perfectly right. The only trouble is that Freud stayed in that zone and analyzed this intermediate thing. He didn't consider the self-awareness or world-awareness; he didn't consider what we can do to be in touch again.

This loss of contact with our authentic self, and loss of contact with the world, is due to this intermediate zone, the big area of *maya* that we carry with us. That is, there is a big area of fantasy activity that takes up so much of our excitement, of our energy, of our life force, that there is very little energy left to be in touch with reality. Now, if we want to make a person whole, we have first to understand what is merely fantasy and irrationality, and we have to discover where one is in touch, and with what. And very often if we work, and we empty out this middle zone of fantasy, this *maya*, then there is the experience of *satori*, of waking up. Suddenly the world is *there*. You wake up from a trance like you wake up from a dream. You're all there again. And the aim in therapy, the growth aim, is to lose more and more of your "mind" and come more to your *senses*. To be more and more in touch, to be in touch with yourself and in touch with the world, instead of only in touch with the fantasies, prejudices, apprehensions, and so on.

If a person confuses *maya* and reality, if he takes fantasy for reality, then he is neurotic or even psychotic. I give you an extreme case of psychosis, the schizophrenic who imagines the doctor is after him, so he decides to beat him to the punch and shoot the doctor, without checking up on reality. On the other hand, there is another possibility. Instead of being divided between *maya* and reality, we can integrate these two, and if *maya* and reality are integrated, we call it art. Great art is real, and great art is at the same time an illusion.

Fantasy can be creative, but it's creative only if you have the fantasy, whatever it is, in the *now*. In the *now*, you use what is available, and you are bound to be creative. Just watch children in their play. What's available is usable and then something happens, something comes out of the being in touch with what is *here* and *now*.

There is only one way to bring about this state of healthy spontaneity, to save the genuineness of the human being. Or, to talk in trite religious terms, there is only one way to regain our soul, or in American terms, to revive the American corpse and bring him back to life. The paradox is that in order to get this spontaneity, we need, like in Zen, an utmost discipline. The discipline is simply to understand the words *now* and *how*, and to bracket off and put aside anything that is not contained in the words *now* and *how*.

Now what's the technique we are using in Gestalt Therapy? The technique is to establish a *continuum of awareness*. This continuum of awareness is required so that the organism can work on the healthy gestalt principle: that the most important unfinished situation will always emerge and can be dealt with. If we prevent ourselves from achieving this gestalt formation, we function badly and we carry hundreds and thousands of unfinished situations with us, that always demand completion.

This continuum of awareness seems to be very simple, just to be aware from second to second what's going on. Unless we are asleep, we are always aware of something. However, as soon as this awareness becomes unpleasant, most people will interrupt it. Then suddenly they start intellectualizing, bullshitting, the flight into the past, the flight into expectations, good intentions, or schizophrenically using free associations, jumping like a grasshopper from experience to experience, and none of these experiences are ever *experienced*, but just a kind of a flash, which leaves all the available material unassimilated and unused.

Now how do we proceed in Gestalt Therapy? What is nowadays quite fashionable was very much pooh-poohed when I started this idea of *everything is awareness*. The purely verbal approach, the Freudian approach in which I was brought up, barks up the wrong tree. Freud's idea was that by a certain procedure called free-association, you can liberate the disowned part of the personality and put it at the disposal of the person and then the person will develop what he called a strong ego. What Freud called association, I call *dissociation*, schizophrenic dissociation to avoid the experience. It's a computer game, an interpretation-computer game, which is exactly an avoidance of the experience of what *is*. You can talk 'til doomsday, you can chase your childhood memories to doomsday, but nothing will change. You can associate—or dissociate—a hundred things to one event, but you can only experience one reality.

So, in contrast to Freud who placed the greatest emphasis on resistances, I have placed the greatest emphasis on *phobic attitude, avoidance, flight from.* Maybe some of you know that Freud's illness was that he suffered from an immense number of phobias, and as he had this illness, of course he had to avoid coping with avoidance. His phobic attitude was tremendous. He couldn't look at a patient— couldn't face having an encounter with the patient—so he had him lie on a couch, and Freud's symptom became the trademark of psycho-analysis. He couldn't go into the open to be photographed, and so on. But usually, if you come to think of it, most of us would rather avoid unpleasant situations and we mobilize all the armor, masks, and so on, a procedure which is usually known as the "repression." So, I try to find out from the patient what he *avoids.*

The enemy of development is this pain phobia—the unwillingness to do a tiny bit of suffering. You see, pain is a signal of nature. The painful leg, the painful feeling, cries out, "Pay attention to me—if you don't pay attention, things will get worse." The broken leg cries, "Don't walk so much. Keep still." We use this fact in Gestalt Therapy by understanding that the awareness continuum is being interrupted—that you become phobic—as soon as you begin to feel something unpleasant. When you begin to feel uncomfortable, you take away your attention.

So the therapeutic agent, the means of development, is to inte-grate *attention* and *awareness.* Often psychology doesn't differenti-ate between awareness and attention. Attention is a deliberate way of listening to the emerging foreground figure, which in this case is something unpleasant. So what I do as therapist is to work as a catalyst both ways: provide situations in which a person can experi-ence this being stuck—the unpleasantness—and I frustrate his avoid-ances still further, until he is willing to mobilize his own resources.

Authenticity, maturity, responsibility for one's actions and life, response-ability, and living in the now, having the creativeness of the now available, is all one and the same thing. Only in the now, are you in touch with what's going on. If the now becomes painful, most people are ready to throw the now overboard and avoid the painful situation. Most people can't even suffer themselves. So in therapy the person might simply become phobic and run away or he might play games which will lead our effort *ad absurdum*—like making a fool out of the situation or playing the bear-trapper game. You probably know the bear-trappers. The bear-trappers suck you in and give you the come-on, and when you're sucked in, down comes the hatchet and you stand there with a bloody nose, head, or whatever. And if you are fool enough to ram your head against the wall until you begin to bleed and be exasperated, then the bear-trapper enjoys himself and enjoys the control he has over you, to render you inadequate, impotent, and he enjoys his victorious self which does a lot for his feeble self-esteem. Or you have the Mona Lisa smiler. They smile and smile, and all the time think, "You're such a fool." And nothing penetrates. Or you have the drive-us-crazy, whose only interest in life is to drive themselves or their spouse or their environment crazy and then fish in troubled waters.

But with these exceptions, anyone who has a little bit of goodwill will benefit from the Gestalt approach because the simplicity of the Gestalt approach is that we pay attention to the obvious, to the utmost surface. We don't delve into a region which we don't know anything about, into the so-called "unconscious." I don't believe in repressions. The whole theory of repression is a fallacy. We can't repress a need. We have only repressed certain expressions of these needs. We have blocked one side, and then the self-expression comes out somewhere else, in our movements, in our posture, and most of all in our voice. A good therapist doesn't listen to the content of the bullshit the patient produces, but to the sound, to the music, to the hesitations. Verbal communication is usually a lie. The real communication is beyond words. There is a *very* good book available, *The Voice of Neurosis*, by Paul Moses, a psychologist from San Francisco who died recently. He could give you a diagnosis from the voice that is better than the Rorschach test.

So don't listen to the words, just listen to what the voice tells you, what the movements tell you, what the posture tells you, what the image tells you. If you have ears, then you know all about the other person. You don't have to listen to *what* the person says: listen to the sounds. *Per sona*—"through sound." The sounds tell you everything. Everything a person wants to express is all there—not in words. What we say is mostly either lies or bullshit. But the voice is there, the gesture, the posture, the facial expression, the psychosomatic language. It's all there if you learn to more or less let the content of the sentences play the second violin only. And if you don't make the mistake of mixing up sentences and reality, and if you use your eyes and ears, then you see that everyone expresses himself in one way or another. If you have eyes and ears, the world is open. Nobody can have any secrets because the neurotic only fools himself, nobody else—except for awhile, maybe, if he is a good actor.

In most psychiatry, the sound of the voice is not noticed, only the verbal contact is abstracted from the total personality. Movements like—you see how much this young man here expresses in his leaning forward—the total personality as it expresses itself with movements, with posture, with sound, with pictures—there is so much invaluable material here, that we don't have to do anything else except get to the obvious, to the outermost surface, and feed this back, so as to bring this into the patient's awareness. *Feedback* was Carl Rogers' introduction into psychiatry. Again, he only mostly feeds back the sentences, but there is so much more to be fed back— something you might not be aware of, and here the attention and awareness of the therapist might be useful. So we have it rather easy compared with the psychoanalysts, because we see the whole being of a person right in front of us, and this is because Gestalt Therapy uses eyes and ears and the therapist stays absolutely in the now. He avoids interpretation, verbiage production, and all other types of mind-fucking. But mind-fucking is mind-fucking. It is also a symptom which might cover something else. But what is there is there. Gestalt Therapy is being in touch with the obvious.

IV

Now let me tell you something about how I see the structure of a neurosis. Of course I don't know what the theory will be next because I'm always developing and simplifying what I'm doing more and more. I now see the neurosis as consisting of five layers.

The first layer is the cliché layer. If you meet somebody you exchange clichés—"Good morning," handshake, and all of the meaningless *tokens* of meeting.

Now behind the clichés, you find the second layer, what I call the Eric Berne or Sigmund Freud layer—the layer where we play games and roles—the very important person, the bully, the cry-baby, the nice little girl, the good boy—whatever roles we choose to play. So those are the superficial, social, *as-if* layers. We pretend to be better, tougher, weaker, more polite, etc., than we really feel. This is essentially where the psychoanalysts stay. They treat *playing* the child as a reality and call it infantilism and try to get all the details of this child-playing.

Now, this synthetic layer has to be first worked through. I call it the synthetic layer because it fits very nicely into the dialectical thinking. If we translate the dialectic—thesis, antithesis, synthesis—into *existence*, we can say: *existence, anti-*existence, and *synthetic* existence. Most of our life is a synthetic existence, a compromise between the anti-existence and existence. For instance, today I had the luck to meet somebody who has not this phony layer, who is an honest person, and relatively direct. But most of us put on a show which we are *not*, for which we don't have our support, our strength, our genuine desire, our genuine talents.

Now if we work through the role-playing layer, if we take away the roles, what do we experience then? Then we experience the *anti*-existence, we experience the nothingness, emptiness. This is the *impasse* that I talked about earlier, the feeling of being stuck and lost. The impasse is marked by a phobic attitude—avoidance. We are phobic, we avoid suffering, especially the suffering of frustration. We are spoiled, and we don't want to go through the hellgates of suffering: We stay immature, we go on manipulating the world, rather than to suffer the pains of growing up. This is the story. We rather suffer being self-conscious, being looked *upon*, than to realize our blindness and get our eyes again. And this is the great difficulty I see in self-therapy. There are *many* things one can do on one's own, do one's own therapy, but when one comes to the difficult parts, especially to the impasse, you become phobic, you get into a whirl, into a merry-go-round, and you are not willing to go through the pain of the impasse.

Behind the impasse lies a very interesting layer, the *death* layer or *implosive* layer. This fourth layer appears either as death or as fear of death. The death layer has nothing to do with Freud's death instinct. It only appears as death because of the paralysis of opposing forces. It is a kind of catatonic paralysis: we pull ourselves together, we contract and compress ourselves, we *implode*. Once we really get in contact with this deadness of the implosive layer, then something very interesting happens.

The *im*plosion becomes *ex*plosion. The death layer comes to life, and this explosion is the link-up with the authentic person who is capable of experiencing and expressing his emotions. There are four basic kinds of explosions from the death layer. There is the explosion of genuine *grief* if we work through a loss or death that has not been assimilated. There is the explosion into *orgasm* in sexually blocked people. There is the explosion into *anger*, and also the explosion into *joy, laughter, joi de vivre.* These explosions connect with the authentic personality, with the true self.

Now, don't be frightened by the word *explosion*. Many of you drive a motor car. There are hundreds of explosions per minute, in the cylinder. This is different from the violent explosion of the catatonic—that would be like an explosion in a gas tank. Also, a single explosion doesn't mean a thing. The so-called breakthroughs of the Reichian therapy, and all that, are as little useful as the insight in psychoanalysis. Things still have to work through.

As you know, most of our role-playing is designed to use up a lot of this energy for controlling just those explosions. The death layer, the fear of death, is that if we explode, then we believe we can't survive any more—then we will die, we'll be persecuted, we'll be punished, we won't be loved any more and so on. So the whole rehearsal and self-torture game continues; we hold ourselves back and control ourselves.

Let me give you an example. There was once a girl, a woman, who had lost her child not too long ago, and she couldn't quite get in touch with the world. And we worked a bit, and we found she was holding onto the coffin. She realized she did not want to let go of this coffin. Now you understand, as long as she is not willing to face this hole, this emptiness, this nothingness, she couldn't come back to life, to the others. So much love is bound up here, in this coffin, that she rather invests her life in this fantasy of having some kind of a child, even if it's a dead child. When she can face her nothingness and experience her grief, she can come back to life and get in touch with the world.

The whole philosophy of nothingness is very fascinating. In our culture "nothingness" has a different meaning than it has in the Eastern religions. When we say "nothingness," there is a void, an emptiness, something deathlike. When the Eastern person says "nothingness," he calls it *no thingness*—there are no *things* there. There is only process, happening. Nothingness doesn't exist for us, in the strictest sense, because nothingness is based on awareness of nothingness, so there is the awareness of nothingness, so there is something there. And we find when we accept and *enter* this nothingness, the void, then the desert starts to bloom. The empty void becomes alive, is being filled. The sterile void becomes the fertile void. I am getting more and more right on the point of writing quite a bit about the philosophy of nothing. I feel this way, as if I am nothing, just function. "I've got plenty of nothing." *Nothing* equals *real*.

Q: Fritz, when I was exploding, outside, you seemed cutting down on me, with being sort of witty, by using your wit on me, and it seems to me that this is what I do—that I explode, that I let myself go, and that you were sort of poking fun at me.

F: Oh, yes. You didn't realize what I did. Yesterday we started out with your being afraid. You let out a lot of passionate energy this morning, and I put more and more obstacles in your way so you could become hotter, more convincing. Do you see what I did for you? (Fritz laughs)

Q: Well, I misinterpreted it—I—

F: Of course. If you had known, it wouldn't have worked. I saw you begin to enjoy yourself so much, in your heightened color, and your saving the world. It was *beautiful*.

Q: Where does all this energy in the implosive layer come from?

F: (he makes hooks of the fingers of each hand, then hooks his hands together and pulls) Did you see what I did? Did you see how much energy I spent doing nothing, just pulling myself with equal strength? Where does the energy come from? By not allowing the excitement to get to our senses and muscles. The excitement goes instead of this into our fantasy life, into the fantasy life which we take for real. You might believe, "I can't possibly do this. I am helpless. I need my wife to comfort me," and you are not willing to wake up and see that you might be able to produce your own comfort, and even comfort other people.

Our life energy goes only into those parts of our personality with which we identify. In our time, many people identify mostly with their computer. They think. Some people talk about the greatness of the homo sapiens, the computer bit, as if our intellect has leadership over the human animal, a notion which has gone out of fashion with Freud. Today we are talking about an integration of the social being and the animal being. Without the support of our vitality, of our physical existence, the intellect remains merely mind-fucking.

Most people play two kinds of intellectual games. The one game is the comparing game, the "more than" game—my car is bigger than yours, my house is better than yours, I'm greater than you, my misery is miserabler than yours, and so on and so on. Now the other game which is of the utmost importance is the fitting game. You know the fitting game in many respects. If you want to play a certain role—let's say you want to go to a party, you want to be the belle of the ball, so you have to put on the costume for this role. You go to a first-class tailor and you play the fitting game. This costume fits me, the tailor has to make the costume to fit me, I have to get accessories that fit the costume, and so on. Now this fitting game can be played in two directions. One direction is, we look upon reality and see where does this reality fit into my theories, my hypotheses, my fantasies *about* what reality is like. Or you can work from the opposite direction. You have faith in a certain concept, you have faith in a certain school, either the psychological school, the Freudian school, or the conditioning school. Now you see how to fit reality into that model. It's just like Procrustes, who had to fit all people into the same size bed. If they were too long, he cut off their legs; if they were too short, he stretched them until they fit the bed. This is the fitting game.

A theory, a concept, is an abstraction, is an aspect of any event. If you take this desk, from this desk you can abstract the form, you can abstract the substance, you can abstract the color, you can abstract its monetary value. You can't add the abstractions together to make a whole, because the whole exists in the first place, and the abstractions are then done by us, from whatever context we need these abstractions.

Now in regard to psychology, I like to point out some of the abstractions you can make from Gestalt Therapy. One is the behavioristic. What we do: we observe the identity of structure and function in the people, organism, and so on, which we encounter. The great thing about the behaviorists is that they actually work in the here and now. They look, they observe what's going on. If we could deduct from the present-day American psychologists their compulsion to condition, and just keep them as observers: If they could realize that the changes which are required are *not* to be obtained by conditioning, that conditioning always produces artifacts, and that the real changes are occurring by themselves in a different way, then I think we could do much toward a reconciliation of the behaviorists and the experientialists.

The experientialists, the clinical psychologists, have one great advantage over the behaviorists. They do not see the human organism as a mechanical something that is just functioning. They see that in the center of life is the means of communication, namely, awareness. Now you call awareness "consciousness," or sensitivity, or just awareness of something. I believe that matter has—besides extension, duration, etc.—also *awareness*. Of course we are not capable yet of measuring the infinitely small quantities of awareness in, let's say, this desk here, but we know that every animal, every plant, has awareness, or you might call it tropism, sensitivity, protoplasmic sensitivity or whatever you want to, but the awareness is there. Otherwise they could not react to sunlight, or to give you another example: If you have a plant, and you put some fertilizer in one place, the plant will grow roots toward this fertilizer. If you now dig out the fertilizer and move it somewhere else, then the plant will grow roots in that direction.

So, what I want to point out is, in Gestalt Therapy we start with *what is*, and see which abstraction, which context, which situation is there to be found and relate the figure, the foreground experience, to the background, to the content, to the perspective, to the situation, and they together form the gestalt. Meaning is the relationship of the foreground figure to its background. If you use the word "king," you have to have a background to understand the meaning of the word "king," whether it's the King of England, the king of a chess game, the chicken à la king—nothing has a meaning without its context. Meaning doesn't exist. It is always created ad hoc.

We have two systems with which to relate to the world. One is called the sensoric system, the other is the motoric system. Now unfortunately the behaviorists, with their idiotic reflex-arc bit, have messed the whole thing up. The sensoric system is for orientation, the sense of touching, where we get in touch with the world. We also have the motoric system with which we cope, the system of action through which we do something with the world. So a really healthy, complete person has to have both a good orientation and ability to act. Now you sometimes get the extreme missing of one side or another, as in the extreme cases of schizophrenia. The extreme cases of schizophrenia are the completely withdrawn persons who lack action, and the paranoiac types who lack sensitivity. So if there is no balance between sensing and doing, then you are out of gear.

Many people rather hang on with their attention to exhaust the situation that doesn't nourish. This hanging onto the world, this fixation, this over-extended contact, is as pathological as the complete withdrawal—the ivory tower or the catatonic stupor. In both cases, contact and withdrawal does not flow—the rhythm is interrupted.

The sickness, playing sick, which is a large part of this getting crazy, is nothing but the quest for environmental support. If you are sick in bed, somebody is coming and cares for you, brings you your food, your warmth, you don't have to go out and make a living, so there is the complete regression. But the regression is not, as Freud thought, a purely pathological phenomenon. Regression means a withdrawal to a position where you can provide your own support, where you feel secure. We are going to work quite a bit with deliberate regression here, deliberate withdrawal, to find out what is the situation in which you feel comfortable, in contrast to the situation you cannot cope with. You find out, what *are* you in touch with, if you cannot be in touch with the world and with your environment.

So let's do another experiment, which might be quite helpful to you. If you're confused or bored or somehow stuck, try the following experiment: Shuttle between *here* and *there*. I want you all to do this now. Close your eyes and go away in your imagination, from here to any place you like. . .

Now the next step is to come back to the *here* experience, the here and now. . . And now compare the two situations. Most likely the *there* situation was preferable to the *here* situation. . . And now close your eyes again. Go away again, wherever you'd like to go. And notice any change. . .

Now again come back to the here and now, and again compare the two situations. Has any change taken place?. . . And now go away again—continue to do this on your own until you really feel comfortable in the present situation, until you come to your senses, and you begin to see and hear and be here in this world; until you really begin to exist. . . Is anybody willing to talk about this experience of shuttling?

P: Initially I went away to a friend's house, it was very nice. I came back. The second time I went to a river-mountain retreat that I go to, and it also was extremely nice. Then I came back. I'm here now, and I realize that working in the future for me is unnecessary. It's more important for me now to be here. The future will take care of itself.

Q: I climbed a mountain with someone with whom I was very much giving and loving and receiving this feeling, and when I came back I still wasn't satisfied because this was not complete in my life. So I will tend to look for that closure.

R: I alternated between three places that are favorite places of nature for me, and I was there alone. And each time I came back, I felt more calm.

S: Fritz, I'm struck by the fact that when I go away, I'm more alive than when I'm right here. I don't operate with as much emotion or as much vitality here—my physical body is much less moved, is much less in reality, than when I go away.

F: You didn't manage to bring any of the vitality back to the here and now?

S: Yes. But not as much. There was still a discrepancy between them.

F: There is still a reservoir left untapped.

T: I feel the same thing that I feel when I go back to my living room at home. Ah, the first time I went back I didn't feel very much, and I came back here and I felt a certain tension. And when I went back the second time, it was the same, and I came back here and I felt more tension. And I went back and I could feel the same tension in my living room as I feel here.

U: I went to a desert island, which was something I escaped to in my dreams as a child. And I appreciated the freedom that I had there. One thing I would do was have no clothes on and be able to swim nude in very clear water. And I appreciated that but at the same time I—I realized, or I think I felt more that I needed people. I'm more aware of my need for people than I was. Ah, I think I brought back some of the—the desire to be free when I came back here. Then the next place I went was on a hike with my husband up Mount Tamalpais—this was when we were courting. And the feelings that go along with that are that he loved me more then than he does now, and there was a great euphoria about our relationship. I brought some of that back with me too, but then I wanted to return to that, which I did. And we were again hiking up Mount Tamalpais, but then I began to appreciate the fact that I wasn't—that he was carrying part of—part of me in the relationship and I think I bring back that awareness now too, to the present situation—both the joy and the realization that I have to carry myself along.

F: Well, I think a number of you experienced quite a bit of integration of these two opposites, *there* and *now*. If you do this with any uncomfortable situation, you can really pinpoint what's missing in this here-and-now situation. Very often the *there* situation gives you a cue for what's missing in the now, what's different in the now. So, whenever you get bored or tense, always withdraw—especially the therapists among you. If you fall asleep when the patient doesn't bring any interesting things, it saves *your* strength, and the patient will either wake you up or come back with some more interesting material. And if not, you at least have time for a snooze.

Withdraw to a situation from which you get support, and then come back with that regained strength to reality. You know Hercules is the famous symbol of self-control. You know, that obsessional character who cleaned out the Augean stables and so on. Now the most important story may be of Hercules' attempt to kill Anteos. As soon as Anteos touched the ground, he regained his strength, and that's what happens in the withdrawal. Of course the optimum withdrawal is the withdrawal into your body. Get in touch with yourself. Turn your attention to your physical existence. Mobilize your inner resources. Even if you get in touch with your fantasy of being on an island or in a warm bathtub, or to any unfinished situation, this will give you a lot of support when you return to reality.

Now normally the *élan vital*, the life force, energizes by sensing, by listening, by scouting, by describing the world—how is the world there. Now this life force apparently first mobilizes the center—*if* you have a center. And the center of the personality is what used to be called the soul: the emotions, the feelings, the spirit. Emotions are not a nuisance to be discharged. The emotions are the most important motors of our behavior: emotion in the widest sense—whatever you feel—the waiting, the joy, the hunger. Now these emotions, or this basic energy, this life force is apparently differentiated in the organism by what I would like to call the hormonic differentiation. This basic excitement is differentiated, let's say by the adrenal glands, into anger and fear: by the sex glands into libido. It might, in case of adjustment to a loss, be turned into grief. Then this emotional excitement mobilizes the muscles, the motoric system. Every emotion, then, expresses itself in the muscular system. You can't imagine anger without muscular movement. You can't imagine joy, which is more or less identical with dancing, without muscular movement. In grief there is sobbing and crying, and in sex there are also certain movements, as you all know. And these muscles are used to move about, to take from the world, to touch the world, to be in contact, to be in touch.

Any disturbance of this excitement metabolism will diminish your vitality. If these excitements cannot be transformed into their specific activities but are stagnated, then we have the state called anxiety, which is a tremendous excitement held up, bottled up. *Angoustia* is the Latin word for narrowness. You narrow the chest, to go through the narrow path; the heart speeds up in order to supply the oxygen needed for the excitement, and so on. If excitement cannot flow into activity through the motoric system, then we try to desensitize the sensoric system to reduce this excitement. So we find all kinds of desensitization: frigidity, blocking of the ears, and so on—all these holes in the personality that I talked about earlier.

So, if we are so disturbed in our metabolism, and have no center from which we can live, we have to do something, we want to do something to collect again the wellspring, the foundation of our being. Now there is not such a thing as total integration. Integration is never completed; maturation is never completed. It's an ongoing process for ever and ever. You can't say, "Now I've eaten a steak and now I am satisfied; now I'm no more hungry," and for the rest of your life there is no more hunger. There's always something to be integrated; always something to be learned. There's always a possibility of richer maturation—of taking more and more responsibility for yourself and for your life. Of course, taking responsibility for your life and being rich in experience and ability is identical. And this is what I hope to do here in this short seminar—to make you understand how much you gain by taking responsibility for every emotion, every movement you make, every thought you have—and shed responsibility for *anybody* else. The world is not there for your expectation, nor do you have to live for the expectation of the world. We touch each other by honestly being what we are, not by intentionally *making* contact.

Responsibility, in one context, is the idea of obligation. If I take responsibility for somebody else, I feel omnipotent: I have to interfere with his life. All it means is, I have a duty—I believe I have the duty to support this person. But responsibility can also be spelled *response-ability*: the ability to respond, to have thoughts, reactions, emotions in a certain situation. Now, this responsibility, the ability to *be* what one *is*, is expressed through the word "I." Many agree with Federn, a friend of Freud, who maintained that the ego is a substance, and I maintain that the ego, the *I*, is merely a symbol of identification. If I say that I am hungry now, and in an hour's time I say I am not hungry, this is not a contradiction. It is not a lie, because in between I have eaten lunch. I identify with my state right now, and I identify with my state afterward.

Responsibility means simply to be willing to say "I am I" and "I am what I am—I'm Popeye, the sailor man." It's not easy to let go of the fantasy or concept of being a child in need, the child that wants to be loved, the child that is afraid to be rejected, but all those events are those for which we are not taking responsibility. Just as I said in regard to self-consciousness, we are not willing to take the responsibility that we are critical, so we project criticism onto others. We don't want to take the responsibility for being discriminating, so we project it outside and then we live in eternal demands to be accepted, or the fear of being rejected. And one of the most important responsibilities—this is a *very* important transition—is to take responsibility for our projections, re-identify with these projections, and become what we project.

The difference between Gestalt Therapy and most other types of psychotherapy is essentially that we do *not* analyze. We *integrate*. The old mistake of mixing up understanding and explanatoriness is what we hope to avoid. If we explain, interpret, this might be a very interesting intellectual game, but it's a dummy activity, and a dummy activity is worse than doing nothing. If you do nothing, at least you *know* you do nothing. If you engage in a dummy activity, you just invest time and energy in unproductive work and possibly get more and more conditioned to doing these futile activities— wasting your time, and if anything getting deeper and deeper into the morass of the neurosis.

It would be wonderful if we could be so wise and intelligent that our rationality could domineer our biological life. And this polarity of mind vs. body is not the only polarity. There are other things to the human being than these two instruments. This identification with the intellect, with explanation, leaves out the total organism, leaves out the body. You *use* your body instead of *being* some-body. And the more all the thinking goes into the computing, into manipulation, the less energy is left for the total self. Since you have bracketed off your body, the result is that you feel like being nobody, because you have no body. There's no body in your life. No wonder so many people, if they are out of the routine of their daily work, get their "Sunday neurosis" when they are really faced with their boredom and the emptiness of their lives.

Gestalt Therapy is an existential approach, which means we are not just occupied with dealing with symptoms or character structure, but with the total existence of a person. This existence, and the problems of existence, in my opinion are mostly very clearly indicated in dreams.

Freud once called the dream the *Via Regia*, the royal road to the unconscious. And I believe it is really the royal road to integration. I never know what the "unconscious" is, but we know that the dream definitely is the most spontaneous production we have. It comes about without our intention, will, deliberation. The dream is the most spontaneous expression of the existence of the human being. There's nothing else as spontaneous as the dream. The most absurd dream doesn't disturb us as being absurd at the time: We feel it is the

real thing. Whatever you do otherwise in life, you still have some
kind of control or deliberate interference. Not so with the dream.
Every dream is an art work, more than a novel, a bizarre drama.
Whether or not it's *good* art is another story, but there is always lots
of movement, fights, encounters, all kinds of things in it. Now if my
contention is correct, which I believe of course it is, all the different
parts of the dream are fragments of our personalities. Since our aim
is to make every one of us a wholesome person, which means a
unified person, without conflicts, what we have to do is put the
different fragments of the dream together. We have to *re-own* these
projected, fragmented parts of our personality, and *re-own* the
hidden potential that appears in the dream.

Because of the phobic attitude, the avoidance of awareness,
much material that is our own, that is part of ourselves, has been
dissociated, alienated, disowned, thrown out. The rest of our potential is not available to us. But I believe most of it *is* available, but as
projections. I suggest we start with the impossible assumption that
whatever we believe we see in another person or in the world is
nothing but a projection. Might be far out, but it's just unbelievable
how much we project, and how blind and deaf we are to what is
really going on. So, the re-owning of our senses and the understanding of projections will go hand in hand. The difference between
reality and fantasy, between observation and imagination—this differentiation will take quite a bit of doing.

We can reassimilate, we can take back our projections, by projecting ourselves completely into that other thing or person. What is
pathological is always the *part*-projection. *Total* projection is called
artistic experience, and this total projection is an identification with
that thing in question. I give you one idea, for instance. In Zen, you
are not allowed to paint a single branch until you have become that
branch.

So, I want to start out with a simple experiment to produce
magic, to transform ourselves—metamorphose ourselves into something we are apparently not, to learn to identify with something we
are not. Let's start with something very simple. Will you all observe
me. I'm going to make some faces and expressions and I want you,

without words or sounds, to copy my expressions and see whether you can really feel that you become me and my expressions. Now watch this. Go along with it. The main thing is the facial expression. . .

Now I tell you how I did it. I imagined a situation and went into that situation, and I had the impression—I think most of you got quite a bit of the feeling of identification, not so much thinking, just simply following.

Now let's take another step. You come up here and talk to me—just say anything. (as the person speaks, Fritz imitates his words, voice inflection, and facial expressions) Pair up and do this, and again try to really get the feel of being this other person. . .

Now I want each one of you to transform yourself into something a little bit more different. Say, transform yourself into a road. . .

Now transform yourself into a motorcar. . .

Now transform yourself into a six-months-old baby. . .

Now transform yourself into the mother of that baby. . .

Now transform yourself into that same baby again. . .

Now the same mother. . .

Now the same baby. . .

Now be two years of age. . .

Now transform yourself into your present age, the age you are. . . Can everyone perform that miracle?

Now, I want to show you how to use this identification technique with dreams. This is quite different from what the psychoanalysts do. What's usually done with a dream is to cut it to pieces, and follow up by association what it means, and interpret it. Now we might possibly get some integration by this procedure, but I don't quite believe it, because in most cases this is merely an intellectual game. Many of you may have been brainwashed by psychoanalysis, but if you want to get something real from a dream, do *not* interpret. Do *not* play intellectual insight games or associate or dissociate freely or unfreely to them.

In Gestalt Therapy we don't interpret dreams. We do something much more interesting with them. Instead of analyzing and further cutting up the dream, we want to bring it back to life. And the way to bring it back to life is to re-live the dream as if it were happening now. Instead of telling the dream as if it were a story in the past, act it out in the present, so that it becomes a part of yourself, so that you are really involved.

If you understand what you can do with dreams, you can do a tremendous lot for yourself on your own. Just take any old dream or dream fragment, it doesn't matter. As long as a dream is remembered, it is still alive and available, and it still contains an unfinished, unassimilated situation. When we are working on dreams, we usually take only a small little bit from the dream, because you can get so much from even a little bit.

So if you want to work on your own, I suggest you write the dream down and make a list of *all* the details in the dream. Get every person, every thing, every mood, and then work on these to *become* each one of them. Ham it up, and really transform yourself into each of the different items. Really *become* that thing—whatever it is in a dream—*become* it. Use your magic. Turn into that ugly frog or whatever is there—the dead thing, the live thing, the demon—and stop thinking. Lose your mind and come to your senses. Every little bit is a piece of the jigsaw puzzle, which together will make up a much larger whole—a much stronger, happier, more completely *real* personality.

Next, take each one of these different items, characters, and parts, and let them have encounters between them. Write a script. By "write a script," I mean have a dialogue between the two opposing parts and you will find—especially if you get the correct opposites—that they always start out fighting each other. All the different parts—any part in the dream is yourself, is a projection of yourself, and if there are inconsistent sides, contradictory sides, and you use them to fight each other, you have the eternal conflict game, the self-torture game. As the process of encounter goes on, there is a mutual learning until we come to an understanding, and an appreciation of differences, until we come to a oneness and integration of the two opposing forces. Then the civil war is finished, and your energies are ready for your struggles with the world.

Each little bit of work you do will mean a bit of assimilation of something. In principle, you can get through the whole cure—let's call it cure or maturation—if you did this with every single thing in one dream. Everything is there. In different forms the dreams change, but when you start like this, you'll find more dreams will come and the existential message will become clearer and clearer.

So I would like from now on to put the accent on dreamwork. We find all we need in the dream, or in the perimeter of the dream, the environment of the dream. The existential difficulty, the missing part of the personality, they are all there. It's a kind of central attack right into the midst of your non-existence.

The dream is an excellent opportunity to find the holes in the personality. They come out as voids, as blank spaces, and when you get into the vicinity of these holes, you get confused or nervous. There is a dreadful experience, the expectation, "If I approach this, there will be catastrophe. I will be *nothing*." I have already talked a bit about the philosophy of nothingness. This is the impasse, where you avoid, where you become phobic. You suddenly get sleepy or remember something very important you have to do. So if you work on dreams it is better if you do it with someone else who can point out where you avoid. Understanding the dream means realizing when you are avoiding the obvious. The only danger is that this other person might come too quickly to the rescue and tell you what is going on in you, instead of giving yourself the chance of discovering yourself.

And if you understand the meaning of each time you identify with some bit of a dream, each time you translate an *it* into an *I*, you increase in vitality and in your potential. Like a debt collector you have your money invested all over the place, so take it back. And on the other hand, begin to understand the dummy activities where you waste your energies like, let's say, when you're bored. Instead of saying, "I'm bored," and find out what you're actually interested in, you suffer and stay with what is boring to you. You torture yourself with staying there, and at the same time, whenever you torture yourself you torture your environment. You become a gloom-caster. If you *enjoy* the gloom-casting, if you *accept* it, that's fine, because then the whole thing becomes a positive experience. Then you take responsibility for what you're doing. If you enjoy self-torture, fine. But there's always the question of accepting or not accepting, and accepting is not just tolerating. Accepting is getting a present, a gift. The balance is always gratefulness for what *is*. If it's too little, you feel resentful; if it's too much, you feel guilty. But if you get the balance, you grow in gratefulness. If you make a sacrifice, you feel resentful; if you give a present, you give something surplus and you feel fine. It's a closure—completion of a gestalt.

Q: We practice, in living with each other, what some people would call the amenities. Could you draw a line between taking responsibility and practicing the amenities?

F: Yah. You take responsibility for playing a phony role. You play polite to keep the other person happy.

Any time you use the words *now* and *how*, and become aware of this, you grow. Each time you use the question *why*, you diminish in stature. You bother yourself with false, unnecessary information. You only feed the computer, the intellect. And the intellect is the whore of intelligence. It's a drag on your life.

So the simple fact is that against the—excuse this expression—evil of self-alienation, self-impoverishment, there's only the remedy of re-integrating, taking back what is rightfully yours. Each time you change an *it* or a *noun* into an *I* or a *verb* you get, let's say, a ten-thousandth of your potential back, and it will accumulate. Each time you can integrate something it gives you a better platform, where again you can facilitate your development, your integration.

Don't try to make a perfectionist program out of it, that you *should* chew up every bit of what you're eating, that you *should* make a pause between the different bites so that you can complete one situation before you start the other; to change *every* noun and *it* into an *I*. Don't torture yourself with these demands, but realize this is the basis of our existence and discover that this is how it is. It is how it should be and it should be how it is.

Dreamwork Seminar

INTRODUCTION

Basically I am doing a kind of individual therapy in a group setting, but it's not limited to this; very often a group happening—happens to happen. Usually I only interfere if the group happening comes merely to mind-fucking. Most group therapy is nothing but mind-fucking. Ping-pong games, "who's right?," opinion exchanges, interpretations, all that crap. If people do this, I interfere. If they are giving their experience, if they are honest in their expression—wonderful. Often the group is very supportive, but if they are merely "helpful," I cut them out. Helpers are con men, interfering. People have to grow by frustration—by skillful frustration. Otherwise they have no incentive to develop their own means and ways of coping with the world. But sometimes very beautiful things do happen, and basically there are not too many conflicts, everybody who is in the group participates. Sometimes I have people who don't say a single word through the whole five-week workshop and they go away and say that they have changed tremendously, that they did their own private therapy work or whatever you want to call it. So anything can happen. As long as you don't structure it, as long as you work with your intuition, your eyes and ears, then something is bound to happen.

Two years ago I read a paper at the American Psychological Association. I claimed all individual therapy to be obsolete, and pointed out the advantages of the workshop. I believe that in the workshop, you learn so much by understanding what's going on in this other person, and realize that so much of his conflicts are your own, and by identification you learn. Learning equals discovery. You discover yourself, and awareness is the means of discovery.

Now I'm slowly coming to the insight that workshops and group therapy also are obsolete, and we are going to start our first Gestalt kibbutz next year. A Gestalt kibbutz is so far the following fantasy, though we have already some actual materials available. I expect to have a permanent number of people, about 30. The division between staff and seminarians will be obsolete. The main thing is, the community spirit enhanced by—let's call it for the time being, for lack of a better expression, therapy. The whole thing is meant to be growth experience and we hope that in this time we can produce *real* people, people who are willing to take a stand, people who are willing to take responsibility for their lives.

In our work here, with Gestalt Therapy, we distinguish two types of work. One is the seminar, and one is the workshop. The workshop is a very limited number of people, up to fifteen, and there we *work*. The large week-end seminar has another purpose—to get you acquainted with what we are doing, and in spite of this, I hope you still will learn *something*. Now these lecture-demonstration seminars are not therapeutic workshops. They're a kind of sampling situation, and any growth experience or therapeutic experience is purely coincidental.

In order to give some idea of what Gestalt Therapy is, there are always a number of people who volunteer to work with me, and I want to clarify my position. I am responsible only for myself and for nobody else. I am not taking responsibility for any of you—you are responsible for yourselves. Fortunately or unfortunately, I've lately gotten such a reputation as a therapist that I can't possibly live up to it. It was about three years ago when I finally could accept what people always told me, that I was a genius. This lasted only three months, and I discovered that I didn't have it in me to be a genius any more. It really doesn't matter one way or another.

I am not God, I am a catalyst. I am well enough versed in understanding projections and so on, to be able to differentiate when it's observation, or whether I have to take a role in this person's life—they make me a wailing wall, or a papa, or a scoundrel, or the wise man. My function as a therapist is to help you to the awareness of the here and now, and to frustrate you in any attempt to break out of this. This is my existence as a therapist, in the therapy role. I haven't managed it yet for many other segments of my life. You see, like every other psychologist or psychiatrist, I solve my problems to quite an extent *outside*. The fact that I'm so happy in integration means that my own integration is incomplete.

So if you want to go crazy, commit suicide, improve, get "turned on," or get an experience that will change your life, that's up to you. I do my thing and you do your thing. Anybody who does not want to take the responsibility for this, please do not attend this seminar. You came here out of your own free will. I don't know how grown up you are, but the essence of a grown-up person is to be able to take responsibility for himself—his thoughts, feelings, and so on. Any objections?. . . Okeh.

Basically, I would say that we encounter two types of clients or patients, and roughly speaking there are the ones who come with goodwill, and the others, those who are clever. The clever people are usually recognized by a specific kind of smile, a kind of smirk, a smirk that says, "Oh, you're an idiot! I know better. I can outwit you and control you." And whatever one tries to do will run off, like the water off the famous duck's back, and nothing will penetrate. These people need quite a bit of work. Very many people do not want to work. Anybody who goes to a therapist has something up his sleeve. I would say roughly 90% don't go to a therapist to be cured, but to be more adequate in their neurosis. If they are power mad, they want to get more power. If they are intellectual, they want to have more elephantshit. If they are ridiculers, they want to have a sharper wit to ridicule, and so on.

Now we are going to have some of these here, and in the short time we have at our disposal, I will very often throw them out from this hot seat. But when you find somebody who is really suffering and is bothered by the aridness of his existence, then with his cooperation we can do a relatively quick job.

Two weeks ago I had a wonderful experience—not that it was a cure, but at least it was an opening up. This man was a stammerer, and I asked him to increase his stammer. As he stammered, I asked him what he feels in his throat, and he said, "I feel like choking myself." So, I gave him my arm, and said, "Now, choke me." "God damn, I could kill you!" he said. He got really in touch with his anger and spoke loudly, without any difficulties. So, I showed him he had an existential choice, to be an angry man or be a stutterer.

And you know how a stutterer can torture you, and keep you on tenterhooks. Any anger that is not coming out, flowing freely, will turn into sadism, power drive, and other means of torturing.

So we don't need any more the year-long therapies. On the other hand, I am often very much over-estimated in what I am doing. I am not perfect, I am a son-of-a-bitch, I am sometimes very nice, I am not omnipotent, I cannot produce any magic, so I have got very much my limitations and very often I find somebody coming forth who has no other aim than to show what a nincompoop I am. I know this anyhow, that in certain situations I am impotent, I am helpless, and I don't *have to* win.

So, apart from this limitation, that I reserve the right to break off whatever we do—in some cases I even throw people out—but within this limitation I am *available*, and please, I am available only within these working hours. Outside these working hours, I am not available. I know some people have the compulsion to interfere with other people's lives, and have to act out their very interesting life, have to run about broadcasting of their tragedies, and so on. They have to choose other victims for that purpose. Apart from this, I am open for work, and I especially prefer to work with dreams. I believe that in a dream, we have a clear existential message of what's missing in our lives, what we avoid doing and living, and we have plenty of material to re-assimilate and re-own the alienated parts of ourselves. In Gestalt Therapy we write the "self" with lower case s, not capital S. Capital S is a relic from the time when we had a soul, or an ego, or something extra special; "self" means just yourself—for better, for worse, in sickness, in health, and nothing else.

I use six implements to be able to function. One is my skill, one is kleenex. Then there is the hot seat. This is where you are invited if you want to work with me. And there is the empty chair which will implement quite a lot of your personality and other—let's call it for the time being—intrapersonal encounters. Then I have my cigarettes—right now I have got a very nice one, a Shaman cigarette—and my ashtray. Finally, I need someone who is willing to work with me—someone who is willing to stay in the *now* and do some work with dreams. So, I'm available. Who really wants to work with me and not just make a fool of me?

SAM

Sam: (speaks rapidly) My name is Sam. . .[1]

Fritz: I have met Sam before. We met before.

S: A—across the table, eating.

F: Yah. But you never worked with me.

S: No. . .

F: Now please don't change your posture. What do you notice about his posture?

X: He's up pretty tight.

F: He's a closed system. And not only is he a closed system, but the right side goes to the left and the left side to the right. So, how mixed up can you get? He hasn't said anything yet but you can see how much he expresses with the posture. . .

S: Yeah, I feel very secure. (laughter)

F: Will you do me a favor? See how you feel when you open up. Yah. . .

S: I feel my heart pounding.

F: Ahah. Now we get stage fright. Not quite so secure. And— you see I will often give you some remarks in between—anxiety, as it's called in psychiatry, is considered a very difficult problem. It's actually nothing but stage fright. If you are in the *now*, you have security. As soon as you jump out of the now, for instance into the future, the gap between the now and the then is filled with pent-up excitement and it's experienced as anxiety. . .

S: I still feel my heart pounding.

F: Yah. Close your eyes and enter the now, namely the experience of your heart pounding and so on. Stay with your body. What do you experience now?

S: A very. . . My whole body, I can feel my heart pound. . . I feel myself breathing. . .

F: Yah? What are you experiencing?

S: Let's move on.

F: What's your objection to staying in the now? "Let's move on" means, again, towards the future. What's your objection to sit-

---

[1] Three periods (. . .) indicate a pause of five seconds or more.

ting there?. . . Do you have any experience like being stuck or feeling impatient or bored or anything?

S: I feel like this will be my only chance with you and I better make the most of it, and not spend time on anxiety.

F: Ahah. Will you put Sam in the empty chair and talk to Sam. "Sam, that's your only chance. Make the best out of it." (laughter). . .

S: Yeah. . . You're sitting there looking pretty stiff. . . What did you go up there for?

F: Change seats. Now the term I have for this is "write your script." You invent a script or dialogue between two opponents. This is part of integrating the fragmented parts of your personality, and these usually go in opposites—for instance, topdog and underdog. So talk back to him. Is it a he or she who sits there?

S: (defensively) It's a he.

F: You don't know how many people have a she as topdog where there's a "Jewish mother."

S: Well, I'm not so sure any more. (laughter) I don't know why I came up here. Just to see if—see if he could get at me, I guess. . .

[2] That's a hell of an attitude. (laughter) You think you're up here to fight with Fritz?. . .

No. No, I don't want to fight with Fritz. . . I don't know why I'm up here. . . Who are you, anyway?. . . What's it to you?. . . What's it to you?. . . (sigh). . .

F: You notice I always let the "patient" do all the work. What's your right hand doing?

S: Playing with my left hand.

F: Okeh. Can you invent a dialogue between your right hand and your left hand? Have them talk to each other.

S: I'm going to hold onto you, left hand. It makes me feel good.

I wanna hold on to you, too.

Well don't let go.

O.K.

I just—hey look, left hand. I just saw my left foot move. (laughter) I wonder what that means.

---

[2] A deeply indented paragraph indicates a change of seats between the "hot seat" and the "empty chair," when the person is in dialogue with himself.

Hey ah, right thumb, look at my left thumb. I'm gonna touch you. And I love you.

That feels very comforting.

You know left—left hand, ah, I'm gonna hold you.

That's very nice.

I don't feel like holding you any more. Now look what you're doing. You're pressing your thumb against your fingers. Looks like eyes. Doesn't it, left hand?

Yeah. You look more like an eye than I do.

Yeah.

F: Can you play the eyes now? Go to the audience. Do you have eyes, or has the audience eyes? Do you feel that you're being looked at, or do you have your own eyes and can do some seeing? Or as I call this type, many people are mirror-draggers. They always drag their mirrors around with them and use other people for reflection. They usually have no eyes themselves. . .

S: Hmm. . . I don't feel ah, governed by all your eyes.

F: What do you see?

S: But I'm really not looking at you either. Kind of a—just comfortable to look out and see everybody. But I'm not really looking at you. Scanning. . . There's my wife. . . I think you all are kind of curious. . . Yeah, and yet you care. . . But not too much.

F: Now play them. Take this chair. "I'm curious but I don't care too much about you."

S: I'm curious but I don't care too much about you. Really what I'm doing is waiting for *my* turn up there. You are kind of an interesting looking fellow, though. A bit closed. You don't look like you let go very much. . . Probably have a hard time getting any work done the way you're acting. But I suppose you don't know any other way to act.

F: Change seats again.

S: I wouldn't exactly call that a caring comment.

F: What would you call it?

S: (quietly) I don't think you're on my side, the way I feel. You're just taking care of number one. I'd call that a selfish comment.

(impatiently) Well, you are using up a lot of time. Nothing's happening. Let's get on with the—pretty soon he'll come to me. I'm number 20 or so. How long you gonna sit up there?

Just, just lay off! /F: Say this again./[3]

[4]Lay off. /F: Louder./

Lay off! /F: Louder!/

Lay off! /F: Louder./

LAY OFF!. . .

What are you getting so excited about? (laughter) No one's trying to get you. Relax. . .

F: How do you feel now?. . .

S: (sighs) Hmm. I'm holding my breath.

F: How does the world appear to you? The audience. . .

S: Curious, interested, caring, attentive.

F: Do you see anything?. . .

S: Some smiling faces. . .

F: Anything else? Do you see any colors?

S: Now, I do. /F: After I—/[5] After you mentioned it.

F: Ahah. Do you see any lights?

S: Now I do.

F: But not before.

S: No. Before, I saw a lot of interesting people.

F: I think you saw your mirror again. You used them for mirroring you. They exist only as far as they are of interest to you.

S: Yeah. Could be.

F: Okeh. You noticed already something here in Sam—something very interesting—that he has no eyes. In the course of our development we put up a game, a role, instead of actualizing ourselves, and during this process most people develop holes in their personality. Most people have no ears. At best they only listen to the abstractions, to the meaning of the sentences. Usually they don't even hear that. Many have no eyes. They have their eyes projected. They always feel they are being looked at. Other persons have no heart. Many people have no genitals. And very many people have no center, and without a center you wobble in life. Now these are a bit

---

[3]Fritz's instruction to repeat a sentence is enclosed between slashes (/ /) immediately following the sentence.

[4]The indented paragraph is also used for this repetition and does not indicate a change of seat in this context.

[5]Slashes (/ /) are also used to set off words spoken by one person while another person is speaking.

more complicated to investigate but I'm sure that we'll come across these holes in the personality during our work here.

LINDA

Linda: I dreamed that I watch. . . a lake. . . drying up, and there is a small island in the middle of the lake, and a circle of. . . porpoises—they're like porpoises except that they can stand up, so they're like porpoises that are like people, and they're in a circle, sort of like a religious ceremony, and it's very sad—I feel very sad because they can breathe, they are sort of dancing around the circle, but the water, their element, is drying up. So it's like a dying—like watching a race of people, or a race of creatures, dying. And they are mostly females, but a few of them have a small male organ, so there are a few males there, but they won't live long enough to reproduce, and their element is drying up. And there is one that is sitting over here near me and I'm talking to this porpoise and he has prickles on his tummy, sort of like a porcupine, and they don't seem to be a part of him. And I think that there's one good point about the water drying up, I think—well, at least at the bottom, when all the water dries up, there will probably be some sort of treasure there, because at the bottom of the lake there should be things that have fallen in, like coins or something, but I look carefully and all that I can find is an old license plate. . . That's the dream.

Fritz: Will you please play the license plate.

L: I am an old license plate, thrown in the bottom of a lake. I have no use because I'm no value—although I'm not rusted—I'm outdated, so I can't be used as a license plate. . . and I'm just thrown on the rubbish heap. That's what I did with a license plate, I threw it on a rubbish heap.

F: Well, how do you feel about this?

L: (quietly) I don't like it. I don't like being a license plate—useless.

F: Could you talk about this. That was such a long dream until you come to find the license plate, I'm sure this must be of great importance.

L: (sighs) Useless. Outdated. . . The use of a license plate is to allow—give a car permission to go. . . and I can't give anyone permission to do anything because I'm outdated... In California, they just paste a little—you buy a sticker—and stick it on the car, on the old license plate. (faint attempt at humor) So maybe someone could put me on their car and stick this sticker on me, I don't know...

F: Okeh, now play the lake.

L: I'm a lake... I'm drying up, and disappearing, soaking into the earth... (with a touch of surprise) *dying*... But when I soak into the earth, I become a part of the earth—so maybe I water the surrounding area, so... even in the lake, even in my bed, flowers can grow (sighs)... New life can grow... from me (cries)...

F: You get the existential message?

L: Yes. (sadly, but with conviction) I can paint—I can create—I can create beauty. I can no longer reproduce, I'm like the porpoise... but I... I'm... I... keep wanting to say I'm *food*... I... as water becomes... I water the earth, and give life—growing things, the water—they need both the earth and water, and the... and the air and the sun, but as the water from the lake, I can play a part in something, and producing—feeding.

F: You see the contrast: On the surface, you find something, some artifact—the license plate, the artificial you—but then when you go deeper, you find the apparent death of the lake is actually fertility...

L: And I don't need a license plate, or a permission, a license in order to...

F: (gently) Nature doesn't need a license plate to grow. You don't have to be useless, if you are organismically creative, which means if you are involved.

L: And I don't need permission to be creative... Thank you.

LIZ

Liz: I dream of tarantulas and spiders crawling on me. And it's pretty consistent.

Fritz: Okeh. Can you imagine I am Liz and you are the spider? Can you crawl on me now? How would you do this?

L: Up your leg and...

F: *Do* it, *do* it... (laughter)

L: I don't like spiders.

F: You are a spider now. It's your dream. You produced this dream. . .

L: (very quietly) All these people, they're covering me up.

F: Yah. Now, is there anybody here who you would like to take the role of a spider?

X: You mean to be a spider on her? /F: Yah./. . .

L: I don't see anyone that reminds me of a spider. (laughter)

F: In that case let's be satisfied with the dialogue. Put the spider in that chair and talk to the spider. . .

L: (sighs) I don't know what to say except to get it off of me.

F: Now be the spider. . .

L: I wanna get somewhere and you're in my way and so I'll crawl over you. . . That was very symbolic. (chuckles). . .

F: What do you say?. . .

L: I feel as though you're inanimate and it doesn't matter if I crawl all over you. /F: Again./ I feel as though you are inanimate and it doesn't matter if I crawl all over you.

F: Say this to the group. . .

L: I don't feel that way toward the group.

F: You feel this towards Liz?. . . Towards whom do you feel this?. . .

L: I don't feel that way. I think the spider feels that way.

F: Oh, you're not the spider.

L: No.

F: Can you say this again, "I am not the spider?"

L: I'm not a spider.

F: Go on. "I am not a spider."

L: I am not a spider.

F: Which means you're not what?

L: Aggressive.

F: Go on.

L: I'm not aggressive.

F: Give us all the negations; all of what you're not. "I'm not a spider, I'm not aggressive—"

L: I'm not. . . ugly, I'm not black and shiny, I don't have any more than two legs—

F: Now say all of this to Liz. . .

L: You're not black and shiny, you only have two legs, you're not aggressive, you're not ugly.

F: Change seats. Talk back.

L: Why do you crawl on me?

F: Go on, change seats on your own and write a dialogue.

L: Because you're not important.

But that's not true. I am important.

F: Now keep going. Now something begins to develop.

L: Who says you're important?

(quietly) Everybody tells me I'm important and so therefore I must be... It's healthy to be important and feel worthy. /F: Hmm?/ It's mentally healthy to be—feel self-important and worthy.

F: Sounds like a *program*, not like a *conviction*. (laughter)

L: (chuckling) It *is* a program.

F: Change seats again.

L: When are you going to *believe* that you are beautiful and healthy and all these things?

Someday when somebody like Mr. Fritz gives me a pill and I'll feel all better.

F: Now let the spider say the same—"I am ugly and I want to be beautiful." Let the spider say the same.

L: I am ugly and I want to be beautiful. To a spider-lover I probably am... But a lot of people don't appreciate spiders.

F: Okeh, go back and give the spider some appreciation.

L: Spiders are necessary because they keep the insect—the flying insect population down. (laughter) Spiders are fantastic because of the webs that they can build.

F: Talk to the spider directly in terms of *you*. "You are important because you—"

L: You are important because you keep the insect population down and you are important because you build beautiful webs... and you're important because you're alive.

F: Now change seats again... I would like you to try and let the spider return the appreciation.

L: You're important because you're a human being, and there are fifty zillion of you and so what makes you so important? (laughter)

F: Now you notice already the hole here in her personality— self-appreciation; lack of self-confidence. Other people have feelings of worthiness or something. She's got a hole. . .

L: But it's up to her to fill the hole.

F: No, it's up to the spider.

L: What can the spider do about it?

F: Well, find out. Let the spider give her some appreciation. . .

L: Spiders can't think of anything.

F: The spider plays stupid. Yah?

L: No. No. She does some neat things but they aren't—she doesn't do them as well as almost anybody she can think of.

F: Are you by any chance suffering from the curse of perfectionism?

L: Oh! *Yes.* (chuckles)

F: So whatever you do is never good enough.

L: Right.

F: Say this to her. . .

L: You do things adequately but never right, never perfectly.

F: Tell her what she *should* do, what she should be like.

L: She should. . .

F: "*You* should—" Never gossip about anybody who is present, especially when it's about yourself. (laughter) Always make it into an encounter. Talk *to* her.

L: You should be able to do anything and everything and do it perfectly. You're a very capable person, you've got the native intelligence to do it and you're too lazy.

F: Ah! You got the first appreciation—you are capable. At least she admits that much.

L: Well she was born with that. She didn't—(laughter)

F: Immediately you say something good about you, here comes the spider and shits on you. Do you see this?

L: Well I think that's true.

F: Yah. Now we have got here the typical topdog, underdog situation. The topdog is always righteous—sometimes right, but not too often—and *always* righteous. And the underdog is willing to believe the topdog. Now the topdog is a judge, is a bully. The underdog usually is very canny and controls the topdog with other means like *mañana* or "You're right," or "I try my best," or "I tried so hard," or "I forgot," things like that. You know that gimmick?

L: Oh yeah.

F: Okeh, now play the topdog-underdog game. The topdog sits here and the underdog there.

L: Why don't you ever do, ever—anything perfectly?

Because I try to do too many things. (laughter) I don't have enough time to spread myself around, and I like to read. . .

Why do you like to read? To escape?

F: What a *mean* topdog. (laughter)

L: Yes, but it's also to improve my mind. (laughter). . . I have to get some enjoyment out of life, besides being perfect.

F: Say this again. Say this again. . . Say this again. . . I dare you. . .

L: I have to get some enjoyment out of life besides being perfect.

F: This time I want to introduce a new element. Let the topdog go on talking to her, and I want her each time to answer back "fuck you" and see what happens.

L: You have a responsibility to yourself to fulfill yourself and get the most out of life and experience the most things and so on. . .

Fuck you. . . But the topdog's right. . .

F: Say this to—

L: But you're right.

F: Who is it? Papa, or Mama, or both together?

L: Grandma.

F: Grandma. Ahah. So put Grandma in that chair. . .

L: Everything you say is true. . . but I don't want them. . .

F: I'd like to try to work on a hunch and I might be completely wrong. Say "Grandma, you're a spider. . ."

L: (convincingly) Grandma, you're a spider. . .

F: Change seats. . .

L: (grandmotherishly) No I'm not, dear. I just want what's best for you. (laughter)

F: That is a stock phrase of the topdog as you probably recognize. . . Change seats again. Now I would like you to close your eyes and enter your self. What do you experience right now? Begin to feel something?

L: Feels like a spider.

F: What do you feel? What do you experience personally?

L: Do you mean physically?

F: Physically, emotionally, so far we have mostly think-think, talk-talk, things. . .

L: I feel like I'm—there's a spider sitting on me and I want to go do something.

F: What do you experience when the spider sits on you?

L: It feels like black up here.

F: No reactions to the spider?. . . If a spider really would crawl over you now what would you experience?

L: Adrenalin and jump and scream.

F: How? (Liz half-heartedly brushes away spider) Again. Spider's still there. . .

L: (monotonously) I'd jump up and down and scream for Walter to come and get it off of me.

F: Can you hear your dead voice? Are you aware that you are talking literature? Say this again and see whether we can believe you. . .

L: I'd scream and—

F: How?. . . How would you scream?

L: I c—I don't know if I could do it. I can hear it though when I do it. It just comes out.

F: How?. . .

L: (sighs) I feel too structured to scream.

F: Say this to your grandmother now.

L: I feel too structured to scream.

F: Okeh, apparently we would have to do quite a bit of work to get through this block of yours, through this armor. But I would like to spend a few minutes on a phony game. Are you willing to cooperate? I want you to write a script, a good girl and a bad girl talking to each other. "I'm a good girl, I do everything my grandmother wants me to do," and so forth. The bad girl says "fuck you" or whatever your bad girl would say.

L: I'm a good girl and I use all my potentials to the greatest degree: all my—as my grandmother would say—God-given creative abilities, my God-given intelligence and appearance and whatever. And I'm just a very nice person and I get along well with everybody. . .

That's very nice for you but you're not gonna get any kicks out of life because I have a very good time and you can go fuck yourself. (to Fritz) All I can think of is things that bad girls are supposed to do to have fun. But I don't—

F: Tell *her* that. Don't tell me.

L: See what you've done to me?. . . You don't enjoy yourself and I don't enjoy myself and we wallow around in it. I can't be bad and you can't be good. . .

F: Now this is a point which we would call the impasse. This is where she's stuck. Okeh, be the good girl again.

L: Well, if you'd listen to me we'd at least get some kicks being good. You have no self-discipline whatsoever and the greatest joys in life are productive ones. . .

The greatest joys in life should just be in experiencing it. . . Live a little here and now. . .

F: May I have a private consultation with you? Your bad girl—is she really so bad?

L: I think other people would think so.

F: Yah? Ask them. . .

L: Walter, would you think my bad girl so bad?

W: Ask them. Don't ask me. (laughter)

L: Chicken.

X: I want to know which way you feel best up there now.

L: Neither one.

F: Yah. This is the impasse. You're stuck. . .

X: Your bad girl isn't bad enough.

L: That's because she's only speaking in generalities. (laughter)

P: I think she's fine.

Q: I do, too.

R: Her bad girl's pretty great.

S: I think the good girl's a god-awful bore.

T: She's awfully self-righteous. The bad girl would be easier to get along with.

U: The bad girl would be much more fun.

V: The bad girl is almost unable to be bad. She's really too good to be called bad.

W: I was hoping you'd feel better being the bad girl after you got up there.

L: Well the bad girl really doesn't feel too self-righteous which is one of the things that the good girl would like to give up.

X: What is bad?

Y: Or good, for you?

L: Being unproductive and using your greatest potential—

F: Ahnh-ah. Bad is what Grandmother disapproves of, and good is what Grandmother approves of. When Grandmother feels bad she calls you bad, and when Grandmother feels good she calls you good. She simply killed your soul, and the whole potential of your soul is missing. It's all mind.

L: My soul?

F: No, there is only mind. So there's just a little bit of your potential used. I don't see any usage of your emotions, of your femininity, of your joy, *joie de vivre*. All that is waste-land so far. You are a "good girl." And behind the good girl there is always the spiteful brat. It's the worst possible diagnosis, because in order to be "good" you have to be a hypocrite—to be the good child, the obedient child—and all the opposition goes into spiting yourself. Life always works in polarities like this. On the surface you're open and compliant, while underneath you're sabotaging me, spiting me. A good girl is the girl that pleases poppa, momma, society. A bad girl is the girl who *dis*pleases. So, the only way a good child can assert itself is through spite. Spite, in this case, is *identity*—identical with being somebody, being something. So this is where you are stuck, between compliance and spite. Okeh.

L: Thank you, Fritz.

F: You notice that everything deals with the present. All talking *about* is out, all interpretation, all mind-fucking is discouraged. What is, is. A rose is a rose is a rose. Very strictly, phenomenologically, is she in touch with herself, is she in touch with her environment, is she in touch with her fantasy? And then you notice something else, this change of seats. I believe we are all fractionalized. We are divided. We are split up in many parts, and the beauty of working with a dream is that in a dream every part—not only every person, but every part is yourself.

CARL

Carl: The dream is a dream that's recurred twice.

Fritz: Those are the best, the most important dreams—the recurrent dreams. If I may say a word here about them. Freud coined a term "compulsive repetition." And he thought this compulsion of repetition leads to petrification and death instinct. And I believe it's just the opposite. If something comes up again and again, it means that a gestalt has not been closed. There is a problem which has not been completed and finished and therefore can't recede into the background. So if anything, it's an attempt to become alive, to come to grips with things. And very often these repetitive dreams are nightmares. Again, it's the opposite from Freud who thought that dreams are wishful thinking. In the nightmares you find always how you frustrate yourself. All right.

C: Well, it's a dream that I had when I was very young—I was about eleven—and the dream was after I had gotten a typhoid injection that had given me a very high fever. And I had this nightmare that night. And I also had it not so long ago, about three or four days after the death of a dog that I was very attached to—the same dream. And—

F: Tell the dream in the present tense.

C: It's pretty hard because I've thought about it several times as to where I'm located in the dream, but I'll try to do that. The scene is a ridge of mountains out here, and a flat desert with white sand. The sky is almost a black-blue—very dark sky, with the moon casting a very pale light over everything. And there's a train track crossing the desert in a perfectly straight line. And the train is coming along. And the sound that I hear is not the sound of a train whistle but rather a very high-pitched sort of electrical frequency whine or whistle-like sound but very steady. It hasn't got a dimension to it.

And I feel that I am in the sand—not directly in front of the train, but in the sand. I feel my head level is in the sand. I can see. And it's quite rich and often quite frightening, mainly because of the sound which is sort of infinite. And it starts and never ends. It just is there. And it drives very heavily on me. And the train sort of never ends. And I'm pretty sure it's death of some sort that's being represented in there. I'm not sure, though. I'm not positive. But the fear—I don't know if I can express this—it's not the convulsive fear of an imminent catastrophe. It's not like the spiders or the tarantulas or anything like I'm ready to flip out. It's much more of a very deep penetrating fear that's steadier. And as I think back on my life I think that those two dreams are the only real feelings of fright I've ever had. And I don't know if I can elaborate on the dream any more than that. I can't think of any other objects. There are no other people in the dream and—

F: Yah. So can you play the desert? "I am the desert. . ." What kind of existence would you lead if you were a desert?

C: If I were a desert I would be sand, I would have no construction. I would just be fluid sand that wove into itself all the time and was blown by the wind. I would roast during the day and be cold at night. Ah—I would go on and on and on without a beginning and without an end. . .

F: And if you were this ridge of mountains?. . .

C: If I were a ridge of mountains I would, again, roast during the day and be cold at night. I would have more character and cons—constancy. I would be more or less, sort of a backbone.

F: And if you were this train.

C: That's the one that I really feel is—if I were the train I would go, and go, and go, with tremendous drive and tremendous direction but never really accomplish—not the end so much that is being set out for as—*an* end that's important. I would just go, and go, and go, kind of. . .

F: Just a merry-go-round. /C: Yes./ As I said before, I see the neurosis as consisting of five layers. This dream is a *very* typical dream of the death layer or implosive layer, where people contract and nothing happens. The desert, as he has already interpreted, is death. There's no life visible. But at least we see something stirring— the power of the train. There's some energy somewhere. It's not leading anywhere, but there is power there. Behind the implosive layer—when we get through the impasse there—you'll find an explosive layer. And there are at least four types of explosions that a—let's call it a healthy person for the time being—must be able to experience. These are: *anger, joy, grief* and *orgasm*. I especially say orgasm and not sex because there is plenty of sex without explosion. Now these explosions in themselves are not the meaning of life or existence. They are kind of an energy that bursts, so to say, a dam, and links up with the authentic person. So that the feeling, the ability to participate, to be emotionally involved, becomes possible. Once you're through the explosive layer, the authentic person, the real person comes through. Now you see here he is stuck in the implosive layer. It also tries to come into connection with real danger of death. So can you play the train. "I'm a train. . ."

C: I'm a train and I'm going somewhere, but it's nowhere. It has direction—/F: "*I* have direction."/ I have direction. I have *enormous* direction, straight on a track. But there's no home, there's no resting place at the end. There's always a straight track and a direction of power, a direction to be going with power. . . I'm a train and a train doesn't relate with people. /F: "*I*—"/ I don't relate with people when I'm a train. I go down the track. . .

X: Do you carry people?

C: Nope.

F: Did you notice the glee that came? (laughter) It was nearly a smirk. "No, I don't carry people. . ." Now I'm interested, what is your left foot doing to your right?. . .

C: Sort of exercising my knee.

F: You're exercising your knee. . . Could you see whether your knee can do some exercise on its own. /C: Yeah./ (Carl exercises knee). . . Okeh, so be the tracks now. . .

C: I am the tracks. I'm lying on my back and life is running over me. . .

F: So at least we have the word "life" now for the first time, really. Now have a conversation between the tracks and the train. . .

C: I feel like I can just let my imagination go and come up with things but they don't feel right. But they are right? Is that what you want, or do you want me to try to pin it down to me?

F: You mean you want to bring associations? I don't get—

C: Well, what I'm doing is just playing. I mean I feel like I can make connections but they're just happening. They don't feel legitimate. They don't feel like they're drawn from me—myself.

F: Okeh, in other words maybe you're not so completely dead. Maybe you are somewhat creative. So let's—

C: Well, that's what it is. It's nothing but my own creation. All right. I'm the train and that's the tracks. I ride straight ahead on you and follow where you lead—straight ahead to nowhere. . .

I direct you, but I direct you passively. Your force directs you but I channel where you go—I channel where your force goes.

That's right. You control where I go and all my force is

channeled into where you tell me to go. But I'm the power. I'm the life. You're inanimate. You're dead. All you do is direct me. . .

I just got people into it. Shall I pull them in and do with it?

F: Oh! That's wonderful. (some laughter) So it's not all dead. Now we get people in.

C: What I feel is that. . .

F: Well you got the first existential message already. A dream to me is an existential message, so apparently you already have gotten the first message. We need people. Mechanics don't do the whole thing by themselves. Okeh, put people in.

C: Well, I feel like the train is me and the tracks are my mother. Well that was the association at any rate. And that would be that— playing my mother or the tracks—

I direct you. I am inanimate, I am dead, but nevertheless I structure your life force. And although you are the life, I lead you in such a way that you are not unique, you're not your own thing. . .

F: You know something? I don't recognize your mother's voice. I think you're talking literature. So play your mother.

C: I direct you.

F: This is how she speaks?. . .

C: I can't come out with the way she speaks.

F: Now go back and tell her that.

C: I can't revive or reconstruct how you speak, Mother.

F: What does she answer?. . . You see, we pick up every experience and feed the experience back. Carl Rogers first found the feedback technique but he always feeds back mostly sentences. We feed back the experience—the part that is alive.

C: I can't reconstruct how you—how you speak, Mother.

F: What would she answer?

C: (accusingly) It's because you never listen to me. (laughter and applause)

No, it's because you never spoke to me. You always spoke *at* me—trying to direct me away from myself.

F: You see, the desert begins to bloom—something alive, some real things come in now.

C: (as mother again) I never try to direct you. That's what you always say. You never want to listen to me. You're just selfish. I only want what's best for you. (chuckles)

F: Say this again.

C: I only want what's best for you.

F: Talk back.

C: Yeah, but you're about as far away from knowing what's best for me as, as ah—you're pretty far away from knowing what's best for me.

But you never agree with me. You never do what I say, ever. Like if I say to do something, that's the kiss of death. You always do the other thing.

That ought to teach you to keep your mouth shut. (laughter) Ah, you've gotta try to pick up on where *I* am, or who I am, and let me lead my life and not try to control it.

F: Say this again.

C: And not try to control it. That's where it's at.

F: Now let's go back to the dream. And what would happen if the train would leave the straight and narrow path—would jump the rails?

C: Well, the desert will encircle it and it doesn't stay night all the time. But the scene is different. The scene is just of creativity. The problem that just comes to my mind is that I don't often feel constricted. I did. I feel I broke away from it—that I am creative, I do my own thing. I don't feel bound. I see how this thing's set up but I think I saw it as a young boy, so I left home early and I developed counter-techniques to the "Jewish mother" scene which were equally devastating when I applied them to the world. But they worked for that scene.

F: Now I noticed—you say you are not restricted—but all the movements you do are usually just in your hands. Once or twice you've made a little bit of an excursion but otherwise—ah, I don't quite get your posture. It looks to me a little bit of a cross between a turtle and a football tackle. (laughter) /C: A ram./ Yah. That you fight with your head first.

C: Yeah, I do sit forward. It feels more comfortable, though. I do lead with my head.

F: Yah. . . So let's finish up with some discussion between your head and the rest of your body. . .

C: Body, you—you're apart from me. You don't really represent me.

But sometimes I represent you completely. Sometimes I am who you are and there is no you.

That's true but that's either black or white. There's no to-getherness between us. Either we're a body or we're a head. When we played football you were the body. That was all we were.

F: Did you play football?

C: Yeah. And when we play lawyer we're all your head. We're a machine—just a head machine.

F: Yah, I have a suggestion to make. You should do two things. One is to get involved in expressive dancing to mobilize you. And the other is to get some treatment from Ida Rolf or one of her pupils. Ida Rolf has a method of re-aligning the body, called structural integration. There's too much of becoming the ram, the tackle, the train, the blind energy. Of course this is what the tackler is—there's no differentiation of the body. If you would dance you wouldn't be effective as a football tackler. But the fact is that you choose that. So in order to get whole again, to be somebody, to get out of the death layer—if you can re-own your body, I think you will find this very valuable. You see, the third layer—the implosive layer—is just the opposite of the explosive. In implosive we implode, we contract, we pull ourselves together and then you become a *thing*. /C: A train./ Yah, a thing instead of something alive. Okeh.

NORA

Nora: In my dream I was in an incomplete house and the stairs have no rails. I climb up the stairs and get very high, but they go nowhere. I know that in reality it would be awful to climb that high on these stairs. In the dream it's bad enough, but it's not that awful, and I always wonder how I could endure it.

Fritz: Okeh. Be this incomplete house, and repeat the dream again.

N: Well, I climb the stairs and the stairs have no rails on the side.

F: "I am an incomplete house, I have no. . ."

N: I am in an incomplete house and I'm climbing the stairs and—

F: Describe what kind of house you are.

N: Well it has a—

F: "I am—"

N: I'm the house?

F: Yah, you're the house.

N: And the house is—

F: *"I am—"*

N: I am the house and I'm incomplete. And I have only the skeleton, the parts and hardly the floors. But the stairs are there. And I don't have the rails to protect me. And yet I do climb and—

F: No, no. You're the house. You don't climb.

N: Yet I'm climbed on. And then I end somewhere on the top, and it—and it leads nowhere and—

F: Say this to Nora. You're the house, and talk to Nora.

N: You're climbing on me and you're getting nowhere. And you might fall. Usually you fall.

F: You see? That's what I try to do—to climb on you and I get nowhere. It took a long time before you even could identify with the house. Now say the same thing to some people here, as the house. "If you try to climb on me. . ."

N: If you try to climb on me, you'll fall.

F: Can you tell me more what you're doing to them, if they're trying to live in you and so on?. . . (Nora sighs) Are you a comfortable house to live in?

N: No, I'm open and unprotected and there are winds blowing inside. (voice sinks to whisper) And if you climb on me you'll fall. And if you'll judge me. . . I'll fall.

F: You begin to experience something? What do you feel?

N: I want to fight.

F: Say this to the house.

N: I want to fight you. I don't care about you. I *do*. I don't *want* to. (crying). . . I don't want to cry and I don't want you—I don't even want you to see me cry. (cries). . . I'm afraid of you. . . I don't want you to pity me.

F: Say this again.

N: I don't want you to pity me. I'm strong enough without you, too. I don't need you and—I, I *wish* I don't need you.

F: Okeh, let the stairs have an encounter with the non-existent railings. "Railings, where are you to hold onto?"

N: Railings, I can live without you. I'm climbable. It would be nicer to have you though. It would be nicer to be complete, to have something on top of the concrete and to have nice polished rails.

F: What kinds of floors have you got?

N: Concrete. Concrete floors, just uncovered. . .

F: Pretty tough, hmmm? With a solid foundation.

N: Yeah.

F: Can you tell this to the group, that you have solid foundations?

N: You can walk and it's safe and you could live with it if you don't mind being a little bit uncomfortable. I'm dependable.

F: So what do you need to be complete?. . .

N: I don't know. I—I don't *think* I need, I—I just feel I—I want more.

F: Ahah. How can we make the house a bit warmer?

N: Well, cover it, close—put windows in it; put walls, curtains, nice colors—nice warm colors.

F: Okeh, can you be all the supplement—all of what's missing, and talk to the incomplete house. "I'm here to complete you, to supplement you."

N: I'm here to complete you. You are pretty good but you could be much better and much nicer to live in if you have me— you'd be warmer and brighter and softer—have nice colors, have maybe carpets and curtains, some soft and bright things and maybe some heating.

F: Change seats. Be the incomplete house.

N: Well you're luxury. You can do without luxury, too. . . And I don't know if I could afford you.

Well if you think I'm worthwhile then you could—then you'll try and get me. And it will make you feel nicer, better.

Well, aren't you really false? I mean aren't you actually only covering?. . .

You're the structure.

Yes, I am.

Well if you think you could manage to live without me just go ahead. Why don't you?

F: What is the left hand doing? Did you notice? Yah, do this some more. You see, we find something similar in psychosis, too. The psychotic has a language which we often don't understand, a language of his own. Now, in a not psychotic person, we mostly understand the movement of what's going on. But still better if we let the "patient" express what this means.

N: Well—

F: No, it was your left hand.

N: I'm not pushing you away. I'm tickling you. . .

F: Ahah. . . Now change seats again.

N: I really feel I'm stubborn and I'm persistent and I don't think I really need you. I mean, it would be fine if you're there—maybe even if you're there I'll try to remember how it was before. . .

I want to convince you, and I've got to try harder. . .

We could all live in concrete houses without walls.

F: What are you doing with your left hand? (Fritz rubs his face) This is what you're doing, yah?

N: Rubbing my face.

F: Let your fingers talk to your face.

N: I'm rubbing you. . . to get your attention. . .

Who are you?. . . I'm thinking too hard.

F: You're thinking too hard. Okeh. Nora, what do you feel about this little bit of work we did here? Terrified? /N: No./ Did you get an existential message?

N: It was great.

F: You got something, yah? Let me say something more about the dream altogether. You see, the whole idea of repression is nonsense. If you look, everything is there. Now the most important thing to understand is the idea of projection. Every dream or every story contains all the material we need. The difficulty is to understand the idea of fragmentation. All the different parts are distributed all over the place. A person, for instance, who has lost his eyes—who has a hole instead of eyes, will always find the eyes in the environment. He will always feel the world is looking at him.

Now Nora's projection is the incomplete house. She doesn't experience herself in the beginning as an incomplete house. It is projected as if she is living in this house. But she herself is the incomplete house. What's missing is warmth and color. As soon as she becomes the house, she admits that she has solid foundations and so on. If you're capable of projecting yourself totally into every little bit of the dream—and really *become* that thing—then you begin to reassimilate, to re-own what you have disowned, given away. The more you disown, the more impoverished you get. Here is an opportunity to take back. The projection often appears as something unpleasant—as a spider, or as a train, or as a dead house, an incomplete house. But if you realize, "This is my dream. I'm responsible for the dream. I painted this picture. Every part is me," then things begin to function and to come together, instead of being incomplete and fragmented. And very often the projection is not even visible, but it's obvious. If I have a staircase without railings it's obvious that the railings are somewhere in the dream but they're missing. They're not there. So where railings should be, there's a hole. Where warmth and color should be, there's a hole. So we find here a very brave, maybe stubborn person who can make it. Okeh.

I'd like to point out one of the most difficult problems to handle in therapy, and this problem is characterized by the word *it*, or the noun. "My memory is bad." "The thought slipped out." "The matches are needed for lighting cigarettes." What happens in the *it*, in the noun? I mentioned before the death layer, and though I am to quite an extent in disagreement with Freud's death instinct as Freud uses it, this petrification does often occur in the way of becoming something dead: a living organism becoming a thing, a process becoming a noun, a freezing of a high potential, a predictability, an easy use of words rather than experiencing living processes. This is one way that we are dead without knowing it.

If it were only this, we still could possibly handle it with a certain amount of comfort, or handle ourselves. But the thing goes further. The *it*, the noun, goes into the projection. It's been externalized. So first it's been killed and then it's been put outside of our organism. So it seems as if we have lost *it*, or this bit of life, completely. And once a projection has occurred, or once we have projected some potential, then this potential turns against us. As I mentioned before, instead of having eyes, we are *being seen*. We feel under observation. We feel either persecuted by the eyes—especially by judging eyes—or, if this is coupled with attending, instead of having our attention free to observe and explore and discover the world, we *need* attention; we want to be attended *to*. Instead of listening, we project the listening. We talk and expect other people to listen to us, but we are not even willing to listen to ourselves. Instead of having our own excitement mobilized, we expect the world to be exciting.

So, you see then how, in the *it*, these two difficulties combine. And both are meant to relieve us of our most valuable property. This property is the word—a very misused word—*response-ability*. Responsibility means the ability to respond: the ability to be alive, to feel, to be sensitive. Now we often have made of this responsibility the idea of obligation, which is identical with being a megalomaniac, omnipotent. We take over responsibility for somebody else. But responsibility simply means "I am I; I have taken and developed in myself what I can be." In other words, responsibility is the ability to respond and be fully responsible for oneself and for *nobody else*. This is, I believe, the most basic characteristic of the mature person.

Now, May here, wanted to come up and work. She told me that she has a wall between herself and the world. Of course here we have an *it* to work with. She says she has got a *thing*: something outside, something May is not responsible for. It just happens that she's a victim of circumstances.

If we alienate something that is really our own—my own potential, my life—then we become impoverished: Excitement, living, becomes less and less until we are walking corpses, robots, zombies. And I'm sure you know plenty of people who identify with their duty rather than their needs, with their business rather than with their family.

Now let's see what we can do with these ideas. So, we have to see whether you can re-identify this alienated part, and the means is playing that part which we have alienated. This wall is part of the self-alienation, of the disowning of something, of some potential, and we have to do the opposite of alienation—identification. The more you really become this thing again, the easier it is to assimilate and make our own again what we have thrown out. So could you please play the wall that is between you and me? Wait a moment. You are not ready. I can see that you are preoccupied with psychosomatic symptoms, so we can't expect that a full involvement can take place, because there is something going on *within* May. So, withdraw into your symptoms and describe what you experience right now. Start with the awareness continuum, with staying with the *now* and the *how*.

MAY

May: (weak monotone) Yes. I feel afraid and I'm shaking and my face is hot, and it's hard for me to breathe, and when I started talking I began to tense up.

Fritz: Close your eyes and tense up. Take responsibility for tensing up. See how you tense up; which muscles tighten?

M: It's in the top part of my body and in my chest and arms and hands. And it restricts my voice.

F: Can you tighten still more?. . . Yah. . . Okeh, now interrupt this, a little bit at least. Now you see what you're doing to yourself? We are often doing many things to ourselves instead of doing these to the world. Now let's make an experiment. Could you stand up please, May. Now could you tense—tighten *me* up as you tightened yourself up. Now just crush me. . . crush me. . . (May crushes Fritz, then sighs) Now sit down. . . How do you feel now?

M: (breathes heavily) I can't *stand* it.

F: Yah? What happened?

M: There were lights flashing in my eyes and I got so tense I just snapped.

F: Stay with your hands.

M: They're trembling.

F: Let them tremble. . . What else do you feel?

M: I feel numb.

F: Say this again.

M: I don't feel anything, I'm numb.

F: Now close your eyes and get into the numbness. . . How do you feel numb?

M: (whispers) I feel gray, grayish cold. . . I still feel closed in. . . It's just all gray. . .

F: You look as if you're in a hypnotic trance. Have you ever been hypnotized?

M: Have I ever been hypnotized? /F: Yah./. . . Yes.

F: Can you go back to the moment when you had been hypnotized? Who is hypnotizing you?

M: I can't go back.

F: You cannot go back. Who prevents you?. . .

M: I know I have been hypnotized but I cannot visualize it. I know who did it.

F: Can you talk to this person?

M: (sighs) It's very hard to see. Yes.

F: Ask him to help you to remember.

M: Doctor Peters, will you help me remember being hypnotized?

F: What does he answer?

M: Yes, May... You came into my office and you were going to have a baby. And I asked you if you would like to have your baby with hypnosis, and you said yes. So we worked on it, and that's the way your baby was born.

F: And you don't know how your baby was born?...

M: Yes, I can remember, but it was with hypnosis.

F: What are you feeling now?...

M: I, my head is very heavy. There's a pressure up here. My hands are almost disconnected from me.

F: Before we go into this I would like you to play a phony game with me. I want you to play the hypnotist, this doctor, and hypnotize me right now. How would you do that?

M: I don't know how I would do it. I can tell you the words he used.

F: Yah. You can be as phony as you like to, but I would like you to play this doctor, and I am May. What would you do about me? "Doctor, I want to get rid of my smoking. Can you hypnotize me? Get me out of it."

M: All right, May. Ah, throw your cigarette in the fireplace there and lean back and close your eyes and relax... Now, May, I want you not to think of anything; just to let your mind relax and your body relax... And relax, relax more and more... You're very, very relaxed now... That's how I would do it.

F: How do you feel now?

M: Relaxed more. (laughter)

F: How are your hands?

M: Well, they're shaking a little, but they're back. (laughs) I can feel them...

F: So, let's go back to the wall. Will you play the wall now...

M: I will not let you come in contact with anyone.

F: Say this to me. You're the wall and I'm May.

M: May, I will not let you contact anyone completely. You can know them and you can see them but you can never fully come in contact with them as a human being, as a person, and I refuse to let you do this. . .

F: Why not? (plays despondent) What have I done to deserve that?

M: Just being there you deserve it. I'm a very mean wall and I will not let you out.

F: Okeh, change roles now. Now be May. The wall has just spoken to her. . .

M: Like, you keep me from ever enjoying anything completely. I'd like to. . . I've got to find a way through you, wall. . .

And the wall says, All right, I'll retreat just a little bit; just enough to make you feel a little bit more comfortable, but I'm always there. . . And when you don't expect it, then I'll really get big again and crush you down.

F: Say this again to me.

M: (strongly) Oh, when you don't expect it I'll get *big* again and I will *crush* you.

F: Can you play a witch?

M: A witch?

F: Yah. "I'll go back there and wait for you and I'll get big and pounce on you." A real mean witch. (laughter)

M: To them?

F: Mm. To me, too. To your child, to your—

M: No, I can only do it to myself.

F: You can only do it to yourself. What kind of person is this who is doing this?

M: A strong person. . . ah, strong and wise and sort of a controlling person.

F: Could you close your eyes and look at this person. Describe this person. Is it a he or a she you're playing there?

M: It's a she—it's me.

F: Where did you get this pattern from?. . . You see I just can't believe that you are constitutionally so mean. . .

M: (quietly) I don't know where I got it, I can't see anyone. . .

F: What do you feel now?. . . Did you put the wall between you and your memory?

M: Yeah.

F: Yah. . . So let's go back to the dialogue between the wall and you. . .

M: I can't talk about it, or I *can't* talk, to the wall. I can't talk. . .

F: So we have to call in my assistant again. You just stymied Fritz. He's impotent, he's helpless, you say you can't, so you make me feel absolutely impotent and helpless. And here sits Fritz impotent and helpless. Play him now. . .

M: Talk to him or play him?

F: Play him first, and again develop dialogue.

M: May, see if you can—see if you can play the wall. . .

Oh, Fritz, I can't play the wall. Won't. . . I can't go beyond that point.

F: Do this again.

M: I can't go beyond this point right here. (whispers) I can get this far.

F: Talk to your wall, that far. Talk to that. . .

M: This is the wall right here, and behind this wall is me.

F: Tell this to the wall—or let the wall tell you, "I'm here to protect you."

M: You are—you are in front of me, wall, and behind you I am safe.

And the wall says, Yes, and you will never be able to get through me. If you do, then you will be vulnerable and people can come in. And this wall keeps people out.

F: *I* keep people out. . .

M: I keep people out with this wall. I keep people out.

F: Now, you just told me something. You're afraid that you might be vulnerable. Can you play a vulnerable person?

M: I don't know.

F: You don't know. What would be the harm that might be inflicted on you?

M: If I were a vulnerable person, people would hurt me.

F: How?

M: By taking me into their confidence, and I'd. . . Ah. . . by rejecting me if I loved them.

F: How? How are they rejecting you?

M: By doing the same thing that I would do, by cutting me off.

F: How?

M: Saying "Go away. Don't bother me."

F: Say this again.

M: (louder) Go away and don't bother me.

F: You just said it to the flies. Say this to them.

M: Go away and don't bother me.

F: Say this to me.

M: Go away and don't bother me.

F: Say this to your child.

M: (more quietly) Go away and don't bother me. . .

F: And now?

M: They go away.

F: And then?

M: Then I'm alone.

F: And you're safe?

M: I'm safe. . . Yeah, he's here.

F: So? The wall is still there.

M: Yeah.

F: Now the wall's coming closer isn't it?

M: At times it gets very close.

F: Now again, have it out with this close wall.

M: (sighs) You get so close that I. . . I cannot breathe sometimes, and I become very much afraid. And yet, and yet I cannot get through you. . . I will not let myself get through. . . I could move in and actually crush myself.

F: Okeh. Now come over here and crush me, again. . . Really *mean*. Crush me.

M: No, I don't want to crush you. Just me.

F: I want you to crush me. . . You want me to crush you?

M: No. . .

F: Okeh, you still have to be content with yourself. Go on; how would you crush yourself?

M: I don't know. I ah, I don't know what I'm doing. . .

F: That's a lie. You know quite well what you're doing. How are you crushing yourself?. . .

M: I'm not—I'm keeping a wall there, and I'm not letting myself get through it.

F: How do you crush yourself?. . . How do you crush your-self?. . .

M: I'm closing myself up and not talking.

F: How do you crush yourself?. . . Yah? What happened right now?

M: I don't crush myself at all.

F: You don't crush yourself at all. You played a game.

M: Yeah.

F: Yah. What do you feel now?. . . I noticed you stopped tor-turing me with your game. . .

M: (lively) Well, right now? I don't know, I just kind of feel sort of silly.

F: Look at the audience. (May laughs). . . Look at them.

M: They're all there.

F: Say this to them.

M: (excitedly, almost crying) You are all there, and I can see your eyes, and your faces looking at me. And you all have beautiful faces. . .

F: Could you go down and touch somebody you see.

M: I could touch all of you. (May goes and touches and hugs people and begins to cry)

F: Well, you see what happened on the private stage, on the stage of imagination, how powerful the imagination of self-hypnosis can be?. . . *There ain't any walls.*

M: (laughs) You're right. . .

F: Okeh. Thank you.

You see, May got quite a little bit of integration by identify-ing with her wall. Next time she does something, this little increased confidence will assist her and she will need less environmental support. And the simplest way, really, to do it is to listen to when-ever you use the *it*. This is the simplest way. And just reformulate your sentence. Start on the pure verbal level until the experience comes: It's not an *it*, there, but *I*.

MAX

Max: I have a fragment of a dream, Fritz.

Fritz: Well let's start right away. Until you understand the meaning of what we are doing you will see this as a kind of technique. And a technique that is not understood becomes a gimmick. So right now we'll use, in your sense, a certain amount of gimmicks. Now the gimmick I'd like to use with you is to change *having* into *being*. Instead of "I *have* a fragment of a dream" you say "I *am* a fragment of a dream."

M: I am a fragment of a dream.

F: Now stay with this sentence and assimilate it. Could it make sense to you that you are a fragment of a dream?

M: Well, I'm a fragment of a whole. /F: Yah./ Only part of me is here. . .

F: You feel your reality; you're not a dream. . .

M: I feel the chair, I feel heat, I feel the tenseness in my stomach and in my hands—

F: *The* tenseness. Here we've got a noun. Now *the* tenseness is a noun. Now change the noun, the thing, into a verb.

M: I am tense. My hands are tense.

F: Your hands are tense. They have nothing to do with you.

M: *I* am tense.

F: You are tense. How are you tense? What are you doing? You see the consistent tendency towards reification—always trying to make a thing out of a process. Life is *process*; death is *thing*.

M: I am tensing myself.

F: That's it. Look at the difference between the words "I am tensing myself" and "There's a tenseness here." When you say "I feel tenseness," you're irresponsible, you are not responsible for this, you are impotent and you can't do anything about it. The world should do something—give you aspirin or whatever it is. But when you say "I am tensing" you take responsibility, and we can see the first bit of excitement of life coming out. So stay with this sentence.

M: I am pushing down on the chair with my arms.

F: Are you sure? Do you experience this?. . . Do it until you really feel *you* are doing it, fully and a hundred percent responsible for what you are doing.

M: I am holding my hands stiffly. . . I am holding my whole body stiffly. My back is stiff—I am holding it stiffly.

F: Can you imagine what amount of energy is required to keep yourself so stiff, playing the corpse?

M: I can't go on because I am stiff.

F: Who's responsible for you being stiff?

M: *I* am holding myself stiff. I have not relaxed myself yet.

F: You have not relaxed yourself yet. See the split? "*I* am relaxing *myself.*"

M: But I'm not, as yet.

F: You feel you ought to relax.

M: I feel I can't go on until I relax.

F: You cannot go on. Who told you to go on?

M: I am telling myself that I want to go on.

F: "I am telling myself to go on." You're manipulating yourself. So you set up the king pin and then you try to knock it down. You make yourself stiff, and then you tell yourself to relax. You see all this energy that is wasting through this game?

M: I just relaxed myself.

F: You relaxed yourself?

M: I am more relaxed.

F: Did you do it, or did it happen?

M: It happened.

F: That's what I am talking about. Any deliberate change is doomed to failure. Change has to come by itself through organismic self-regulation. If you're hungry, you're hungry. If you eat when you're not hungry then you'll probably get a stomach ulcer... I notice you're alive from the elbow down. You are like a dumpling and there's just a little bit sticking out—your hands. Otherwise you keep completely to yourself. Just become aware of this—how little expanding you are towards life. Now how do you feel about these remarks of mine?

M: I didn't like the word dumpling but I—it was true.

F: You see when you expressed this you smiled. But you are sitting on the not-liking. It produces already a certain amount of discomfort and you can't invest your exciting energy in what's going on because you are too busy holding something back. And some people are really collectors of grievances and do nothing else in their life but collecting grievances and not letting them out. You can imagine how little vitality they have left for living.

The discomfort is coming out quite frequently. Discomfort is always a symptom of dishonesty. If you don't express yourself honestly, you feel uncomfortable. The very moment you express yourself adequately, the discomfort goes.

M: (tight and quick speech) I don't, most of the time I didn't. I mean you just picked something that happened right now because I'm nervous.

F: You're nervous. /M: Yeah./ Can you give me your symptoms?

M: The feeling that blood flows in my veins. I feel them—I feel the blood flowing, and my heartbeat, and I have a sudden ache in my back down here, and I feel stiff, just stiff. That's nervousness... Could I go ahead with the dream?

F: Ask Fritz. Put Fritz in that chair and ask him.

M: Fritz, could I go ahead with the dream?...

　　You decide for yourself. (laughter)

　　I'm in an open field and in the far distance I see some collection of things piled up. And then I get closer to it, and it's just a ruined city—when I get close to it, it's a ruined city. Huge pieces of concrete lying one on top of the other. And the dream has somehow disconnected parts. It happened during a complicated night I suppose. But in the next picture I'm in a cave and I'm standing in the cave. I don't see myself in the dream. And there are two other men in the cave. And as I look at them I see they are walking in the cave—it's very shady, it's very dark—they look like apes, they walk like apes, back and forth. I suddenly realize they are basically deformed. There's something very deformed about each one of them.

　　And then in the corner sits a woman, and then I realize the woman is also totally deformed. She has no chin and her right side is completely squashed in. And these men walk back and forth, and then suddenly the next thing is this woman—she lies on the floor with her legs open and the men are going over her and they're screwing her. And the scene gets more and more grotesque and then I get drawn into it. And I go and fuck her, too. And I'm almost ready to throw up. Something was choking me.

　　And then there was silence. I don't know how long it takes, and there was another dream that followed immediately and I was in an open field again. And I was going with a child, with a child in my hand. And I was trying to take him around and trying to teach him something. And I tried to talk to him and I tried to talk to him, and suddenly I realize he doesn't understand a thing. He has no mind. And I started screaming at him "You must understand! You must understand!" But he didn't understand a thing. . . (quietly) That's it.

F: What interested me mostly was you spoke about the right side being maimed and yet all the time you were only talking with your right hand. The left was completely passive. . .

M: My left hand is weak. I can do very little with it. My right hand's a lot stronger. . .

F: Okeh, now get your own Fritz again, and let him direct your dream work.

M: There's a conflict because I'm more interested in the two men and the woman. I'm interested in what they are. So if I were Fritz I would go along with that, do that.

X: Could you speak a little louder?

M: (snaps) I said I can't be my own Fritz, I said. . . You asked me an impossible question. I can't do it. I've tried to do it, in fact, in my mind over the past 24 hours.

F: Say this to Fritz. . .

M: I've tried over the past 24 hours to try to identify myself and be one of these two men or the woman, and talk to myself. And I just couldn't do it. They refused to say a word. They were just looking at me, totally silent. I was getting mad at them, I was screaming, and they wouldn't respond. I tried to play them; I'd just be sitting there and watching me, with total silence, a total death.

F: So what does Fritz say to that?

M: Fritz, Fritz says. . . "All right, could you talk to death?". . . (whispers, with feeling) God *damn* it.

F: Say this again.

M: God damn it, I said. /F: Again./
God damn it. /F: Again./
God *damn* it! (strikes arm of chair with fist). . .

F: What do you experience now? Something's going on.

M: I experience what I experienced the evening before the dream. I was going to have brain surgery. It was the first time that I was totally, completely afraid of death. I had a car accident and I was just a healthy man and I suddenly had to go into brain surgery. And I was frightened to death. (whispers) And that sensation came back now absolutely. It's the first time I became aware of it as something totally in the present. You know, it's just there on the next corner. And I was afraid. I've n—I was never afraid before. And that sensation came back to me right now. . . Of sheer fear, just—

F: Talk to death. . .

M: But they—they—they are death. I don't know what to say to them!

F: Talk to death. You said you're afraid of death. I don't know what death means to you.

M: What are you going to do to me? All right, suppose you take over. What'll you do to me?

(laughs gently) I'll empty your mind. You'll be like that child; you will be without mind. . .

You see he stopped me. He stopped me right there. . . I started thinking. . .

F: You're using your mind again?

M: Yes. I just slipped into it.

F: Could you play a person without a mind?

M: The child! (lively) He was *totally* joyous. He was joyous, he was running around playing, /F: Play it./ collecting flowers—

F: Play him. (laughter)

M: (excitedly) He was going around, he was just collecting flowers, he was having fun, he was running around the hills, he was laughing, smiling, doing all the things.

F: Play him.

M: I am a child.

F: *Play* him.

M: A man without a mind doesn't talk, so I can only *do* things. I can only do things. . . (softly) No, he was laughing. (laughter) He was laughing and smiling.

F: *Play* him. (laughter)

M: (excitedly) No room, not enough room. I have to run—I just have to run. To play him I have to run up the hill and collect flowers.

F: See the difference between this mindless child and the thinker?

M: Yeah. I'm not unaware of it. . . It's very true in the dream, I screamed in my dream. I screamed at the child like that. I screamed "There's no time. There's no time. You must understand." And he goes around collecting flowers. (laughter and applause)

F: Get the message? (laughter) Well you see this is what I'm concerned with. I, *this* Fritz can't go home with you. You can't have me as a permanent therapist. But you can get your own personalized Fritz and take *this* along with you. And he knows *much* more than I do because he's your creation. I can only guess or theorize or interpret what you're experiencing. I can see the scratch, but I cannot feel the itch. I'm not in you and I'm not arrogant enough to be a psychoanalyst and say that I know what you experience, what you feel. But if you understand the idea of this purely personal Fritz, you can get yourself a chair, couch or whatever you have, and whenever you're in trouble go and talk to this imaginary Fritz.

MARK

Mark: I experience you as waiting for me to begin. I have the feeling that we're both sitting here waiting for something to happen.

Fritz: So, *how* do you experience *waiting*? What is this phenomenon called waiting? What's going on in you while you are waiting?

M: When I'm waiting, I start thinking about, ah. . . whatever you might say or do, so I'll know how to act.

F: *How* do you think?. . . Or as I call it, how do you rehearse?

M: Well, I try to imagine what you might say. . . I try to select exactly the right response. . . I try out different phrases and words and. . . put them up there and see how they look.

F: Well, you see this is a wonderful example of *anti*-spontaneous action. You prevent yourself from being spontaneous by having to rehearse, and go over, or to say whatever will be the right thing, and so on. So you kill off all possibility of being spontaneous.

Now the first thing I notice about any person is whether he is a closed or open system. You see, Mark is a closed system. His hands are closed, his legs are closed, so I don't know whether I can have communication with him. (Mark opens his posture) Now, as soon as I say this, he destroys the phenomenon of closedness, and he puts up a show of openness. We'll see how long this putting up a show will last, whether he returns to closedness. I doubt whether one can open a closed system so quickly, just by pointing it out.

M: This dream—it's just a very short fragment. As an avocation I write songs, and I had an agreement with a certain singer that he was going to record a song of mine, and I had not heard from him since that agreement about a year ago, and in the dream—

F: This is the dream?

M: No. In the dream—

F: Oh. You bring associations.

M: Well, just a little preface to the dream. The dream itself—

F: What do you know about your need to put prefaces onto your actions and speeches?

M: For the convenience of the people here, so that they will—I figured that they might like to have some background to the dream.

F: Ahah.

M: The dream itself—in the dream itself, he was talking to me, and he said, "Well, you know we had a great problem with the arrangement."

F: Now, I can already use this little bit. Can you play him, talking to you?

M: (propitiatingly) Well, we had a problem with the arrangement.

F: Now change seats. So what do you answer?

M: I'd have to invent the answer, I didn't have an answer in the dream.

F: Say this to him.

M: I didn't have an answer in the dream. That's all I recall.

F: Now take this seat again. Talk to Mark again.

M: (challenging) Do you accept what I said?

F: Change roles. Write a script now, between you and your friend.

M: No, that doesn't seem like a suitable answer. You promised me you were going to record it. I think it sounds like a cop-out.

F: You don't want him to fade out so quickly. (laughter) But you notice the friend is already pushing back a bit. And I notice that each time I say something that seems to be like disapproval, you try to change what you are doing. . . Okeh.

M: I don't know—I don't know, we were recording, I promised— like I'm a busy man and we had a problem we couldn't surmount, and went on to other things.

F: Do you hear your voice?

M: Yes.

F: What does your voice sound like?

M: I heard a whine at the end.

F: Ahh. You notice a change from how you started out.

M: I know you're a busy man, but this was very important to me and I regard a promise as a commitment. Besides which, I know you were very affected by the song and you—it seems as if that commitment is just going by the wayside. And I'd like an explanation.

Now look, if you want to make a federal case, you can, but that's as much of an explanation as I'm going to give you.

F: What is your right hand doing?

M: It's rubbing the space between these two fingers. I feel as if I have closed the conversation with that last statement.

F: Say this to him.

M: I feel as if I closed the conversation with that last statement.

F: You are smiling. (laughter) What's so funny about this closure?

M: To say it to you, and then for you to give me the order to say it to him, and then for me to say it to him, struck me as being funny. I think it struck me as being funny.

F: Can you tell me, "Fritz, you're funny"?

M: Fritz, you're funny. Fritz, you *are* funny. (laughter)

F: Can you elaborate on this?

M: Well, when you were announced as being Cyrano, you sort of made a nose and took great pleasure in that. And when Sally said she loves a man who likes to fondle his beard, you sort of jumped up and rubbed your beard a *lot*. That was a funny magnification of each of those moments. You are also very sad, by the way. . . That's funny, too.

F: Will you please play the sad Fritz. (Mark pantomimes sad Fritz with audience laughter, and then sits waiting). . .

F: How does the atmosphere change? Do you notice the change in the atmosphere?

M: It seems to be sort of tentative. I'm—I'm waiting for you, and they're waiting for us, I think.

F: How do you know they are waiting?

M: I assume they are. There's an interaction here which is silent, and—

F: You *assume*.

M: I assume that they're waiting for a continuation. I was just experiencing the silence of the. . .

F: I just want to underline the word *assume*. You don't *know*.

M: No. I don't—I said afterwards that I—

F: Did you, by any chance, experience at that moment some waiting?

M: Waiting? I don't know whether it was waiting or just observing you and me looking at each other, which might be an experience in itself, without waiting for something else.

F: Okeh, let's go back to the dream, now. What else was in the dream? Was this the whole dream?. . . To what degree do you recognize yourself in your friend? Can you play him once more. Can you tell Mark, "I am such and such a guy"?

M: I'm a singer, and I—in a social situation I heard Mark sing this song, and was very much touched by the song, as I demonstrated to him, and he said, "Well, if you feel that way, I might even let you sing it," and I said, "I'm going to record it."

F: Now this is the basic question for me in every dream: What are you avoiding?

M: I made a small attempt to contact him in the year since, but I think a more aggressive effort to remind him of this commitment would have been appropriate, but I didn't make it.

F: So you avoid closing the situation, closing the gestalt. You still run around with this unfinished business. So this would be the short-range avoidance. And the long-range avoidance—well, that's— Can you sing this song?

M: Yes.

F: Will you please do so.

M: (sings softly and slowly in a low voice)
Roses white, and roses red
Wishes and puppies do come true.
But they have to be tended
They have to be fed
Or little brown dogs, and wishes too

Fade and die, and when they are dead
What can you say?
And what can you do?
But sing them a song
And drop on their head
Roses white, and roses red.

F: (gently) And what do you need him for? You can sing your own songs.

M: I can sing it, and I enjoy singing it. I would like to have other people have the opportunity to hear it.

F: Do you know how to work a tape recorder?

M: Yes.

F: So what do you need him for then? You can work a tape recorder yourself. Okeh. Can you *play* this song? Can you play this rose? "I am a red rose—" Give it some words.

M: I'm a red rose, growing next to a white rose. I need to be tended, and like anything else, taken care of.

F: To whom are you saying this? To whom are you talking?

M: I'm not aware that I'm saying it to anyone.

F: Do me a favor and say it to *someone.*

M: I am a red rose, and I'm like a puppy, and anything else that's alive. I need to be—while I'm growing, I need to be tended, and taken care of—and if you know this, and if I belong to you, then it is your job to take care of me, and if you don't, all that you will have to do is throw another red rose on top of me, or a white rose.

F: Again, I want you to change roles. Be now the person who is doing exactly what Mark wants him or her to do. Be this person, and take care of Mark. (Mark pantomimes tending and caring for a rose, tenderly)

F: What do you experience?

M: I care. . . for this. I'm doing my task, related to this.

F: Now change again, be the rose again.

M: A nice feeling. I'm without the awareness of anything specific. Suddenly, I'm being taken care of.

F: Okeh, I want to finish here. There is still a lot to do, I would say. Mark still needs. . . Let me give you some short idea about Mark, because it came out here *very* beautifully. As I said before, growth and maturation is the transcendence from environmental support to self-support. The child needs the environment to take care of him, and as you grow up, you learn more and more to stand on your own feet, to provide your own *means-whereby* to live, and so forth. Now it came out clearly here, that Mark still needs people to take care of him, he needs environmental support for his songs, for being nourished, so there is still something of the mature person missing. And where is this missing part? It is in what we call the projection, still in the outside world. But you notice, when he took care of the rose, it was a very loving care. He tried to pooh-pooh it by saying that he does it out of duty, but I found in his movements something *very* tender, something *very* much involved. This is what I see here.

JIM

Jim: I have just a fragment of a dream. There's no voices in the dream.

Fritz: Now, the first look is that Jim is open in his undercarriage, but closed up here—he is covering his genitals with his hands. So this is the first thing I see. Now, this is very important, which part is closed up, whether the total personality, or the lower or the upper carriage. The lower carriage is mostly for support, and the upper carriage for contact. This is how we stand up on our own feet, and this is where we reach toward the world, with our hands. So I see already a lot just by Jim sitting there: his posture, the way he moves his head, and so on and so on.

J: You already have me pretty well shook up. (laughter) This has nothing to do with my dream, but that's a heck of a comment to make, because—

F: You see the lack of ambidexterity in his gestures? He uses only the right hand and it always points to himself; he is relating himself to himself. That's what Kierkegaard said in the beginning— the relation of the self to the self. If you live like this, how much can you achieve?

J: I'm afraid to move.

F: That is exactly what I wanted to point out. (laughter)

J: Now I know why my dreams are short.

F: Would you enlighten me? I don't know why your dreams are short.

J: I just have the typical recurring dream which I think a lot of people might have if they have a background problem, and it isn't of anything that I think I can act out. It's the distant wheel—I'm not sure what type it is—it's coming towards me, and ever-increasing in size, *always* increasing in size. And then finally, it's just above me and it's no height that I can determine, it's so high. And that's—

F: If you were this wheel, what kind of existence would you lead, and what would you do with Jim?

J: What kind of a relationship would I, as a wheel, have?

F: You have just described the wheel, growing in size. . .

J: Right. I am just about to roll over Jim.

F: How would you do this?

J: How would I do it? By continuing in my pathway—in my current path, I'd continue to go, and roll over Jim.

F: Talk to Jim. . .

J: As the wheel?

F: Yah.

J: I don't know what the wheel is trying to say to Jim.

F: Okeh. I'm going to help you to tell me whether I understand this wheel correctly. I'm here, I'm rolling, rolling along, getting more and more powerful, and nothing can stand in my way. I'll just go over you, Jim, whether you like it or not. . . This would be *my* wheel—now, what would *your* wheel be like?

J: I'd say, you're not going over me.

F: Say this to the wheel.

J: (tentatively) You're not going over me. I'm not going to let you.

F: Did you listen to your voice? If you were this wheel, would this voice stop the wheel? (laughter)

J: No.

F: What does the wheel say to that voice of Jim?

J: *Tough.* (laughter)

F: What does Jim say?

J: Jim has that instinct to, perhaps—I don't know. My first impulse would be to—that Jim would say it louder, or—I don't know. The first impulse would be to try to—

F: Did you notice how often the words "I'm not sure, I don't know" occur here? Again and again, we hear, "I don't know, I am not sure, what would I do?" Does this have any meaning, that I heard so often these expressions?

J: Does it have any meaning?

F: To you. Yah. The fact that I heard this kind of expression so often.

J: Yes, it has a lot of meaning in *my* life, that I'm very indecisive, and cannot make any commitment to act.

F: Now, where is your power, in the dream?

J: I don't see what power I have, when I have—in other words, I see a size that's beyond—beyond any—it's like the wheel is just too tremendous to even contemplate any opposition.

F: Yah. Now, play the wheel again. This time, try to identify with the wheel and play the wheel. Get up and play the wheel. . . And I'm Jim. . .

J: I am the wheel, and I—I'm—you have no chance. I'm coming over you and I—and—you're not to move.

F: Did you feel any power? Did you feel any indecisiveness right now when you played the wheel?

J: No. . . I felt determination.

F: That's right. This is where you have invested and projected your potentialities, so much so that in your deliberate personality, there is very little left. Now play this wheel again. Elaborate. Oh! You even have two hands, now. Notice, you even begin to *use* these hands.

J: I am a wheel, and right now I don't feel like the wheel is as big as I thought it was. (laughter) You're putting a little bit of doubt in Jim's mind as to really the strength of this wheel, and I can't act the wheel. . .

F: Okeh, now sit down—Now you talk to the wheel again.

J: (hesitantly) Ahhh. . . (laughter). . . You're a lot of talk. /F: Say this again./

You're a lot of talk. /F: Again./
You're a lot of talk. /F: Again./
You're a lot of talk.

F: Now say this to the wheel.

J: You're a lot of talk. You appear big, but when I stop to

evaluate how big you are, you're really not that determined to be as powerful as I thought you first were.

F: Notice how much of your unsureness has left you? How much you have already re-owned from the projection of the wheel?

J: Yeah. I think I—as large as it is, right now, I think I'd do whatever I could. In other words, I've always had the feeling that— what *could* I do?—but now I know at least I'd do whatever I could— to stop the wheel. . . And, ah—on this thing here, I'm sterile, and that entered into my marriage—that's the very thing I was ashamed of, and you know you said I covered my genitals.

F: The big wheel. Yah?

QUESTIONS I

Q: What if you don't remember any dreams? What does this mean?

F: I have a *theory* about it. You don't want to face your existence. To me, a dream is an existential message of what part of your personality is missing, and in the dream you can clearly see how you avoid. Very typical are nightmares, where you run away. You can be pretty sure that people who don't want to recall their dreams are phobic people. And if you refuse to remember your dreams, you refuse really to face your existence—to face what's wrong with your existence. You avoid coping with unpleasantness. Usually these are the people who more or less *think* that they have come to terms with life. You do dream, but you don't remember it. You dream at least four dreams per night. We know this. If a person can't remember their dreams, I let them talk to the missing dreams—"Dreams, where are you?" and so on.

Q: What happens if you have a very short dream?

F: Often I ask somebody to relate a dream. It is very long and complicated, and before the dream ends, a whole hour is gone and you are more confused than when you started to work. So a short dream is often better than a long dream. If you have a long dream, I would take only a tiny segment.

I believe that every part of the dream is a part of yourself—not just the person, but every item, every mood, anything that comes across. My favorite example is this: A patient dreams he is leaving my office and goes to Central Park. And he goes across the bridle path, into the Park. So I ask him, "Now play the bridle path." He answers indignantly, "*What*? And let everybody shit and crap on me?" You see, he really got the identification. I let the patient play all these parts, because only by really playing can you get the full identification, and the identification is the counteraction to the *alienation*. *Alienation* means "That's not me, that's something else, something strange, something not belonging to me." And often you encounter quite a bit of resistance against playing this alienated part. You don't want to re-own, take back, those parts of yourself which you have pushed out of your personality. This is the way you have impoverished yourself. This is the advantage of this role-playing, and if I let the patient do *all* the roles himself, we get a clearer picture than when we use Moreno's technique of psychodrama, pulling people in who know very little about you—because they bring in *their own* fantasies, *their own* interpretations. The patient's role is falsified by the uniqueness of the other people. But if you do everything yourself, then we know that we are within yourself. Also, in psychodrama you usually have to confine yourself to people, while the empty chair can be used for playing the role of all kinds of things—wheels, spiders, missing railings, headaches, silence. There is so much invested in these objects. If we can bring these things back to life, then we have more material to assimilate. And my whole technique develops more and more into *never, never interpret*. Just back-feeding, providing an opportunity for the other person to discover himself.

Q: I'd like you to comment on a feeling one carries over into the waking state as a result of dreams. I know that I dream every night but I remember very few of them. But I've learned from my feeling during the ensuing days. If I feel anxious and so on, I feel intuitively that I've had some anxiety-producing dreams, and some days I feel very exhilarated and exalted and I can vaguely remember a very rewarding dream.

F: Yah. What you are avoiding is to say, "What is the anxiety about?" My guess would be that you have to perform on that day, and you didn't allow yourself to rehearse in the dream, to prepare for that event, that you lack spontaneous action, that you have to prepare. Anxiety is always the result of leaving the now.

Q: In my case, some dreams are repetitious for years and years, and I've had one where there was no action, just scenes. That has a message?

F: Yah. You avoid the action.

Q: Would people who are not fragmented, who are well-integrated, dream?

F: Yah. But there you don't find nightmares any more. There you find attempts to fill the holes in their personality, to cope with unfinished situations—directly and immediately. The more fragmented the person is, the more nightmarish their dreams are. A very good idea is always to look at what is avoided in the dream, and then fill in the holes, see what's there.

It often goes like this. I remember a patient who had visual blindness—you see, his eyes were projected. He always experienced that the Lord was looking at him. So of course he had no eyes left, so he couldn't see. And one day he dreamed he was in the audience, and there was this stage—there was *nothing* on the stage. I got him to go on stage; he says, "There is nothing there." I said to look further, and then he says, "Yah, there is some carpet there." So I asked him to describe the carpet.

"Oh, there are colors! And there are curtains!" And then he woke up, (snap) like that, with a mini-satori. "Ah! I can see!" He suddenly got his eyes. This doesn't mean that the eyes will *stay* with him, but at least he discovered that he could see, that he didn't always have to be the target of eyes. This is a typical example: Where other people had eyes, he had nothing.

Q: Could you make a few comments on existential problems. What are they, exactly? Can you elaborate on this.

F: I give you one example. Maybe this can show it. A person can be embarrassed about a certain act. Right? But some people have an *existential* embarrassment. They are embarrassed to exist, to be. So they always have to justify their existence. In other words, the idea of existence is much wider than just the treatment of symptoms, or character features. Many people don't even have the feeling that they actually exist, and to go any further we would have to go into the whole philosophy of nothingness, which I think is beyond the scope of this seminar. But for the time being, just take existential philosophy as a philosophy which is concerned with *being*. The first question, of course, is: How is there being rather than not-being? Most philosophies are interested in *explaining* life, or creating certain ideals how a person *should* live.

Let me give you one example of the philosophy of nothingness as compared to the other philosophies. We don't know what happened in the past, and when we try to fathom, how is the beginning of the world, or so on, we hit nothing. Now this nothingness for many people has a certain feeling of uncanniness. They feel there is a void. So they put something there, and every religion quickly invents something, how the world came about. This is usually the way of philosophy, to explain. Now this explanatoriness, of course, gets in the way of understanding. They give you some reason, some justification, some bit of elephantshit. I would say the best definition of existentialism was given with the sentence by Gertrude Stein, "A rose is a rose is a rose." What is, is.

Q: There is an existential problem—from the psychological point of view. In psychology, the problem of the here and now without— I'm trying to create a bridge between philosophy and psychology.

F: There is no problem about the here and now. You can *make* a problem out of it, by forgetting that you are here and now. Are *you* here, now?—No. You are here, but you are essentially *not* here. You are in your computer. This is your now-ness. I doubt that you are here breathing, or seeing me, or aware of your posture, so your being is restricted. Your existence might be revolving around your thinking. Many people in our time exist only as computers. They think, and think, and think, and construct one explanation, and another explanation, and the understanding is missing. Have you ever read Steinbeck's *The Grapes of Wrath*? The woman there, at the end of the book, the mother—she *understood*. She was *all there*.

Q: Is there any way to tell if a dream would be a compensation, and the meaning would be opposite, or if it is a straight message?

F: It's always a cryptic message. If it would be a straight message, you wouldn't need to dream it. Then you would be honest, which means that you would be healthy and sane. You can't be honest and neurotic at the same time.

Q: You said that a dream is always a cryptic message. I once had a dream. I thought it was a very simple message, and the next day the sequences of the dream were very specific outlines to follow in terms of my experience, and so I don't see dreams as always being cryptic, and I saw that as a kind of psychological preparation for what was going to happen, or did I not see it all—that there was some other thing in back of it?

F: Yah. There is something buried. We do many things which are actually part of the *trance* in which we live. You see, very few of us are awake. I would say the majority of modern man lives in a verbal trance. He doesn't see, he doesn't hear, and it takes quite awhile to wake up. First, in therapy—you noticed quite a few small awakenings here—what I call the mini-satori. Possibly one day one is fully awake, and then one has satori. Very often there is a waking up, and then sliding back into the trance of persecution, or verbalism, and what you talk about is definitely a part of this being in trance, even if you act out this dream in reality.

Q: The acting out, I can accept—I can accept that. But the events that occurred, I was unable to control them physically. That's what I'm trying to say, that when I realized what was happening to me in a situation over which I had no control, it was then and only then that I recalled the dream. So I didn't see it as a cryptic message. That's what I was trying to say. I saw it as a very real relationship, and preparation for this lack of control.

F: You look at me as if you expect an argument.

Q: I'm arguing with myself, trying to decide—

F: Ahnh-ah. I hear definitely some challenge.

Q: All right. You still think that all dreams are cryptic messages?

F: Yah.

Q: If the child is naturally left-handed, and his parents force him to be right-handed, does that have to have psychological effects on him?

F: Yah. Definitely. Because then you put a double load on the right side. The result very often is stammering, stuttering.

Q: I have always noticed that I have a dissatisfaction in showing people my left side. I often sit where people can look at my right side. I had an operation on my nose, to correct the sides so that both would be more even, and my eyebrow on my right side is like arched and sort of stern, and it's always bothered me. I wanted to be more gentle, like the left side. And I'm quite interested in what I could learn about this. Is it a resistance to accepting the right side, the masculine side?

F: You ask me whether you have a resistance. What's *your* opinion?

Q: My opinion is that I have.

F: Okeh.

Q: What is your opinion about meditation?

F: Meditation is neither shit nor get off the pot.

Q: Is it possible to use an unresolved life situation as if it were a dream and work on it in the same way?

F: Yah, just the same.

Q: What does Gestalt Therapy have to say about psychosis?

F: I have very little, yet, to say about psychosis. We are working always with opposites, polarities. But I see the polarities in, for instance—let's take one psychosis, schizophrenia, which is the one most people are interested in. Now, our world consists of three spheres. You understand this is very schematic. The self zone, the inner zone which is essentially—let's call it the biological animal. The outer zone—the world around us—and between the outer zone and the inner zone, there is a DMZ, a demilitarized zone, essentially discovered by Freud under the name of *complex*.

In other words, in this middle zone there is a fantasy life of the conscious, called "mind," which is full of catastrophic expectations, full of fantasies, full of computer activity—verbiage, programs, plans, thoughts, constructions. This intermediate zone takes up all the energy, all the excitement, so that very little is free to be in touch with yourself or the world.

Freud had the right idea of emptying out this middle zone, but in practice in psychoanalysis you *stay* in the middle zone. You are not allowed to touch, to go out, to discover yourself in the whole range of physical experience, in being in touch with the world, and so on.

So now, in schizophrenia, I find—especially through investigation of my own schizophrenic zone—that there is a lot of dead debris where the excitement cannot go. The psychotic has a very large dead layer, and this dead zone cannot be nourished by the life force.

One thing we know for sure is that the life energy, biological energy or whatever you want to call it, becomes unmanageable in the case of psychosis. Instead of being differentiated and distributed, it comes out in spurts. So usually all we do is try to cut out a piece of the brain, or to kill the excitement with tranquilizers. Now if we do this, we dim the level of excitement so that relatively rational behavior is achieved. But this doesn't really cure the patient, because his self then does not receive the amount of vitality it needs to cope with the exigencies of life.

It appears to me that there are some similarities between dreams and psychosis. They both are absurd to the outsider, and both seem real to the person in question. While you are dreaming, it seems the dream *absolutely* is real. The most absurd dream, the most terrible dream, doesn't bring any doubt that this actually happens. We don't know much about psychosis, but we do know quite a bit about dreams.

A very interesting *difference* between dreams and the behavior and mentality of the psychotic is this: Usually the psychotic does not even *try* to deal with frustrations; he just denies the frustrations, and behaves as if these frustrations don't exist. In dreams, however, we see an attempt to overcome these frustrations. You probably know that the majority of dreams are nightmares. The nightmare is a dream where you frustrate yourself, and then you try to overcome that. You are not successful, but as it goes on, especially with work on those dreams, you are capable of overcoming these self-frustrations, and learn to cope with them. So these are a few relationships of dreams and psychosis which I think might be worthwhile investigating. It might be worthwhile also investigating how this absurd language of the psychotic can be made understandable.

We know for sure that a person can go into a mental hospital and get better, go out and get worse again. This shows that an important situational or behavioral factor must be involved. It can't be *just* chemistry. And also the relationship of chemistry to behavior is very little investigated. The craziness is in the mind, in spite of what the chemical physiologists say. It's also of course in the physiology, but primarily everything disturbing that goes on is in your fantasy.

And then we see in the schizophrenic exactly the same polarity that we see in most people. We find people who are in touch with themselves, the withdrawn people, who are out of touch with the world. They have a rich inner life, but they are shut off from he world. And we have also the paranoid schizophrenic who is out of touch with himself, who is always in touch with the world. He is always scanning the world, but desensitized. So again there is just a tiny part of him functioning. So no rational relationship is possible. That is as far as I want to go with talking about this.

JUDY

Judy: May I ask, Dr. Perls, why ah—you know they always say you have symbolic dreams. I never did. I. . . /Fritz: I don't know what symbols are./ I re-lived trauma—Well, I never dreamed anything that was imaginary. I went through trauma that I had actually experienced. And it was exactly as it had occurred. What is the significance of that? Ah, in recent years I've had—it's changed—you know, I don't dream about it any more, but—

F: I don't get any message. You want to say something, but I don't get—Could you be good enough to come up here?

J: If you don't make me talk about the dream. I don't remember any of it very well. . .

F: I hear you—you are saying sentences to me and I would like to get the message.

J: (nervously) Let me fortify myself with a cigarette, before I do. Does anybody have a match? (she gets a light from someone as she walks up to the platform) Thank you.

F: And what is there? (Fritz points to matches she had been holding in her hand all the time; she laughs) And what is there? You see—

J: I read *Sex and The Single Girl* and it said never carry your own matches—

F: (gently) Shut up. She is only manipulating the environment for support. She carries her own matches, but she has to suck you into taking care of her. This is already the first message. . .

J: Yes?

F: Yes? *You're* asking *me*?

J: (invitingly, with poise and control) It's your show, Doctor.

F: (to group) did you notice the twist? It's my show. *I* want something from *her*.

J: (nervous laughter, slightly panicked) I don't think you're going to get it.

F: So, the stage is set. I want something from her. I wouldn't get it.

J: I've heard about you.

F: She's giving me the come-on, so that the hatchet can fall.

J: Whose hatchet, mine or yours?

F: Please make a statement out of this question.

J: Make a statement out of that—out of the hatchet? Uhhhhh. . . Who's gonna deal the blow, you or me?

F: This is a very good illustration. This is what we call the bear-trapper. She's playing the trapping game. Baiting the trap and waiting for you to get trapped, so that—psst!. . .

J: I'm not vicious. . . (Fritz starts to light a cigarette, but intentionally strikes match where it will not light—playing Judy's game— much laughter)

J: You need support, Doctor—can't you light your own cigarette? (Fritz continues to strike match where it will not light. . . finally Judy lights it for him. . . Fritz first looks bored, then closes his eyes and appears to sleep)

J: You're breathing too deeply for one asleep. . . (Fritz continues to keep eyes closed). . .

J: Don't make me kick you! (roars of laughter)

F: Okeh. Thank you very much.

BEVERLY

Beverly: I guess I'm supposed to say something. I don't have any interesting dreams. Mine are sort of patent.

Fritz: Are you aware that you're defensive?. . . I didn't ask you in only to bring dreams.

B: You asked for them last night and I was afraid that would disqualify me. If I could manufacture a few. . .

F: Now you have a very interesting posture. The left leg supports the right leg, the right leg supports the right hand, the right hand supports the left hand.

B: Yeah. It gives me something to hang onto. And with a lot of people out there you kind of get some stage fright. There are so many of them.

F: You have stage fright and there are people outside. In other words you're on stage.

B: Yeah, I suppose I feel that way.

F: Well, what about getting in touch with your audience. . .

B: Well they look very good. They have wonderful faces.

F: Tell this to them.

B: You have very warm faces, very interested, very interest-*ing*. . . with—with a lot of warmth.

F: So then shuttle back to your stage fright. What do you experience now?

B: I don't have any more stage fright. But my husband doesn't look at me.

F: So go back to your husband.

B: You're the only one that looks self-conscious. Nobody else looks self-conscious at me. (laughter) You sort of feel like you're up here, don't you? Or sort of like your youngster's up here?. . . No?

X: (from audience, yells) Answer!

Husband: She's the one who's up there and she's trying to place me up there.

F: (to husband) Yah. You've got to answer. (to Beverly) You have to know what I feel.

B: Well he doesn't usually answer. Did you want him out of character? (much laughter)

F: So, you are a clobberer.

B: You need an ashtray.

F: "I need an ashtray." (Fritz holds up his ashtray) She knows what *I* need. (laughter)

B: Oh, no—you have one. (laughter)

F: Now *I* get stage fright. (laughter) I always have difficulties in dealing with "Jewish mothers." (laughter)

B: Don't you like "Jewish mothers"?

F: Oh, I love them. Especially their matzo-ball soup. (laughter)

B: I'm not a gastronomical Jewish mother, just a Jewish mother. (chuckles) I don't like gefilte fish either. I guess I'm a pretty obvious Jewish mother. Well that's not bad to be. That's all right. Matter of fact, that's good to be.

F: What are your hands doing?

B: Well, my thumbnails are pulling at each other.

F: What are they doing to each other?

B: Just playing. I do this often. See, I don't smoke, so what else are you gonna do with your hands. It doesn't look good to suck your thumbs.

F: That's also the Jewish mother. She has reasons for everything. (laughter)

B: (jokingly) And if I don't have one I'll make one up. (chuckles) The ordered universe. What's wrong with being a Jewish mother?

F: Did I say there's something wrong with a Jewish mother? I only say *I* have difficulties in dealing with them.

There is a famous story of a man who was such an excellent swordsman that he could hit even a raindrop, and when it was raining he used his sword instead of an umbrella. (laughter) Now there are also intellectual and behavioristic swordsmen, who in answer to every question, statement, or whatever, hit it back. So whatever you do, immediately you are castrated or knocked out with some kind of reply—playing stupid or poor-me or whatever the games are. She's perfect.

B: I never realized that.

F: You see? Again the sword. Playing stupid. I want once more to restate what I said earlier. Maturation is the transcendence from environmental support to self-support. The neurotic, instead of mobilizing his own resources, puts all his energy into manipulating the environment for support. And what you do is again and again manipulate me, you manipulate your husband, you manipulate everybody to come to the rescue of the "damsel in distress."

B: How did I manipulate you?

F: You see, again. This question, for instance. This is very important for maturation—change your questions to statements. Every question is a hook, and I would say that the majority of your questions are inventions to torture yourself and torture others. But if you change the question to a statement, you open up a lot of your background. This is one of the best means to develop a good intelligence. So change your question to a statement.

B: Well, th—that implies that, ah, there's a fault to me. Didn't you intend it so?. . .

F: Put Fritz in that chair and ask him that question.

B: Don't you like Jewish mothers? Did you have one that you didn't like?

Well, I like them. They're just a very difficult lot to deal with.

Well, what makes them so difficult?

Well, they're very dogmatic and very opinionated and inflexible and the box that they construct for themselves to grow in is a little narrower than many. They're less easy to therapize.

Does everybody have to be subject to your therapy?

No. (laughter)

(to Fritz) Did you ever switch chairs like this with yourself?

F: (laughing) Oh yes—*Oh*! Even *I* get sucked in! (laughter)

B: You said you had problems with Jewish mothers. (laughter)

Husband: Do you understand now why I didn't answer? (laughter and applause)

F: That's right, because you see how a Jewish mother doesn't say "You shouldn't smoke so much." She says, "You need an ashtray." (laughter) Okeh. Thank you.

MAXINE

Maxine: My dream is that I'm at home at my parents' house and. . .

Fritz: Well, will you first play your voice. "I am Maxine's voice. I am loud, soft, droning, musical, I'm alive. . ."

M: I am Maxine's voice and I am very lifeless. . . little feeling in it, and I feel very different than my voice represents.

F: Okeh, then have an encounter with your voice. Put your voice here, and you sit there. You say, "Voice, I have no relationship with you. You're different from me."

M: Voice, you're different from me. I feel altogether different from—from—from the way you sound. I'm nervous, I'm trembling, and I'm scared to death. . .

F: That's what you feel.

M: My stomach is—my stomach is—is jumpy.

F: Okeh, now be your voice.

M: I—I know that you don't—you don't want me to—to, uh—to express how you really feel, so I'm helping you to cover it up.

F: Now, write a script, which means you change chairs, with every sentence or whenever you feel like answering back. Now the voice says to Maxine, "I want to cover up what you feel," right?

M: But I don't want you to cover up what I feel. I want to—I want you to let my feelings out, I want you to—

F: Say this again. "I want you to let my feelings out."

M: (more lively) I want you to let my feelings out, I want you to let me be a person.

F: Again.

M: I'm sick and tired of—of you covering up for me all the time. I want—I wanna be myself.

F: Say that again, "I want to be myself."

M: I want to be myself. /F: Again./

I would like to be myself, voice! I want you to stop covering up for me. /F: Again./

I want to be a genuine person. /F: Again./

I wanna be myself! *Stop* covering up for me!

F: Let me work on a hunch. Say this to Brian. (fiancé)

M: Stop covering up for me. . .

F: Feel it?

M: No. I'm scared to say it.

F: Say this to him. . .

M: *Don't* cover up for me.

F: Okeh, close your eyes again. Close your eyes again and enter your body. What do you experience?

M: Very nervous. My legs are shaking, and my arms are shaking, and my stomach is nervous.

F: Dance nervousness. Express all that you feel now in movements.

M: I feel sort of tight, in my—

F: Yah. (Fritz holds out his arm) Now tighten me, tighten it more—more—more. Implode me. . . So what do you feel now?. . .

M: I feel more relaxed.

F: Ahah. Because you did to me what you usually do to yourself. This is the golden rule in Gestalt Therapy: "Do unto others what you do unto yourself." I think we are ready for the dream now, so let's have the dream.

M: I was home, and I'm—I'm with my sister, and—and we have a lot of fun together.

F: In the dream? /M: Yeah./ What kind of fun?

M: We talk together, we do things together, we—

F: What do you do together? You see, I can't understand abstract language. I must have something real to work with.

M: We—we escape together, we—

F: You escape together.

M: We escape from people, and—

F: I don't understand the word "people." From whom do you escape?

M: From my parents.

F: Ah. And that's fun.

M: It's fun. And we understand each other. I can tell her—I can take out my hostility on her, I can scream at her, and pick at her. I can't do that to my parents. All I can do is be just—just lifeless with them, just listen to them.

F: Okeh. Have an encounter with your sister.

M: You're a bum. You're no good. I'm better than you are. . .

F: Change seats. What does she answer?

M: I don't like being called a bum. /F: Say this again./
(louder) I don't *like* being called a bum. /F: Again./
(animated) I don't *like* being called a bum! /F: Again./
I'm sick and tired of you calling me a bum all the time!

F: Now you sound real. Do you hear it?

M: I don't like you for it, (high, petulant voice) and I hate you, I don't—

F: I don't believe the hate. "I hate you." I didn't hear *any* hate in there. You're talking literature again.

M: *You're* the bum.

F: Ah! Say this again.

M: *You're* a bum, *you're* a bum, I'm not the bum. *You're* the bum.

F: Change seats. . . What do you experience now?

M: I—I feel like I would like to tear her apart. I'd like to tear her clothes off, and her legs off, and I'd just like to smash her to pieces.

F: Now do it—dance this. Act it out.

M: I can't act it out.

F: Do it! Don't give me that crap. . . You could squeeze me very nicely. Do we have anything she could tear apart? (someone gets some newspapers) And breathe when you do this, and make noises. Make noises.

M: I *can't* tear you apart, Norma. . . I would like to, but—

F: Yah? What's your objection?

M: I—I—You're not the one I'm really angry at.

F: Ahah.

M: I don't want to hurt you.

F: How don't you want to hurt her? (laughter)

M: You're not the one—I don't want to kill you. I don't want to tear you apart. I don't wanna—to make a *vegetable* out of you. Not kill you physically, but I don't wanna—

F: Whom do you want to kill?

M: (softly) I'd like to kill my father.

F: Okeh. Let's call Papa in. (Fritz whistles) You know, of course, parents are *never* good, parents are *always* at fault. If they are tall, they should be small. If they are that, they should be this. So, tell him off. How does he not fit your expectations? What should he be like?

M: He should let me alone.

F: Say this to him.

M: (petulant, complaining) Let me alone, Dad. Go away from me. Let me alone. Let me live my own life and just stop interfering, and leave me alone.

F: Does he hear you?

M: No.

F: So try again. Get communication.

M: I—I feel very sad—when I tell you this.

F: Say this to him.

M: I feel sad when I tell you this, because I really don't want to hurt you. I feel guilty when I try to hurt you.

F: We translate the word "guilty" in Gestalt Therapy by *resentful*, so let's try this on for size. How do you call him?

M: Dad.

F: "Dad, I resent this and this—I resent this and this."

M: Dad, I resent—I resent your trying to make me—fill your needs—

F: Such as—

M: I resent your telling me where to live, what to do, because I know that the only reason you tell me this is because of—because of your own needs. You want me to live near you. You want me to. . .

F: What are you blocking, right now?

M: I'm trying to think—I'm trying to think how to word what he wants me to do.

F: Okeh, play *him*. Let him say, "Maxine, I want you to live near me. . ."

M: All that I want from you, Max—All that I've given to you, I've done so much for you—All that I want from you in return is to be a good daughter. I want you to do what *other* people do. I want you to—I want you to practice pharmacy, this is what your degree is in, but instead you're throwing it *all* away. If you would do this, by the time you're forty, you could *retire*, you could have *all* the money you want. (laughter)

I don't *want* to be a pharmacist. I never *did* want to be a pharmacist.

F: Play Papa again.

M: *I* never told you to study pharmacy. You can do anything you want to. I don't care what you do. All I told you is to do something where you make a lotta money and you have a good reputation.

F: Can you do something phony? Yah?

M: Yes.

F: Go on playing Papa, and then go back and each time you answer, "Fuck you!" (laughter)

M: Each time I answer my father, I say, "Fuck you"?

F: Yes. Right. He is sermonizing, isn't he? So let him preach, and each time he tries to bullshit you into something, tell him "Fuck you."

M: I'm a sick man, and—and—I just can't put up with—with the way you treat me. You're gonna *kill* me.

F: Now he changed his tune. Now he plays the tragedy queen. (laughter) Tell him that.

M: Dad, you're playing the tragedy queen. You play the poor helpless old man, "Feel sorry for me."—That's what you tell me. "Feel sorry for me." A weak old man. I—I'm sick and tired of it. I—I can't help it if you're a weak old man if that's what you are.

(snores) He falls asleep. (laughter)

Goddamit, Dad, I'm so mad at you—every time I wanna express anything or tell you anything, you completely—you won't—you won't even listen to anything—anything I have to say is irresponsible—

F: Put more—put your whole self into it.

M: Anything I *ever* have to say to you, you consider irresponsible, not worthwhile—

F: (mimicking her tone) Nyahnyahnyahnyah.

M: Nyahnyahnyah. I'm getting sick and tired of being treated like a child. I'm not a child!

F: Well, your voice doesn't tell it, doesn't say so. Your voice is the voice of a petulant child. Try my medicine. Tell him "Fuck you."

M: Fuck you, you old bastard. (roars of laughter and applause)

How can you say such terrible things to your father! I never said those things. I never brought you up to talk that way. You're going to the dogs—it's all the education you've been getting. (laughter)

You're a narrow-minded—You're so narrow-minded you can't see anything, except /F: Nyahnyahnyahnyah./ your own way.

F: Nyahhh. Do you hear your voice? Okeh, go on talking to him, but listen to your voice.

M: I wish I could tell you what I really thought of you.

F: Yah. This sounded real. Say this again.

M: I wish I could tell you what I really thought of you.

F: Who prevents you? He isn't here. He isn't here in reality. Take the risk. . .

M: If you wouldn't die, and blame it on me, I—I'd really tell you a few things.

F: Okeh. He is dead, now.

M: *Thank God!!* (laughter)

F: Now you can talk real.

M: I feel like it's all my fault that he died.

F: Oh, this is *his* voice. Come on, switch. I want to hear what he says. "It's all your fault."

M: It's all your fault. I was—I was sick and helpless. I've got all kinds of diseases, I've got all kinds of ailments, and because you shout at me, because you make me—because you won't—uh—because you're ungrateful, because you won't help me, because you wouldn't be with me when I needed you, I died. And it's your fault.

F: Okeh, switch. "It's my fault."

M: Yeah. So I'm a slob. Does that make you happy now? Do you feel proud of me? Is that what you want? Think your daughter's a slob? O.K. I admit it, I'm a slob, and I'm gonna go on being a slob, too.

Well, I showed you. I died, and you'll be sorry. Someday you'll be sorry.

F: Again.

M: You'll be sorry someday.

F: When?

M: Someday you'll be sorry when you realize—when you grow up and realize how you have treated me—when you realize that all because of you, I died, you're going to be sorry.

F: Okeh. Now say this to someone in the audience. Say this to Brian. (fiancé) Put it on for size. . . "One day, you'll be sorry, for how you mistreated me." (laughter)

M: (laughs nervously) Please don't laugh at me. (clears throat) Someday you're going to be sorry for it. You'll be sorry, because— because you didn't treat me right. You'll lose me.

F: Tell him what you resent about him. . . What do you experience now?

M: I feel—uh—shy—and—like I—like I have no right to talk with you. (sighs)

F: What do you feel? What do you experience? What do you feel *physically*?

M: Lifeless, nothingness. Death. I feel like I have no reason to live. . .

F: So instead of going forward, you go back, yah? Okeh, come back to me. How do you feel about me?

M: I'm scared of you.

F: What do you want to do to me?

M: I'd like to be your friend.

F: Well, if you are scared, that means you project some aggression on me.

M: I'm afraid you'll get too close to me.

F: Ahah. How close can I come?

M: I don't know. (laughs) That's what I'm scared of.

F: Okeh, let's go back and say this to Papa. . .

M: Daddy, I'm scared you'll get too close to me. And I'm afraid you'll get your hooks into me. I'm afraid that you'll just make me a blob—a nothing. . .

F: So play that Papa, "I'm going to get hooks into you."

M: I'm going to *getcha*.

F: Yah. This is where your power is now. Come on. Play the witch.

M: (strongly) I'm stronger than you are. I'm gonna get you, and I'm going to put you in a cage, for life. (hands outstretched and clutching)

F: Well, this looks more like strangling.

M: I'm gonna strangle you. . . /F: Yah./ I'm gonna make you just like your mother. I'm gonna make you—I'm gonna reduce you to the level of—I'm gonna make you *just* what *I* want you to be. You're gonna fulfill just—you're gonna fulfill all my needs. You're gonna be my slave. I'm gonna take all feeling away from you, until the only thing you feel is what *I* feel, and the only thing that you're receptive to are *my* feelings, and—and—you take care of *my* feelings. Forget about yours. They aren't important. They're immature. They're childish.

F: How do you feel in that role, as the manipulator?

M: I don't like it.

F: Do you feel any strength?

M: Yes.

F: Do you recognize yourself as the manipulator? (she shakes her head) No. Then it's of no value. . . What do you experience now?. . .

M: I'm angry at my father.

F: Okeh.

M: You're not gonna do this to me, Dad. I'm not gonna letcha.

F: Say this again.

M: (louder) You're *not* gonna do this to me.

F: I still don't hear any anger. I still hear complaining. Nyahnyahnyah. So far, all the strength is still in him, and you're still on the defensive.

M: Dad, I'm not gonna let you do this to me. I don't know—I can't stop you when you're around me. If I can't stop you when you're around me, I'm just gonna get away from you. I'm gonna put the distance between us—the miles between us—so great that you can't do this to me. I'm not gonna let you. If I have to run away from you, that's what I'm gonna do.

F: Say this, "I won't let you—"

M: I won't let you. /F: Louder./
I won't let you! /F: Louder./
Goddamit! (screams) *I won't let you!*

F: Louder. Say it with your whole body.

M: I WON'T LET YOU!

F: Again, I still don't believe you. It's all literature still—wailing, complaining. . . I don't feel any confidence yet.

M: I can't say it louder.

F: He's still the stronger one.

M: Then I'll run away from him.

F: Yah. Now this is something you still have to work through—to really stand up to him. Not like a cry-baby, but as a grown-up woman.

M: I know what you mean. Thank you.

F: I want to tell you about my latest hobby. Jerry Greenwald, an ex-pupil of mine, wrote a very beautiful paper. As all psychologists of course he has to put in letters, numbers, and names, so he puts in T people and N people. T people are *toxic* people, and N people are *nourishing* people, and my suggestion to you is listen very carefully when you encounter anyone, whether he is toxic or nourishing. If he is toxic, you feel blaaaah, exhausted, irritated; if he is nourishing, you grow, you want to dance, embrace him. So any sentence—anything anybody says or does can be either toxic or nourishing. Anything that gets its support from the self is nourishing. Anything that is manipulated, conjured up, deliberate, is in most cases toxic. It's false, it's hypocrisy, it's a lie.

Those of you who are therapists, if you get a toxic patient, find out *how* he wants to poison you. How much energy do you spend? Do you strain to listen to your patients? Do you feel responsible for all the crap he talks and how he wastes the first 40 minutes with nonsense in order to bring in during the last five minutes something that puts you on tenterhooks, and makes it difficult for you to dismiss him? Or do you hear that he is putting you to sleep, and are you a good therapist and fall asleep until he wakes you up?

Of course, there is often a mixture, but sometimes you get really 100% poisonous people. If you are poisonous, that means that you have got a dybbuk, a demon, in you, somebody who poisons you, whom you have swallowed whole. The Freudian idea that we introject the person we love is wrong. You always introject people who are *in control*.

I really have a thing going right now with the poison and nourishment. You can be sure if you are in company or in a group, and you feel all exhausted and drained afterwards, you got a lot of toxic sentences. If you are refreshed and alert, you got a lot of nourishment. And very often the toxic is sugar-coated, dipped in saccharine. Now you notice how full of toxic Maxine's father is. He has poisoned her with all these threats—so she keeps away from him. But she is not yet immunized. You know what I am talking about?

M: I know what you're talking about.

F: I think for the first session you ever had—you were very brave and cooperative, but we didn't quite get through. We can't always do therapy in twenty minutes.

Q: You said that you go from the explosion to the authentic level. Can't the explosion in joy or sex or anger be authentic, /F: Yah./ and why do you differentiate this from the authentic level?

F: Because the authentic level will show itself *first* in those explosions.

Q: So they're related.

F: Oh, definitely. That's what I said. It's the link-up. The implosion goes *out*, the conflicting energies go out in the explosion. You noticed here how, in every case, they keep themselves back. Here, the voice is covering up. It's always the inner struggle. When she squeezed herself, imploded—she felt very uncomfortable. When she exploded mildly into squeezing me—she is very strong—she felt much better, much more herself.

I found it very interesting what I learned from Stan Grof this summer about what they are doing with LSD therapy in Czechoslovakia, which completely confirms my theory about the implosive layer, the death center. Despite all the deterioration, they apparently have had the courage to get through to the death center and stick to it, and then the recovery came, instead of all the symptoms coming back. I find it a beautiful confirmation of my theory—a kind of proof apart from my own experience.

ELAINE

Fritz: Do you realize something is going on in your body?

Elaine: Yes.

F: What do you experience?

E: My stomach is fluttering, and my heart is ticking, but I really don't feel—I'm starting to relax now. . . I had a dream that I wanted to talk to you. I was on. . .

F: Did you hear the tears in your voice when you said "I was on"? Did you hear the tears? This is what I like to draw your attention to—the voice. All the things the voice tells you—every second.

E: Well, I was in my bed and, uh—

F: Please tell the dream in the present tense.

E: Yes. I am lying down, and. . . I'm sleeping, and a priest, a Catholic priest—comes, and he is draped in black robes, and he comes to the bed and, ah, he asks me to come with him. And I'm frightened, at first, because I have no control of the situation. And he asks me—

F: May I interrupt for a moment? Tell the group, "I have to be in control of the situation."

E: I have to be in control of the situation.

F: Tell this to a few people here.

E: I have to be in control of the situation. (crying haltingly) I have to be in control of the situation. Uh, ah—he comes to me draped in robes, and he asks me to come, and I wasn't in control— I'm not in control.

F: Now you notice this kind of rushing. So Elaine acts as if she has emotional blindness. She experiences something—crying or so— something is going on, but she has to go through to the dream as if nothing must disturb her achievement. Apparently she is goal-oriented. Okeh.

E: And he asks me to come with him, and, I'm frightened, and I say "I can't come, now" and he's very stern, and he says "You must come, now." And I say, "I can't, I'm not ready yet." And then—I—seem to move, out—as I'm talking to him. I'm not, I don't feel I'm in my body. (begins to cry) My body is in the bed, and I'm out. . .side—but I can't move with him, because I can't leave my body in the bed, and so I tell him I have to go back, I have to go back into my body because I'm not ready. (less distressed) And I do—I move back, and he leaves immediately. When he leaves, I'm sitting at a table with my body, and at this table is some—it's a long table and it's wood and my family is sitting there—my mother, my father, myself, my brother. And, first my brother walks up to move into the other room, to die, (calmly) and I'm not affected by this. The death means nothing to me, that he's going to die. And I almost feel guilty, in the dream, that I feel nothing for his death. And then, my mother and father walk back from the room, and my father—I'm trying to hold him up. I'm lifting him, and (voice breaks) he has no bones, he has no structure, he's just an amoeba and I can't lift him, and I pick him up, and he (begins to cry) *can't stand.* There's no way I can hold him up—I *tried.* And (softly) that happens to him. . . He comes to his death also—(very rapidly) he's moving to his death and then there's just my mother and I that are left, and I'm sitting at the table, waiting for my death. . .

F: So, let's start with having an encounter with the priest. You sit there, put the priest in this chair, and talk to him.

E: I'm terribly frightened. . . of all the things you told me, about my death, and I *want* to understand it, but you've given me *nothing,* and (crying) no means to understand it. . . and I've asked you. . . and I have no means of. . . finding it, through you, and yet you insist on coming back into my life. . .

F: Play him. "I am your priest."

E: (coolly) I am your priest. . .

F: What are you doing now? Are you rehearsing?

E: No. . . I'm. . . feeling an authoritarian figure to talk to her.

F: Say this to her. "I am an authority."

E: (weakly) I am an authority. . . I am an authority. I'm an authority, and you must listen to what I tell you.

F: Say this again.

E: I *am* an authority, and you must listen to what I tell you.

F: Louder.

E: I am an authority (cries) and you must listen to what I tell you.

F: The priest is crying?. . .

E: No, but I had a realization of myself when I said—

F: So be yourself again. . .

E: I. . . Do you know what just came to me just now?

F: Say this to him.

E: (weakly) I am the priest. . . *I* am the priest. Elaine is the priest.

F: Ahah, now say this to the audience.

E: (coolly) *I* am the priest. Elaine is the priest.

F: Actually—and this is the decisive point—every bit of the dream is yourself. The fragmentation of the human personality is coming out nowhere better than in the dream. If you free-associate to a dream or look for actual facts, you destroy what you can get from a dream or fantasy. Namely, the re-integration of your dis-owned personality. I want to emphasize this again and again. Gestalt Therapy has an integrative approach. We integrate. We are not ana-lytically oriented. We don't cut things up further and look for rea-sons and insights. The experience that Elaine just had is typical. With this little bit, she already realized that she *is* the priest. And every bit of the material, if you really play it fully, becomes part of yourself again, and instead of being more and more impoverished, you be-come richer and richer and richer. So be our priest. Be my priest. . .

E: *I'm* going to direct *you*.

F: Yah. You are in control, aren't you?

E: Yes. Now I am. And—I'm going to help *you* guide *your* being, not me. That's when I'm the priest—or, I *am* the priest.

F: You are afraid of your power, your wish to be a priest?

E: Yes.

F: Tell this to the audience, too.

E: I'm afraid of my power, (cries) and wish to be a priest. . . I *am*.

F: Well, I don't understand your crying, there. Let's go a step further. What's your power of crying?

E: I very seldom cry in front of people, or in situations, very seldom.

F: What do you achieve with crying? What's your power of crying?

E: Ahh. . . my power of crying. I'm humble, I'm being humble, that I want to have humility, that I want to be humble.

F: You put on a performance of a cry-baby.

E: Am I doing this now?

F: It's an old joke of mine that tears are a woman's second-best weapon. (laughter) Do you know what the best weapon is?—Cooking. (laughter) So what do you experience now? /E: Humility./ Humility. /E: Yes./ Can you exaggerate humility—dance it, act it out?. . . (Elaine gets up and moves around slowly with shoulders bent). . . How does it feel?. . .

E: I know how it does *not* feel—more than I know how it feels. I usually stand very erect, and tall. And here I feel very little, and small.

F: So let's go on a little bit more with the encounter with the priest. Put him there again. Tell him again, "I'm not ready for you."

E: I'm not ready for you. . . and I don't know. . . how to *deal* with you. . .

But I insist that you deal with me, and it has to be now, because you can't wait. You really *haven't* got much time to wait.

F: Say this again.

E: You *haven't* got much time to wait. You've waited long enough.

F: Change chairs.

E: There are too many things that I have to take care of yet. I'm—*not* going to deal with you, because. . . there are too many *practical* things I have to take care of. I don't have—I don't have the *time*.

F: Yah. You get the existential message?

E: Yes, I'm getting?—am I getting what's going on?

F: Yah. From the dream—do you get the message, what the dream says? What does the dream say?

E: It's telling me that I'm living at two poles—at the ends of the poles—and I'm not coming together, in the middle. It's like, I'm living in the. . . I'm not living in the now as you say.

F: You notice the whole dream is preoccupied with the future, and most of all with the *end* of the future—death. And the fear of death means the fear of life. Does this mean anything? You get a little?

E: Yes. Oh, yes. I—my intensity for life has become so great, emotionally /F: Yah./ that I'm very intense about so many things that I become involved in, *because* of my preoccupation, it seems to me, with death, that every moment—um, with so many things that I do, there's such turmoil going on in my body. . .

F: Okeh, put the turmoil in this chair. Talk to your turmoil. . .

E: You have no—My tur—. . . You have no, no means of—I have no means of *dealing* with you.

F: Umhm. Say this again.

E: I have no means of *dealing* with you. . . There's. . . no way. . . for me to come in contact. *You're* controlling *me*.

F: Yah. Now be the turmoil that controls you. "Elaine, I am your turmoil. I control you."

E: I will keep you moving. /F: Say this again./
I will keep you moving. /F: Again./
Uhuh, moving. /F: Again./
I will keep you moving. /F: Say this to the audience./
I will keep you moving. /F: Say this to a few people here./
I will keep you moving. I will keep you moving. I will keep you moving.

F: So how do you do this? How do you keep people moving?. . .

E: By letting them become involved—in what I'm saying. /F: Umhum./ But I'm in control.

F: Umhum. Now talk again to the group and give us a speech of about a minute. "I am control mad. I have to control the world, I have to control myself—"

E: I'm control mad. I have to control people. I have to control myself. I have to control the world. When I control the world, then I can deal with it, but when I'm in control, I have no means of dealing with it. So then I become lost, so I'm—

F: "And then I become lost." Let me pick this up. Close your eyes, and *get lost*. . . What happens when you get lost?

E: (relaxed) Oh, I'm. . . slowly moving, I'm at peace with myself.

F: Say this again.

E: I'm. . . I'm slowly moving, at peace with myself. /F: Yah./ Swirling. . . soft. . . Absence of tension.

F: Does it feel good?. . .

E: In contrast. Yes.

F: Yah. . . So what happened when you got lost? When you are not in control?. . .

E: It's. . . I can—I can describe it—it's a movement of the sea when the tide and the surf is slowly rolling, and—only—I am a part of the movement and the swirl, it's not violent. And I slowly move, in a circle. I am turning, my body is slowly turning, as the sea turns—that's how I feel.

F: So the catastrophic expectation that something terrible will happen if you don't control is not quite correct?

E: No. This is, what I become then—

F: Yah. I felt you were much more yourself, much less torn. So the control-madness really *prevents* you from being yourself.

E: Yes. Even with my body.

F: Yah. . . Okeh.

JEAN

Jean: It's a long time ago I dreamed this. I'm not sure how it started. I think it first started in the—sort of like the New York subway, and kind of paying—putting a token in, and going to the turnstile, and walking a little way down the corridors, and then kind of turning a corner and I realize that some way or other in here, uh. . . instead of being a subway, it seemed like there were sort of like inclines that started going down into the earth. And it seemed to turn and I realized what was going on, and some way or another just about this point as I discovered this incline, my mother was with me, or maybe she was when I started—I can't remember.

At any rate, it was this incline—it was sort of muddy, sort of slippery, and I thought, Oh! We can go down this! and well, sort of on the side, I picked up a left-over carton—or maybe it was just flattened out or I flattened it out. At any rate, I said, "Let's sit down on this." I sat down on the edge, kind of made a toboggan out of it, and I said, "Mom, you sit down behind me," and we started going down. And it sort of went around and around (quickly) and there were other people it seemed like, waiting in line, but then they kind of disappeared, and we were (happily) just going down and around and it just kept on going down and down and down, and I was sort of realizing that I was going down kind of into the bowels of the earth.

And every once in a while I'd turn around and say, "Isn't this

fun?"—it seems, although maybe I'll discover I didn't have that attitude either. But it seemed like fun. And yet I wondered what would
be down at the bottom of this—going, turn and turn, and then finally
it leveled out and we got up and I was just astounded, because here I
thought, "Oh my God, the bowels of the earth!" And yet, instead of
being dark, it was like there was sunlight coming from somewhere,
and a beautiful. . . oh, kind of like a. . . I've never been to Florida,
but it seemed like a Florida kind of everglades, with lagoons, and tall
reeds, and beautiful long-legged birds—herons—and things like that.
And I don't remember saying anything particularly, except maybe
something like, "Who would ever have expected this!"—or something.

Fritz: Yes. Now, when the dreamer tells a story like this, you
can take it just as an incident or unfinished situation, or wish fulfill-
ment, but if we tell it in the present, as mirroring our existence, it
immediately gets a different aspect. It's not just an occasional happening. You see, a dream is a condensed reflection of our existence.
What we don't realize enough is that we devote our lives to a dream:
a dream of glory, usefulness, do-gooder, gangster, or whatever we
dream of. And in many people's lives, through self-frustration, our
dream turns into a nightmare. The task of all deep religions—especially Zen Buddhism—or of really good therapy, is the *satori*, the
great awakening, the coming to one's senses, waking up from one's
dream—especially from one's nightmare. We can start already on this
by realizing that we are playing roles in the theater of life, by understanding that we are always in a trance. We decide "This is an
enemy," "This is a friend," and we play all these games until we
come to our *senses*.

When we come to our senses, we start to *see*, to *feel*, to *experience* our needs and satisfactions, instead of playing roles and needing
such a lot of props for that—houses, motor cars, dozens and dozens
of costumes, though, when it comes to it, a woman never has anything to wear, so she needs still another costume. Or the man has to
get a new costume when he goes to work and when he goes to see his
sweetheart—all the millions of unnecessary ballast with which we
burden ourselves, not realizing that all property is given to us only
for the duration anyhow. You can't take it with you, and if we have
money, then we have additional worry what to do with the money.

You shouldn't lose it, or should increase it, and so on and so on—all these dreams, all these nightmares, which are so typical of our civilization. Now the idea of *waking up* and becoming real means to exist with what we have, the real full potential, a rich life, deep experiences, joy, anger—being *real* not *zombies*! This is the meaning of real therapy, the real maturation, the real waking up, instead of this continual self-deception and fantasizing impossible goals, feeling sorry for ourselves because we can't play that part we want to play, and so on.

So, let's switch back to Jean. Jean, would you talk again, tell again the dream, live it through as if this was your existence, as if you live it now, see if you can understand more about your life. . .

J: I don't—it doesn't really seem clear until I find myself—the place has become kind of a top of the chute. I don't remember whether at first I was afraid or not, possibly—oh, I should say this is now?

F: You are now on the chute. Are you afraid to go down?

J: (laughs) I guess I am, a little afraid to go down. But then it seems like. . .

F: So the existential message is, "You've got to go down."

J: I guess I'm afraid to find out what's there.

F: This points to false ambitions, that you're too high up.

J: That's true.

F: So the existential message says, "Go down." Again our mentality says, "High up is better than down." You must always be somewhere higher.

J: Anyway, I seem a little afraid to go down.

F: Talk to the chute.

J: Why are you muddy? You're slippery and slidy and I might fall on you and slip.

F: Now play the chute. "I'm slippery and. . ."

J: I'm slippery and muddy, the better to slide and faster to get down on. (laughs)

F: Ahah, well, what's the joke?

J: (continues laughing) I'm just laughing.

F: Can you accept yourself as slippery?

J: Hm. I guess so. Yes. I can never seem to. . . Yeah, you know, always just when I think I'm about to, you know, say, "Aha! I've caught you now!" it slips away—you know, rationalization. I'm slippery and slidy. Hm. Anyway, I'm going to go down because it looks like it would be fun, and I want to find out where this goes and what's going to be at the end of it. And it seems, perhaps only now, I'm turning around and looking to see what I could use to kind of protect my clothes (laughs) or maybe make a better slide. I discover this cardboard—

F: Can you play this cardboard? If you were this cardboard. . . what's your function?

J: I'm just—to make things easier. I'm just kind of lying around and left-over, and aha, I have a use for it.

F: Oh—you can be useful.

J: I can be useful. I'm not just left-over and lying around, and we can make it easier to get down.

F: Is it important for you to be useful?

J: (quietly) Yes. I want to be an advantage to somebody. . . Is that enough for being the cardboard?. . . Maybe I also want to be sat upon. (laughter) /F: Oh!/ What is that part in the book about who wants to kick who? I want to be pitied, I want to be scrunched down. /F: Say this again./

(laughing) I want to be sat upon and scrunched down.

F: Say this to the group.

J: Well, that's hard to do. (loudly) I want to be sat upon and scrunched down. . . Hm. (loudly) I want to be *sat upon* and *scrunched down*. (pounds her thigh with fist)

F: Who are you hitting? /J: Me./ Besides you?

J: I think my mother, who's turning, who's behind me and I look around and see her.

F: Good. Now hit her.

J: (loudly) Mother, I'm scrunching down upon—(hits thigh) ouch!—you (laughs) and *I* am going to take *you* for a ride (laughter) instead of your telling me to go, and taking *me* wherever *you* want to, *I'm* taking *you* along for a ride with *me*.

F: Did you notice anything in your behavior with your mother?

J: Just now? (laughs)

F: I had the impression it was *too much* to be convincing. . . It was spoken with anger, not with firmness.

J: Mmm. I think I'm still a little afraid of her.

F: That's it. You tell her that.

J: Mom, I'm still afraid of you. . . but I'm gonna take you for a ride anyway.

F: Okeh. Let's put momma on the sled. (laughter)

J: (laughs) You sit behind me. You have to sit behind this time. . . Are you ready? O.K.

F: You're taking the lead.

J: I'm in the lead. I'm in control. (laughs)

F: You are the driver.

J: (sadly) The only driving I'm doing is with, you know—downs. (sighs)

F: Do you ride a bobsled?

J: I've never ridden a bobsled. . . but I've skiied. O.K., here we go. I don't know where we're going—at this point. We're just going off because it's some place to go and we're there.

F: Well, you said that this is a journey into the bowels of the earth.

J: Yes. But I'm not really sure of that now, I think. I don't really—it doesn't really dawn on me until I realize just how far we keep going.

F: So, start out.

J: We're going down now. We're sliding down, and then we come to a turn, and now we go round. . . around. . . around. . . and I see if she's still there. (laughs) She's still there.

F: Always make it an encounter. This is the *most* important thing, to change everything into an encounter, instead of gossiping *about*. Talk *to* her. If you don't talk *to* someone, you are giving a performance.

J: Are you still there?

F: What does she answer?

J: Yes. I'm still here, but it's kind of scary.

Don't worry. I've got it all taken care of. (decisively) We're having *fun*. I don't know where this is going, but we're going to find out.

I'm scared!

I think I—don't be scared. It's going down and down and DOWN and DOWN. . . (softly) I wonder what's going to be down there. It'll just be black. . . I don't know what she says.

F: What's your left hand doing?

J: Right this instant?

F: Yah. *Always* right this instant.

J: Holding my head. I'm—

F: As if?. . .

J: Not to see?

F: Ahah. You don't want to see where you are going, don't want to see the danger.

J: Umhm. (softly) I'm really afraid—of what will be down there. . . It could be terrible or just blackness or just maybe even oblivion.

F: I would like you to go now into this blackness. This is your nothingness, the blankness, the sterile void. What does it feel like to be in this nothingness?

J: Suddenly, nothingness is I'm going down, now. . . So I still have a feeling that I'm going down, and so it's kind of exciting and exhilarating. . . because I'm moving, and I'm very much alive. . . I'm not really afraid. It's more—kind of terribly exciting and. . . the anticipation—what I will discover at the end of this. It's not really black—it's sort of going down, somehow there's some light, where it's from, I don't—

F: Yah. I want to make a little bit of a shortcut here, to say something. Are you aware of what you are avoiding in this dream?

J: Am I aware of what I am avoiding?. . .

F: Having legs.

J: Having legs?

F: Yah.

J: Legs to carry me some place.

F: Yah. Instead of standing on your legs, you rely on the support of the cardboard, and you rely on gravitation to carry you.

J: Passively. . . passively through the tunnel—through life.

F: What's your objection to having legs?

J: The first thing that comes into my head is that somebody— the first thing was that somebody might knock me down, then I realized that I was afraid my mother would knock me down. She doesn't want me to have legs.

F: Now, have another encounter with her. Is it true she doesn't want you to stand on your own legs—on your own feet?

J: (complaining) Why don't you want me to stand on my own legs?

'Cause you're helpless. You need me.

I *don't* need you. I can go through life all by myself. . . I can!—She must have said, "You can't."

F: There you notice the same anger /J: Yeah, I did./ and lack of firmness, lack of support.

J: Yeah.

F: You see this is very peculiar how we are built. The lower carriage is for support and the upper carriage is for contact, but without firm support and good support, of course, the contact is wobbly too.

J: I shouldn't be angry.

F: I didn't say you shouldn't be angry, but the anger is still /J: It's too wobbly./ too wobbly, yah.

J: I'm afraid to stand on my own two legs and be angry. . . at her.

F: And *face* her, really. Stand on your legs now, and encounter your mother, and see whether you can talk to her.

J: (softly) I'm afraid to look at her.

F: Say this to her.

J: (loudly) I'm afraid to look at you, mother! (exhales)

F: What would you see?

J: What do I see? I see I hate her. (loudly) I hate you for holding me back every time I wanted to even go across the aisle of the damn department store.

(high-pitched) Come back here! Don't go on the other side of the aisle.

I can't even walk across the damned aisle. Can't go to Flushing when I want to go on the bus. Can't go to New York—not until I go to college. Damn you!. . .

F: How old are you when you play this now?

J: Well, I'm. . . in the department store, I'm only anywhere from six to ten or twelve—

F: How old are you, really?

J: Really? Thirty-one. /F: Thirty-one./ She's even dead.

F: Okeh, can you talk as a thirty-one-year-old to your mother? Can you be your age?

J: (quietly and firmly) Mother, I am thirty-one years old. I'm quite capable of walking on my own.

F: Notice the difference. Much less noise, and much more substance.

J: I can stand on my own legs. I can do *any*thing I want to do, and I can know what I want to do. I don't need you. In fact, you're not even here if I *did* need you. So why do you hang around?

F: Yah. Can you say goodbye to her? Can you bury her?

J: Well, I can now, because I'm at the bottom of the slope, and when I come to the bottom I stand up. I stand up and I walk around and it's a beautiful place.

F: Can you say to your mother, "Goodbye Mother, rest in peace"?

J: I think I did tell her. . . Goodbye, Mother. (like a cry) Good-bye!. . .

F: (gently) Talk to her. Go to her grave and talk to her about it.

J: (crying) Goodbye, Mom. You couldn't help what you did. It wasn't your fault that you had three boys first, and then you thought it would be another boy, and you didn't want me and you felt so bad after you found out I was a girl. (still crying) You just tried to make it up to me that's all. You didn't have to smother me. . . I forgive you, Mom. . . You worked awful hard. I can go, now. . . Sure, I can go.

F: You are still holding your breath, Jean. . .

J: (to herself) Are you really sure, Jean?. . . (softly) Momma, let me go.

F: What would she say?

J: I can't let you go.

F: Now *you* say this to your mother.

J: I can't let you go?

F: Yah. You keep her. You're holding on to her.

J: Mom, I *can't* let you go. I need you. Mom, I don't need you.

F: But you still miss her. . . don't you?

J: (very softly) A little. Just somebody there. . . what if nobody was there?. . . what if it was all empty, and dark. It's not all empty and dark—it's beautiful. . . I'll let you go. . . (sighs, almost inaudible) I'll let you go, Mom. . .

F: I'm very glad that we have this last experience—we can learn such a lot from this. You notice this was no play-acting. This was no crying for sympathy, it was no crying to get control, this was one of the four explosions I mentioned—the ability to explode into grief— and this mourning labor, as Freud called it, is necessary to grow up, to say goodbye to the image of the child. This is very essential. Very few people can really visualize, conceive themselves as adults. They always still have to have a mother or father image around. This is where Freud went completely astray. One of the few things where he was *completely* wrong. He thought a person does not mature *because* he has childhood traumata. It is the other way around. A person doesn't want to take the responsibility of the adult person, and thereby rationalizes, hangs on to the childhood memories, to the image that they are a child, and so on. Because to grow up means to be *alone*, and to be alone is the prerequisite for maturity and contact. Loneliness, isolation, is still longing for support. Jean has made a big step toward growing, tonight.

CAROL

Carol: I'm trying to decide whether to divorce my husband or not, and have been for ten years.

Fritz: It's a real impasse, yah! A real unfinished situation. And this is typical of the impasse. We try *everything* to keep the status quo, rather than to get through the impasse. We keep on with our self-torture games, with our bad marriages, with our therapy where we improve, improve, improve, and nothing changes, but our inner conflict is always the same, we maintain the status quo. So talk to your husband. Put him there.

C: Well, I feel like I've been—I've found out some things, Andy, and I found out who you—who you are to me, and I love you in some ways. You know, I didn't love you when I married you, but I do love you now, in some ways, but—but I feel like I'm not gonna be able to grow up if I stay with you, and I don't want to be a freak.

F: Change seats.

C: That's not fair, Carol, because I love you so much, and we've been together for so long. . . and I want to take care of you. . . I just want you to love me, and—

F: I don't understand. First, he says he loves you, and now you say he wants—he needs love.

C: Yes. I—I really need—I guess I do need love.

F: Is it a trade? A trade agreement—love vs. love?. . .

C: I need you.

F: Ah! What do you need Carol for?

C: Because you're exciting. . . I feel dead without you.

You're a *drag*, Andy. I can't *feel* for *both* of us. . . I'm—I know, I'm scared too, I'm really scared of leaving. I'm scared of leaving, too, but—we're just scared. We both need love. I don't think I can give it to you.

F: Can we start with resentments. Tell him what you resent about him.

C: Ohh, I resent your being such a burden on my back. I resent—every time I leave the house, I have to feel guilty about it. I feel guilty for—

F: Now that's a lie. When you feel guilty, you actually feel resentful. Scratch out the word guilty, and use the word *resentful* instead, each time.

C: I resent not being able to feel free. I want to move. I want—I resent. . . I resent your nagging at me. . .

F: Now tell him what you appreciate in him.

C: All right. I really appreciate—your taking care of me, and your loving me, 'cause I'm—I know nobody else could really love me like you do. I resent your—

F: Now let's scratch out the word "love," and put in the real words instead.

C: Ohh. I resent your smothering me. I resent your keeping me a little girl.

F: And what should he do?

C: You should go to bed with me, and you should screw me. And I don't want to screw you any more, the way you do it. I don't want to. You should do it. Something's wrong, something should be different. I—I really would like to love some—*some*body. I—I'm tired of that place, just being loved. I feel that there's a hole in me, I've chewed a big hole in me. I want to grow up.

F: How old do you feel you are?

C: How old? I. . . I don't have—I don't really know. I know I recognize two voices all the time, and I've been trying not to talk much here so I won't hear them. One is very childish, and one is—one that I like, it sounds adult. It's one I use on the phone a lot. It's sometimes very hostile and sharp.

F: Can you hear your voice now?

C: It's—kind of in the middle. It's—uh—it's—controlled, so it won't be childish.

F: Well, *I* react to your voice right now with sleepiness. You hypnotize me, you put me to sleep. . .

C: (cries) I put myself to sleep, like this, /F: Yah. Yah./ and then I can't seem to go beyond—where I am now—I can grow up, and then when I really think about making a decision—then I put myself to sleep. I either go to sleep or I have five jobs. (laughs) I just go crazy working. And then, once in awhile I have an experience, I think, "Well, I'll think about this," and instead of thinking about it, I just block and I go to sleep. Either sitting here and going to sleep, or go take sleeping pills and go to sleep.

F: Now I want an encounter between Carol and sleep.

C: Ohhh, sleep. O.K. Shall I just be sleep here?

F: No, *there* is Carol. Sleep is *here*.

C: Oh, boy, would I just like to go to sleep. I might be able to take a nap this afternoon, or—if I can just get down to this work, I'll go to sleep. But then maybe I'll stay up some more, or watch television or something. There's nothing to do, I guess I'll just have to go to sleep. I don't think I can go to sleep by myself, so I'll take a pill and then I'll be *sure* to go to sleep, because I have to watch the clock and in a few hours I've got to get up. So start over. O.K., I'm going to go to sleep, and I'm gonna—I'll be sleep.

Oh. I'm sleep. . . It's not like I thought. I'm sleep. (voice dies to a whisper) I'm not really—I'm nothing—I'm—I'm not restful. I'm wan. . . I'm wan. . . I'm moving. . . I'm not peaceful. . . I'm not peaceful. I'm. . . dreaming and I'm talking, I'm hearing sounds. . .

F: Now be Carol again.

C: I'm tense. My back hurts, now. My eyes feel tired. My legs feel tight. And I—well, I fantasize. I fantasize a lot.

F: Yah.

C: And when I'm in bed, I fantasize a lot.

F: For instance?

C: Well, I have my old standards. (laughs) Prince Charming. . . I don't—I don't believe it any more. (cries) It just wouldn't leave me still for six months, and I just don't believe it any more. I'm gonna have to do something on my own—nothing—all this fantasy crap, it doesn't help things, at least not for me. I have to do something myself. I want to, one way or the other, make a commitment in my marriage, one way or the other. Shit or get off the pot—one way or the other, so that I don't spend my energy and time thinking each day whether this will be the day when I make my mind up.

F: Now tell this—talk like this to Carol, "Carol, shit or get off the pot."

C: I've been telling her.

F: Let's have it again.

C: Ohhhhh. (laughs) Oh, Carol, when are you gonna make up your *mind*? What are you gonna do? Do *something*, for Christ's sake. You're just a dull, monotonous rattle—on and on with your goddamn fantasy world. Prince *Charming*. You're not getting so pretty any more. You never were. Take you away, shit. Nobody's gonna come and take you away. Get up and go, if you're gonna go.

F: Change seats. . .

C: Yeah, but at least I know what I've got here. It's not so bad, really, you know, if I just look at things. Stop being so dramatic about it, it's really not bad at all. I'm very lucky. Eugghhlhch! (laughter)

F: Say this again.

C: Eugghhch! /F: Again./
Eyahhgh! /F: Again./
Eyagghh! So reasonable. Oy, vey! You've been so *reasonable*. Well, you sure did a *boner*.

F: Change seats again.

C: I've forgotten who I am again.

F: I should say! I agree. Yah. Well, I want to finish here. All I can say is, you are a beautiful example of being stuck. You are stuck in your marriage, you are stuck with your fantasies, you are stuck with your self-torture—

C: So what does that mean?

F: That you are stuck. . . You want something from me, now. You look at me as if you want something.

C: Oh, I know you can't really help me make my decisions, but—/F: *But.*/ But maybe you can help me understand where I am— like if I'm making any progress.

F: No. You are stuck. You are in your morass.

C: Then, how do you get out of this? How do I get out of this thing?

F: Go further *into* it. Understand how you are stuck. Have you ever seen a film, *The Woman in the Dunes*?

C: Well, how do I go further into it?. . . Think about it?

F: Well, I suggest that you use the words, "I'm stuck," about a hundred times a day. Talk to your husband about how you're stuck, and talk to your friends, until you fully understand how you are stuck.

C: Thank you.

F: Well, what I would like to bring home is, it's really a beautiful example. You can go to psychoanalysis for a hundred years, you can do mind-fucking for a hundred years. Nothing would change. The status quo is maintained. She *is* stuck, and she *wants* to be stuck. If she doesn't get through the impasse, she will remain like this for the rest of her life.

X: What you're saying, the more you go into it, then she finally, as someone said last night, will get tired of it. That, perhaps—

F: This would be telling. I can tell you only this much: It is possible to get through the impasse. If I would say how, I would be "helpful," and it would be of no avail. She has to discover it, all on her own. If she really gets clear, "I'm stuck," she might be willing to do something about it. She is pretty close to realizing, at least, that she is stuck in the marriage. She doesn't realize yet that she is stuck with her self-torture, in her game. "You should/you should not; you should/you should not; yes/but; but in case this happens/then; why doesn't Prince Charming come/but Prince Charming doesn't exist." All this verbiage, what I call the merry-go-round of the being-stuck whirl, the real whirl. I think you got a good example. The only solution is to find a magician with his magic wand. And this doesn't exist. All right.

KIRK

Kirk: I don't have a dream to tell you.

Fritz: Okeh, talk to that non-existent dream.

K: Well, you're not non-existent, you're just—that I have—when you're around—and then you run away as soon as I wake up. And everybody here is learning so much about himself but you copped out. You didn't give me any information I can work with.

F: Change seats. "Yes, I run away. I am your dream, I run away."

K: Well, it wasn't my fault you woke up and forgot. I did my business. I dreamed. You're the one that forgot. I didn't run away.

So it's my fault, again.

F: That must be a Jewish mother dream. "It's my fault again!" (laughter)

K: Shame on you, poor little me. You know.

F: Can you answer without thinking when I snap my finger, to my question? Without thinking. When did you lose your dream?

K: Right after I woke up. . . I had a dream, and I told—this is what Fritz wants to work with, and I woke up, and I didn't have it. . .

F: A life without a dream. . . What happened to your dream?

K: My dream. . . A life without a dream is something very sad.

F: What are your hands doing now?

K: They're massaging the tips. My hands are shaking.

F: Yah. Let's have an encounter; there's something going on there.

K: You're nervous, and I'm—as usual I'm going to protect you, and—get your—your *action* down here, so you won't do anything you shouldn't do with your hands. You're ashamed of their trembling, your left hand trembling—so—ah, I'll close them.

F: Could you give me a number of sentences starting with "I am ashamed of—"?

K: I am ashamed of my physique, I am ashamed of the way I am unable to come across with people. I am ashamed of the way I look. I am ashamed that I'm stupid to be ashamed. I'm ashamed—

F: Say this to Kirk, "Kirk, you should be ashamed of—walking the earth, or of being nervous—"

K: You should be *ashamed* for doing this. You know better. You know that you have worth, you know that there are things you can do well.

F: Go on nagging. Become a real nag.

K: You should be ashamed! It's silly, it's stupid. It's just further evidence that you're—you're—not worth being around. You won't even accept—stand up for things you know that you can do well. You're rotten to be—to feel the way you do.

F: Now, can you nag *us* a bit. Tell us we should be ashamed. . .

K: You should be ashamed. . .

F: Just play a nag.

K: Be ashamed! You're sitting and watching people and why are you even down here? You should know everything. You should be able to take care of yourself. . . and thinking about yourselves, and thinking you have to come down here and take care of yourselves, when there's so much going on in the world that should be taken care of. I know you came down here for your own benefit. This is something very phony.

F: Good. Let's play this phony game. Again go back to Kirk. Say, "Kirk, you should be ashamed of this and that." Then you play Kirk, and each time you talk back, either "Fuck you," or nag back, make a counter-attack.

K: Kirk, you should be ashamed for being. . .

(disgustedly) Oh, shut up! You're always doing that. Just shut up!

Who's gonna tell you if you don't? Somebody has to keep reminding you to keep yourself down, now don't think you're so fucking smart.

Ah, there he goes again! Screaming at me. All day long. All day long. Let me enjoy myself a little.

All I can do is say, over and over again—

F: What are your hands doing now?

K: They want to hit.

F: Ah. Yah. The nagger gets a little stronger now.

K: It's what happens, 'cause—

F: Tell him, "I could hit you."

K: I could hit you! but I really can't hit you, so I nag. My words are hitting. This is safer, because if you really hit, well then you'll destroy, and I wouldn't have any reason. . . not to feel this way. . . if you weren't there to nag me. 'Cause if I hit, I would destroy you.

F: Now say this to your parents. Is this the Jewish mother? Did your mother nag? Is she a nag?

K: No.

F: Who is the nagger? The director, the pusher.

K: God. (resentfully) Your sins are all your fault, but your virtues are gifts of God, so don't—pride goeth before a fall, and all this shit you get all your life.

F: Can you tell God what you resent in him?

K: He's such a fucking phony. (laughter)

F: Tell *him*.

K: (halting) You're—you're—(loud laughter). . . If you *were*, you *are* a phony. Whatever—Godness is, in me, it's phony. It's worse than phony, it's *malicious*.

F: Could you say, "*I* am malicious"?

K: I am malicious. I am malicious.

F: Say this to God, too. "You are malicious."

K: *You* are malicious. . . Except you aren't.

F: I know, now, what you are. You are a *canceller*. You put up the kingpins, and then you knock them down. You put up the king-pins again, and then you knock them down. "Yes—but." It is very important to understand the word *but*. *But* is a killer. You say "yes. . ." and then comes the big "but" that kills the whole yes. You don't give the yes a chance. Now if you replace *but* with *and*, then you give the yes, the positive side, a chance. More difficult to under-stand is the *but* when it's not verbal, and comes out in behavior. You might say "yes, yes, yes," and your attitude is *but*; your voice or your gestures cancel out what you say. "Yes—but." So there's no chance of growing or developing.

K: How do I change, then?

F: Put Fritz in the chair and ask him.

K: How do I change that, Fritz?

   Don't knock down pins, when you set them up.

   Sounds very simple. . .

   It may be simple, but it's hard, that you have to practice.

F: See? "Yes—but." "How simple, *but*"—(laughter)

K: It's simple but it's hard.

F: Yah. You see, even Fritz is a canceller—*your* Fritz. . .

K: Yeah. I wanted you to tell me what to do—

F: So that you can throw it in the garbage can.

K: I *can* do it. . . I just *stop* doing it. . . stop conning myself.

F: Are you nagging again?

K: Yeah. "I oughta be ashamed." Yeah. It's the way I am. . .

F: What's your objection to yourself?. . . Will you do me a favor, and accept everything bad in you, like the trembling and so on. You go on with your nervousness and find it interesting. Say "Yes" to your trembling and leave out the "but." I know it's a gimmick right now, but let's try this gimmick, "I'm trembling. I enjoy it."

K: You relax me, I can't—

F: Ah! You relax the very moment you stop pushing, because then you don't have to be spiteful. Nagging creates a counterforce. This is the basis of the self-torture game—to try to be something you are not. Okeh.

MEG

Meg: In my dream, I'm sitting on a platform, and there's somebody else with me, a man, and maybe another person, and—ah—a couple of rattlesnakes. And one's up on the platform, now, all coiled up, and I'm frightened. And his head's up, but he doesn't seem like he's gonna strike me. He's just sitting there and I'm frightened, and this other person says to me—uh—just, just don't disturb the snake and he won't bother you. And the other snake, the other snake's down below, and there's a dog down there.

Fritz: What is there?

M: A dog, and the other snake.

F: So, up here is one rattlesnake and down below is another rattlesnake and the dog.

M: And the dog is sort of sniffing at the rattlesnake. He's—ah—getting very close to the rattlesnake, sort of playing with it, and I wanna stop—stop him from doing that.

F: Tell him.

M: Dog, stop! /F: Louder./
Stop! /F: Louder./
(shouts) STOP! /F: Louder./
(screams) *STOP!*

F: Does the dog stop?

M: He's looking at me. Now he's gone back to the snake. Now—now, the snake's sort of coiling up around the dog, and the dog's lying down, and—and the snake's coiling around the dog, and the dog looks very happy.

F: Ah! Now have an encounter between the dog and the rattlesnake.

M: You want me to play them?

F: Both. Sure. This is your dream. Every part is a part of yourself.

M: I'm the dog. (hesitantly) Huh. Hello, rattlesnake. It sort of feels good with you wrapped around me.

F: Look at the audience. Say this to somebody in the audience.

M: (laughs gently) Hello, snake. It feels good to have you wrapped around me.

F: Close your eyes. Enter your body. What do you experience physically?

M: I'm trembling. Tensing.

F: Let this develop. Allow yourself to tremble and get your feelings... (her whole body begins to move a little) Yah. Let it happen. Can you dance it? Get up and dance it. Let your eyes open, just so that you stay in touch with your body, with what you want to express physically... Yah... (she walks, trembling and jerkily, almost staggering) Now dance rattlesnake... (she moves slowly and sinuously graceful)... How does it feel to be a rattlesnake now?...

M: It's—sort of—slowly—quite—quite aware, of anything getting too close.

F: Hm?

M: Quite aware of not letting anything get too close, ready to strike.

F: Say this to us. "If you come too close, I—"

M: If you come too close, I'll strike back!

F: I don't hear you. I don't believe you, yet.

M: If you come too close, I will *strike back*!

F: Say this to each one, here.

M: If you come too close, I will *strike back!*

F: Say this with your whole body.

M: If you come too close, I will *strike back!*

F: How are your legs? I experience you as being somewhat wobbly.

M: Yeah.

F: That you don't really take a stand.

M: Yes. I feel I'm. . . kind of, in between being very strong and—if I let go, they're going to turn to rubber.

F: Okeh, let them turn to rubber. (her knees bend and wobble) Again. . . Now try out how strong they are. Try out—hit the floor. Do anything. (she stamps several times with one foot) Yah, now the other. (stamps other foot) Now let them turn to rubber again. (she lets knees bend again) More difficult now, isn't it?

M: Yeah.

F: Now say again the sentence, "If you come too close—". . . (she makes an effort). . . (laughter). . .

M: If—if you. . .

F: Okeh, change. Say "Come close." (laughter)

M: Come close.

F: How do you feel now?

M: Warm.

F: You feel somewhat more real?

M: Yeah.

F: Okeh. . . So what we did is we took away some of the fear of being in touch. So, from now on, she'll be a bit more in touch.

You see how you can use *everything* in a dream. If you are pursued by an ogre in a dream, and you *become* the ogre, the nightmare disappears. You re-own the energy that is invested in the demon. Then the power of the ogre is no longer outside, alienated, but inside where you can use it.

CHUCK

Chuck: (assured confident voice) Would you say the thing about the ogre again? I don't quite get all of it. The ogre outside and the ogre inside.

Fritz: Do you have any nightmare?

C: Yes. . . (laughter). . . (he comes up to work) The nightmare is not recurrent, but it has happened two or three times where—once I recall *very* vividly, when I was driving down the hill from my house—

F: You remember our agreement?

C: Yes. I'm sorry. We're in the present. I'm sorry. O.K. Here we come. I am driving down the hill in my car, on my way to work, and my little boy runs in front of the car and I hit him, and this is pretty frightening. This has happened two or three times.

F: Now play the car.

C: O.K. Over here or where I am?

F: Just play the car—as if you were this car.

C: I'm driving—giving the car a life of its own, that it doesn't have?

F: Yah.

C: I have the life. The car does what I tell it to.

F: Say this to the car.

C: Car, you do what I tell you to. When I turn the wheel, you—when I turn the wheel, you turn, and when you—when I hold the wheel straight, you go straight.

F: What does the car answer?

C: The car answers, "Yes, sir." (laughter) What else can it answer? I run it; it doesn't run me.

F: Say this to the car.

C: Car, I run you, and you don't run me.

F: Now play this boy. Dream the dream from the point of view of the boy.

C: O.K. Here comes Daddy's car down the road, and I love Daddy and I want to run out and—uh, say hello to Daddy, and all of a sudden the car—all of a sudden this car is hitting me. Why?

F: (wryly) Funny boy. The moment the car hits him, he asks "Why?" (laughter)

C: Well, I—mind you, I'm second-guessing the boy. And I don't *know* what he thinks, this is just what—what's coming back to me that he thinks.

F: Okeh. Play the boy once more.

C: O.K. All right. Here comes Daddy in the car, and I love him and I want to talk to him—and he's gonna hit me! He hates me!

F: And?

C: Shall I do this dream, when he hits? Because this doesn't happen—this doesn't happen. I don't hit him. I'm awake before I hit him.

F: So, at what moment do you interrupt the dream?

C: The front wheels are about six inches away.

F: So what are you avoiding?

C: I'm avoiding killing the boy.

F: Yah. Now kill the boy.

C: O.K. All right. I'm driving down the hill in the car, and when I see the boy coming, I'm not going to stop.

F: And?

C: We hit him.

F: And?

C: He's dead.

F: Close your eyes. Look at him. He's dead. . . Talk to him, now.

C: (cries) I didn't mean to do it. I didn't mean to do it. I couldn't stop.

F: Go on talking to him.

C: There's no more to say. . . except I'm sorry.

F: Tell him all the things you're sorry about.

C: I'm sorry I pushed him away when he wanted to—come and be with Daddy and I was too busy to talk to him.

F: Say this to him, now.

C: I'm sorry that I pushed you away—all the times that I pushed you away when I was doing something that was—I felt was very very important to me, and the really important thing was not what I was doing, but the fact that you wanted to—be with Daddy.

F: Now play him.

C: O.K. Ah. . . ah. . .

F: Go back to the time when he wanted to talk to you.

C: O.K. Daddy,—I'm—I'm the boy. Daddy, why is so-and-so—Daddy, what's the mouse when he spins? Things like this.

F: Okeh. Now—

C: Daddy, I want to talk to you. I'll ask anything if you'll just talk to me and notice that I'm here. This is—this is the boy.

F: Okeh. Now, change over. Talk like this to *your* father.

C: All right. For Christ's sake, why do you sit there writing sermons all evening when *I'm* here?

F: Now go on with the dialogue. Let him talk back.

C: Son, you know I've got a service tomorrow. You know every Saturday afternoon is Sermon day. So would you please go away and don't bother me, because I've got to get the thing done... I'm projecting—I'm projecting in my own thoughts because I don't remember the exact words, but it was something like this.

F: Now, go on. Insist that he should talk to you.

C: Daddy, *please* talk to me or let's go—take me to the movies or something. *Anything.* I want to talk to you about what's important to me, and you won't listen. You *won't listen!* (shouts angrily) *You're too goddamn busy to listen!* And *I'm* here.

F: Make him listen.

C: (shouts louder) *For Christ's sake, listen, you son-of-a-bitch.* That'll teach you, that I'm here too.

F: Okeh. Now go back to your son.

C: Who am I? Am I him or—

F: You are you, and he is sitting there. Talk to him now.

C: What I'm doing isn't all that big. Let's go to the beach.

F: You are all the time looking at me. What do you want from me?

C: I want you to help me finish a few scenes.

F: Put Fritz in that chair.

C: O.K.

F: "Fritz, I want you to help me."

C: Fritz, I've got scenes that are unfinished and they've been unfinished for years, and I want some help.

F: Change seats. Play Fritz.

C: From me, you want help? Look, Chuck, this is something *you've* got to do. If you know, if you know what the—if you know what the unfinished scene is, and you know what you ought to do to finish it, what in hell's stopping you? You—all you're—all you're doing is just—uh—playing games with yourself. All you—all you want to do is lay out flat and let me do it for you. Well, I'm not going to. *You're* going to.

F: Yah. You see how you want my support.

C: Yeah, of course I do.

F: Now *this* Fritz in the empty chair is going to give you all the support you need. Now change seats.

C: O.K. This Fritz is—there's a Fritz there, now, and I'm me.

F: Yah.

C: O.K. . . uh. . . Fritz, for Christ's sake help me, will you?—I'm not getting any feedback from you. (laughter) Because I already know what the feedback is, I just gave it. . .

F: You're not going to suck me in. (laughter) You can play helpless 'til doomsday with me. I'm a very good frustrator.

C: O.K. Um. . . Fritz, this Fritz, isn't really going to help me.

F: Oh, yes.

C: No, he isn't. He told me he wasn't. This Fritz just told me to pull my own red wagon. So that's what I've gotta do, is pull my own red wagon.

F: Are you willing to listen to him?

C: Certainly I'll listen to him.

F: Okeh. Find out.

C: I'm him?. . . He hasn't said anything, yet. Except what he's already said, which we all know about.

F: You feel that you are stuck?

C: I'm pretty stuck, right now.

F: Now describe the experience of being stuck.

C: You can go—it's very simple, you can go neither forward nor back. You're there. You're stuck. You don't move. You—ah—I feel—in—in the situation where you're stuck, whatever you do is wrong. Whatever you do is—is—if—if it moves you, it's gonna move you in deeper, not—not out again. So best—best stay stuck and stay very very still. . . And so you're still leaving me stuck. Stuck. You're stuck, I'm stuck. So, you're not gonna unstick me, are you?

F: Certainly not. (laughter) I am a frustrator. I am certainly *not* an alpine rescuer.

C: All right. Where are we stuck at?

F: Ask him.

C: Well, he's being pretty uncommunicative right now. He's not telling me much. Uhh—O.K. I'm gonna be him. You still have to unstick yourself. You still have to decide for yourself what you're gonna do, and what's—what's—meaningful and what isn't. And you're the only one who knows that, so why don't you get off your ass and do it?

Now *me* again. Fritz, you—of course I know what I gotta do, but—if I—if I do something about it, one way or the other somebody's gonna get hurt.

F: Ahah. So you get already the first message. Somebody gets hurt.

C: Because it's like this: If I give up what I—what is meaningful and important to me, to—ah—well, let us say this: I've got a term paper due, Fritz, and it's Sunday afternoon, the thing is due on Monday morning and I haven't gotten it done. If I don't—if I drop this and take you to the beach, or whatever, and don't do the term paper, *I* get hurt, and I have a right not to be hurt, too. If I—if I *don't* do the term paper and do take him to—or if I *do* the term paper and don't take him to the beach, *he's* hurt. So whatever I do is wrong. Whatever I do, somebody's gonna get some pain out of it— either me or him, and sometimes I just take the pain myself, and sometimes I give it back to him, but neither one of us—but neither solution is very satisfactory. So what happens next? What do I do, dump them all over the side? What do I do, give up what's important to me so that you all won't be hurting any more? I can't be Fritz again.

F: Right now, I experience myself as a wailing wall.

C: Eh?. . . O.K. I'll buy it. I'm still looking for support from the environment—like crazy.

F: Yah.

C: *Why* isn't it *out* there? Why do I have to do it *all* myself? Why don't I get a little help?

F: Nyahhhnyahnyah. Say this in gibberish.

C: (does so) Yeah, that's what I'm doing. O.K. I'll buy it.

F: Go on. Go on.

C: O.K. (makes the same gibberish sounds with more crying in them, like a small child, then carries the same sounds into words) Nobody loves me. Nobody'll help me. Nyanyahnhhnyah.

F: How old are you in this role?

C: About three.

F: Three. It's about time that you hit *that* child.

C: Yeah!

F: Now talk to that child, to the three-year-old child. The nyanhnyanh child.

C: Nyah, go peddle your own potatoes somewhere, I'm busy.

Pull your own wed ragon—red wagon—go and play with your friends, I've got things to do. And if you get hurt, I'm sorry. I'm sorry. But I count too.

F: Say this again.

C: I'm sorry—but I *count too*, and don't you forget it.

F: Say this, "I count too."

C: I count too, goddammit, and *remember* it from now on!

F: Say this to the audience.

C: I count too, goddammit, and I—remember it, all of you, from now on. The lot of you!

F: Say it to more people—your wife, your father, and so on. Say this to your whole environment.

C: Remember one thing and dig this real good and wrap onto this real good and hold on tight because this is the way it's gonna be. *I count too!* as much as you do—not any more and not any less, but just as much, and remember it! Now, peddle that. Grab onto them apples and see how you like 'em. *I count too*, goddammit, and *remember it*!

F: Say this to me, too.

C: I count too! I'm just as important as anybody in this room, and don't *you* forget it. . . (as if asking for permission) O.K.? (laughter) And I can finish my own scenes. Can I say that again? (laughter) Because *I* want to remember that. I can finish my own scenes.

F: Yah. Now, I went along with you to quite an extent, except that I don't believe you in your tailored rules, that you have *either* to finish a term paper *or* go out with the boy. I think that's a lie.

C: O.K. . . Of course it's a lie. Because as a matter of fact, in the case that—that I'm generalizing this from, this is exactly what happened. I did go out to the beach with him, and term papers are written—let's face it—at four o'clock in the morning, anyway. They're no good if they're not. And so it—it wasn't either/or, it was both/and, and there's no reason why it shouldn't be this all the time.

F: Exactly. . . Well, I see the existential message from the dream as, "You don't have to wait until you hit your boy, to get in touch with him." You don't have to copy your father.

BILL

Bill: I have a kind of volcano in me that keeps erupting—

Fritz: Okeh. I try to reinforce the empty chair game because this is something you can do so easily at home with yourself. As a matter of fact, somebody suggested to make little Fritzie dolls and—(much laughter) So have a volcano, talk to it.

B: You're just sitting inside. You're just sitting in there and most of the time I don't even know you're there—I just go on enjoying myself and every once in a while you just erupt and I end up shaking and sort of out of control, and I don't understand it.

F: Be the volcano.

B: Well, I'm waiting. I may erupt any time, you'd better watch out.

F: Say this to me.

B: I may erupt any time, you better watch out.

F: Huh?

B: (louder) I may erupt any time—you better watch out.

F: I don't hear you yet.

B: (loud) I may erupt any moment—you better watch out.

F: Okeh. I'm ready.

B: Hrowwerhh! (laughter)

F: What do you feel now?

B: (quietly) Shaky.

F: Close your eyes. Enter your shakiness—enter your body.

B: It doesn't feel all that bad. I don't know why it's shaking. I don't know why I'm shaking.

F: Can you allow the shaking to develop? I can give you the diagnosis—you suffer from over-control. So *de*control yourself— shake a bit. . .

B: (after a long pause) It stopped then.

F: Okeh. Go back and talk to the volcano.

B: Well, you've got a loud bang, but your bark isn't as bad, I guess. If I just let you erupt—stop trying to keep you bottled—

F: Can you make up a fantasy—if you were a volcano and you would erupt fully, what would happen?

B: Fly to pieces—all the parts would go scattering in all directions. Fiery pieces would come crashing down all around. There'd be nothing left.

F: You would destroy everything. So could you tell us if you were a volcano, what would you do with us?

B: I'd blow up—blow the whole place up.

F: Listen to your voice.

B: My voice is absolutely dead.

F: Yah. Who is going to believe you?

B: No one. (laughter) The volcano doesn't hurt anyone else. It blows *me* up. Nobody else is affected at all. They stand there watching me blow up and wonder what it's all about.

F: Can you say this to us?

B: If I blew up in front of you, you'd sit there and watch me blowing up and say, "What the hell is he—what's with him? He's not hurting me any. He's making lots of loud noise and shouting at the top of his lungs."

F: Now, can you play it again?

B: Play what?

F: The volcano! Let us watch you. Give us an exhibition.

B: Of a volcano.

F: Yah.

B: *BLOOOWRRH!*

F: Go on.

B: *ROWRRHH!* Nothing works right.

F: Listen to your voice now—it is a weak, mild voice. You see the fragmentation between yourself as a rather weak person, and the volcano on the other hand. There's nothing between. Go on playing the volcano.

B: I know it doesn't work. I can't, I can't—I would be sure of playing it, at this stage, I would be playing a game, or—it would make no sense.

F: Now listen to your voice again. Play your voice.

B: My voice says, "I'm speaking in a nice, controlled tone, not saying anything that's going to hurt anybody—keeping all emotion out of it."

F: Now be the volcano voice. What would the volcano say?

B: (growls in very loud voice) *TO HELL WITH YOU!*

F: Be your other voice again.

B: There's no real emotion. Why should I expect any? I don't feel anything, really. I'm not angry at you. You haven't done anything to me.

F: Talk like the volcano again.

B: (yells) *What's wrong with you!* (normal voice) Why don't I feel anything—towards you? I want real contact and I don't feel it.

F: I would like you to have a discussion with your volcano voice and your other voice.

B: Volcano voice, you're a big empty bang. You startle people but you don't convince them.

What do you think *you* do? (laughter) You don't even startle them. Well? *Do* something, *show* something—*real*.

Well, I'm just as real as you, but I guess that's not what I want to be either—neither you nor me. I'd like to be a voice that's convincing—that means what it says and sounds like it, means what it says.

F: Ahah. Now we have learned something, that you have no center of confidence. You have split up into a meek and mild voice, and an empty, bully voice, but the center is missing; the confidence is missing. So, let them go on. The meek and mild, and the bully—the shouter.

B: Instead of shouting in that big, loud voice, maybe if you just expressed exactly the way you felt—if you feel convinced of something, say it. Perhaps you're afraid to just use your real self, or expose your real self. You have to expose your big noisy self or else you have to please. . .

But I feel frightened now. I would like to be able to just feel—you know, express what I feel. Maybe I am. I feel nervous.

F: Close your eyes and enter the nervousness. Withdraw and regress into your nervousness. There's not such tremendous excitement as in the volcano but there's some excitement in the nervousness. How do you feel nervousness? Can you feel vibrations anywhere?

B: I feel vibrations and I feel—fingers tingling. I feel almost distant tears could come—very distant.

F: What do you feel in your genitals, especially in your testicles?

B: It's a little hard to describe. . . I think it feels like a small boy—like I used to feel sometimes when I got out of the bathtub.

F: What do you feel in your eyes, your eyeballs?

B: I don't feel so much my eyeballs as I feel contracting around them.

F: Yah. Could you contract a little bit more—or imagine that you were contracting a little bit more? What do you feel in your hands?

B: They're clasping.

F: What do you feel in your testicles?

B: Nothing.

F: Are they there?

B: Yeah.

F: No contraction?

B: No. . .

F: What do you experience now?

B: The tears in my eyes. I feel my hands holding on.

F: Can you tell the audience, "I won't cry"?

B: I won't cry. /F: Again./
I won't cry. /F: Again./
I won't cry. I won't cry.

F: What are your objections to crying?

B: I have no real objections. I'm afraid of what people will think of me if I cry.

F: Okeh. Change seats again and play people.

B: We're not going to think any less of you if you cry. There's absolutely nothing wrong with it. If you feel like crying, then you have something to cry about.

I know all that abstractly, but something in me keeps holding back—sometimes consciously and sometimes unconsciously.

F: Close your eyes again. Give us the exact details of how you hold back your tears. Which muscles do you use, and so on.

B: I'm not feeling it now. I can remember holding them back, tightening my throat, clenching my jaws.

F: Can you do this now? (through his teeth) "I won't cry."

B: I won't cry.

F: Yah. Clench your jaw. Hold it back.

B: I won't cry. I won't cry.

F: What's the situation? What's the occasion?

B: When I'm not crying? /F: Yah./ I was at a funeral. (voice quavers) I'm at a funeral. /F: Who?/ An old man who died whom I liked very much.

F: Go back to his grave and say goodbye to him.

B: (very soft voice) Goodbye.

F: What's his name?

B: Curt.

F: Say, "Goodbye, Curt."

B: Goodbye, Curt. I've really missed you. (almost crying) I wish I could have expressed more how I liked you, when there was time.

F: Let him talk back—give him a voice.

B: I knew you liked me. When I was lonely it would have been nice if I could have seen more of you. I enjoyed the times we were together. It was hard living alone. Being left out of everything. . . You don't have to feel sorry. There's nothing wrong with it, either.

F: Tell him a little bit more what you appreciated in him.

B: He was so gentle.

F: Say this to him.

B: You were *so* gentle. Gentlest person I knew. No hostility toward anyone. Incredible.

F: No volcano there?

B: No. No volcano.

F: Can you see him? Can you see your friend? Go touch him and say goodbye again.

B: Goodbye. (starts to cry) Goodbye. . . (cries) Goodbye. It's hard to say goodbye. It's hard to say goodbye. . . (sobs). . .

F: Come back to us. How do you see us now?

B: I don't. . .

F: Well, I don't feel that your goodbye is finished. You still have to do more mourning there. Pull out your roots again and become free to get new friends.

This is one of the most important unfinished situations: if you haven't cried enough over a beloved person whom you have lost. Freud has done magnificent work about the mourning labor, which in Europe usually takes a year until you take up all the roots from a dead person and can apply yourself again to the living ones.

ELLIE

Ellie: My name is Ellie. . . Well, I feel a fluttering in my chest, now, and I'd like to loosen up.

F: That's a program.

E: What?

F: That is a program—when you say, "I'd like to loosen up."

E: I'm trying, now.

F: "I'm trying." This is also a program. You mix up what you *want to be* with what *is*.

E: Now I'm—I'm moving my arms, to feel at ease. And I would like to talk about my. . .

F: Let me tell you something, Ellie. The basis of this work is the *now*. All the time, you are in the *future*. "I want to work on this." "I want to try this," and so on. If you can work, start every sentence with the word *now*.

E: Now I'm saying to you, Dr. Perls, that I am uncomfortable. Now, I feel my chest going up and down. I feel a deep breath. I feel a little better now.

F: You see, instead of trying to escape into the future, you got in touch with yourself in the now. So of course you feel better. . . What are your hands doing?

E: Reassuring me. They are in touch—I feel them, touching myself. I feel they're keeping me together.

F: Talk to them. "Hands, you are reassuring me—"

E: Hands, you are reassuring me. Hands, you are something I know. It feels good to move my finger.

F: Well, my attention is more with the audience. (to audience) I sense a restlessness. Could you talk about it?

X: We can't hear very well.

F: So, you rather sit with your discomfort of not hearing very well—straining—than to express yourself. Cowards.

X: Could you turn around so we can hear you.

Y: Can you speak up?

E: I will—can you hear me now? /X: Yes./ All right. (clears throat) Ahem.

F: (mocking, like a singer limbering up) Mi, mi, mi, mi, mi. . .

E: I'd rather you'd tell me when you cannot hear than be restless. But I don't want to have to keep consciously thinking of you—I would like to ask you—

F: What are you doing with your left hand?

E: My left hand?. . . is directing.

F: Are you aware of doing this?

E: I was not. I am aware of it now. I want to be—

F: Another program.

E: A program.

F: (brusquely) Thank you—I can't work with you. I ask you to stay with the now.

E: I feel inadequate now. . . I feel now I want something. I feel scared now that I'm not going to get it. I feel—

F: You see, you are again in the future. "I want something, I won't get it." What's your objection to being here, being alive, being in the now? What makes you always jump into the future?

E: There's so much I want, and I'm afraid—I won't have it.

F: In other words, you are greedy.

E: Yes.

F: Tell this to the audience. "I want, I want, I want."

E: I want, I want, I'm greedy, selfish. I'm insatiable. I want what I want, right now. It doesn't feel good not to get it. . . I feel inadequate right now.

F: I don't understand the word.

E: I feel dumb now.

F: Maybe you *are* dumb. . . or do you *play* dumb? How does it feel to be dumb?

E: I don't know what to do. I want to do something, but I don't know how to go about doing it.

F: So play helpless.

E: Please help me, Dr. Perls. /F: (as if he can't hear) Ahnh?/
Please help me, Dr. Perls. /F: Ahnh?/
Please help me, Dr. Perls!. . .

F: Well, I don't have my checkbook with me. (laughter)

E: That's not what I want from you.

F: Oh! You didn't even say what you want—what kind of help you want.

E: I want help in feeling at ease with me being a woman. I want to enjoy sex with my husband more.

F: Ah! When you have sex, are you ever in the now? /E: No./ Where are you when you have sex? Do you have a program—achieving orgasm or something like that?

E: Yes, I do.

F: You want to achieve an orgasm. So again you've got a program.

E: Right. And that's my problem.

F: Your problem is that you plan, you make a program. Instead of fucking, you make programs. If you stay in the now, you can enjoy it. Okeh.

We are all concerned with the idea of change, and most people go about it by making programs. They want to change. "I should be like this" and so on and so on. What happens is that the idea of deliberate change *never, never, never* functions. As soon as you say, "I want to change"—make a program—a counter-force is created that prevents you from change. Changes are taking place by themselves. If you go deeper into what you *are*, if you accept what is there, then a change automatically occurs by itself. This is the paradox of change. Maybe I can reinforce it a bit with a good old proverb which says that "The road to hell is paved with good intentions." As soon as you make a decision, as soon as you want to change, you open up the road to hell because you can't achieve it, so you feel bad, you torture yourself, and then you start to play the famous self-torture game which is so popular with most people in our time.

As long as you fight a symptom, it will become worse. If you take responsibility for what you are doing to yourself, how you produce your symptoms, how you produce your illness, how you produce your existence—the very moment you get in touch with yourself—growth begins, integration begins.

DAN

Dan: I've got a psychosomatic nose, and I—

Fritz: Talk to your psychosomatic nose.

D: I—well, all right. . . I've always thought there was something out of my past, here, that I couldn't understand, and I worked on it, and I can partly control it—

F: What is your right hand doing?

D: Pardon?

F: What did I say?

D: What shall I—

F: Ahah. We had a short encounter previously, where Dan exhibited his unwillingness to listen.

D: I didn't hear the last words. Shall I go on?. . . I've tried to control it, and to some extent I can, ah, temporarily, and then here, last—

F: Did you hear what I said just now about controlling?

D: I heard what you said about my not listening.

F: Did you hear what I said about controlling? And wanting to change?

D: No, sir.

F: Can you switch back about five minutes?

D: To outside, previously. I asked you a question, and you, uh. . .

F: Did you hear that I said five minutes?. . . You notice that whatever I say, you distort, you don't listen, in other words you're not open at all.

D: I'll try to open.

F: "I'll try to open." Another promise. I don't know how I can communicate with you.

D: I had a feeling you thought I was a toxic personality, but if you don't try, what can you do?. . .

F: What would happen if you would listen, if you would have ears? Can you make up a fantasy? What's the danger of listening?. . .

D: Well, if I don't listen but one is unaware of listening, there should be no danger, in listening—there should be no threat. And I see no threat. . .

F: What is the danger of listening?. . .

D: The only danger of listening would be to hear something you didn't want to hear.

F: Ah! Can you say this sentence, "I hear only what I like to hear"? Can you repeat this sentence after me?

D: Ah, you said, "I can hear only what I want to hear."

F: Did I say that?

X: No. . .

F: Is this what you do in life, altogether, always distorting the messages you get from outside?

D: It couldn't be *all* the time, but probably is sometimes.

F: Now, listen carefully. "I hear only what I like to hear."

D: I hear only what I like to hear.

F: Say this to the audience, now.

D: I hear only what I like to hear. /F: Again./

I hear only what I like to hear.

F: Say it louder. Say it to some specific people.

D: I hear only what I *like* to hear. I hear only what I like to hear.

F: Say this to your wife.

D: I hear only what I like to hear.

F: So play her. What would she answer?. . .

D: At times she'd say "Yes, sir," and at other times she'd say, "You're right!"

F: Okeh. Now, play a wife that says only things you like to hear. . .

D: Well, uh—

F: What do you like to hear?

D: I like to hear things that are pleasant.

F: Such as?

D: Well, uh. . . I've done what you've asked me to do about this, or I've tried to do this or that about the boys, and I think that's probably agreeable to you, or—

F: So you expect people to listen to you. Am I right?

D: Well, I expect I should listen to others, and that others should listen to me, too. From what you say, I'm not sure I do, though.

F: It's a wonderful gimmick. If you expect people to listen to you, but you won't listen to what people have to say to you, then you are always in control.

D: It might always be in control, but you wouldn't be very happy.

F: Exactly. And you get your symptoms. Okeh.

DICK

Dick: (rapidly) I have a recurring nightmare. I'm asleep, and I hear somebody screaming and I wake up and the cops are beating up some kid. And I want to get up and help him but somebody's standing at the head, and at the foot of my bed, and they're throwing pillows back and forth faster and faster and I can't move my head. I can't get up. And I wake up screaming and in full sweat.

Fritz: Can you act it out? Tell your dream once more but use your body as well as your voice.

D: I'm sleeping. Suddenly I hear somebody screaming.

F: Wait a moment. Say again "I'm sleeping."

D: I'm sleeping.

F: Do you believe it?

D: No.

F: So act it out.

D: I'm asleep. Suddenly I hear somebody screaming. I wake up and I see some cops beating up on a kid, and I want to get up to help him, and somebody's standing at the head and the foot of my bed and they're throwing a pillow back and forth, (talking rapidly) faster and faster, faster and faster, and I can't move—I want to get my head up and I can't and they're going faster and faster, and I wake up screaming.

F: Can you do this again with your head?

D: (rapidly) They're, they're just throwing the pillow back and forth and it's, it's so fast I can't move my head. It's just faster and faster and faster and I just can't move my head and—

F: Can you be the policeman and beat up the kid like this— faster and faster?

D: (rapidly and very expressively) All right, kid, we caught you now and you're going to go to jail. No more of that bullshit. You're gonna go right into the goddamn reform school. You think you're getting away with a hell of a lot but you're not getting away with anything. You're gonna have to serve your goddamn time and be a good citizen and not fuck up so much.

F: How do you feel in that role?

D: I don't like it.

F: You don't like it?

D: No.

F: Okeh, talk to that guy—to the policeman there.

D: (pleading) The kid wasn't trying to steal because he wanted anything. He just didn't have anywhere to go and nothing to do. He was just caught up in a trap and he just stole a few things. You shouldn't beat him up. If you think he has to serve some time, if he has to pay some kind of a debt, O.K. But you don't have to hit him; you don't have to punish him for that. You can be kind to him; you could show him some comfort, show him some sympathy. You can understand what the hell he's gone through.

F: So be the policeman again. Talk back.

D: Yeah, but he's robbing people, and they've got some respect coming. He should understand what the hell they feel like. They work for their money. If he wants to get something he should go out and try to educate himself and get a job and be productive and get his money the right way. If he's going to go about hurting other people he has to get hurt in turn.

F: Put the kid in this. You're the policeman and the kid is in that scene.

D: (playing kid) I just wanted to—to belong. I just wanted to be part of the gang. I didn't want to hurt anybody. I didn't want to take anybody's money. I didn't want to steal. I just wanted to be part of people. I wanted to belong to the crowd. I just wanted to be accepted by them. That's all. I didn't mean any harm. I could have given the money back, I don't need the money. I don't use it for anything—just screw around with the damn stuff, throw it away, gamble. I don't have it very long. I don't want to hurt anybody.

F: So what does the policeman say?

D: I don't care what you *want* to do, it's what you *have* done. The guy wasn't doing you any harm, you had to rob him just because you wanted to be part of the gang. Well, there are other gangs and other people. They don't all do that. If you want to belong—well, belong to the right people if you don't want to get hurt.

But this is where I live. This is the way life is, over here. We don't have any other groups to go to. We don't have any clubs. Everybody steals and if they don't steal they're not part of things. If you want to belong and you want to be part of it you have to go along with it. That's all. And it's not a matter of feeling anything against the guy you're robbing.

I don't care how you feel. It's what you *do* that counts. If you do something that's wrong you have to be punished for it.

F: Say this to the group now.

D: If you do something that's wrong, you're punished for it.

F: Go on talking like this to us.

D: If you want to be respected and you want to be treated kindly you have to be willing to abide by the laws and you have to be willing to go along with people. If you want to be a free man and you want to go among people with a little respect, then you just have to show them the same kind of respect that you expect them to give you. If you don't, you just get the punishment you deserve.

F: Now play the group. . .

D: We know that life isn't easy in the slums; it's hard to get out, it's hard to figure out what you should be doing that's right. It's hard to go against the code that everybody seems to think is the right one to do. It's hard to be a big shot in that kind of company unless you do these things.

F: Ah! Here we get a new theme. Big shot—you want to be a big shot. Tell this to the policeman.

D: I want to be a big shot. I want to be somebody that other people respect. I want to be as tough as everybody else is. I can take anything you give me; you won't make me do anything. You won't make me talk. I wanna be a big man here.

F: Change seats again.

D: If being a big man means going out and stealing, taking things from other people and breaking the law, then the big man will get punished.

F: How do you feel now in the role of the policeman?. . .

D: I sympathize with him.

F: You're more comfortable now as a policeman. /D: Yeah./ Okeh, go on.

D: We don't care if you're big or you're small or you're thin or you're fat, black or white. You can be anything you want but if you break the law it's our business to stop you. We stop you the best way we know how, that's all. Sometimes it takes a little force, that's all. . .

F: Close your eyes now, become aware of yourself. What do you experience?

D: Weakness in my knees and calves, throbbing in—over my left eye, sort of impotence to be able to do what I want to do.

F: Now, can you say this to this boy.

D: I feel weak in my legs, I feel my head's throbbing, I don't feel capable of doing what I want to do, I don't feel free—I feel you hold me down, you won't let me go where I want to go, be what I want to be.

F: Now take the place of the boy again. Talk back to the policeman.

D: I'm gonna get out of here. I'm gonna do the things I want to do, but I have to have some help. I just can't do it by myself. All I want is somebody to understand. It's *hard*.

F: You see, the very moment he got in contact, in touch with himself, you notice how much of the toughness turned out to be a fake. And the boy, too, is much less spiteful, much less aggressive. They're coming a bit closer. Okeh, be the policeman again.

D: Listen, kid, if you really want to break out of this neighborhood there are plenty of things that we can do to help you: all kinds of counselors, all kinds of workers that are willing to help you along. We've got Big Brother organizations; the probation office has all kinds of routines to help you. You'll spend a little time in jail; they'll tell you how to get by and get out of here.

F: Now slap him again. Hit him up.

D: (yelling angrily and expressively) You don't know what the hell you're talking about, for Christ sake! What do they do in jail? They don't give you any goddamn help. Social workers, my ass! All they do is give you a lot of goddamn eulogizing, proselytizing and tell you what the fuck you're supposed to be doing with your life without helping you!

F: Oh! Now the anger is on the side of the boy. You were the boy; you were not the policeman.

D: (quietly) Yeah.

F: Ahah. What would the policeman now say to this anger of the boy? Now the roles have changed.

D: (toughly) Listen, kid. Unless you straighten out, unless you understand what the hell you're doing, nobody's gonna help you. They try to help you and if every time they try to help you, you think they're just trying to screw you up, you're not gonna get any help at all. If you want to get out of this mess you'd better straighten up and understand who the hell your friends are. These crumbs who think they're your friends—bullshit. They'll stab you in the back for a dime.

F: Okeh, switch roles.

D: Yeah, but they accept me. They know me and they don't ask anything of me other than what I give. (angrily) All you other people, you're always asking for things you can't get or I can't give you. And you want it the way *you* define the damn things, not the way *I* see them.

F: So what do you experience now?

D: Violence.

F: The violence isn't projected any more. You feel it as your own.

D: Yeah. . .

F: So close your eyes again. Now get in touch with your violence. How do you experience violence?. . .

D: (breathlessly) I wanna des—destroy things. I wanna—I wanna break the past. I wanna get rid of all those things that keep me from doing things. I wanna be *free*. I just want to lash out at them.

F: So talk to the past. "Past, I want to get rid of you."

D: Past, you can't hold me up. A lot of kids have gone through the same thing. There are all kinds of slums in the world. Many people have gone to reform school, been in jail. That doesn't mean that they can't accomplish something. I'm getting my Ph.D. I'm *through* with you. I've gotten *out* of it. I don't have to have you around any more. You don't have to bug me any more. I don't have to go back and see what the hell life is like there. I don't have to feel the excitement any more. I can live where I'm living now. I'm going into the academic world—the real world!

F: What does the past answer?

D: Yeah, but you—you know that we're your friends and we understand what you want. Our life is richer. There's more excitement, there's more meaning, there's more to do, more to see. It isn't sterile. You know what you've done. You can't get out of it, you can't leave it.

F: In other words the past experiences the Ph.D. as somewhat sterile? Are you—

D: Ph.D. is—ahh, the Ph.D., what the hell is that?

F: Say this to him.

D: Look. When you have a Ph.D. what have you got? It puts you in the position of being able to do a little bit more in helping to analyze certain problems, and when people are presented with it, they're not going to really do a hell of a lot with it. It's not gonna really make a hell of a lot of difference one way or the other *what* you do.

F: You see, now we enter the existential problem. Now you have got your hang-up, your impasse.

D: Yeah.

F: You want to do something more exciting.

D: I not only want to do something more exciting; I want to do something more meaningful—something *real*. I want to touch it, I want to feel it. I wanna see it grow and develop. I wanna feel that I'm useful. Even in a warm, loving way I want to feel useful. I don't want to move the world. . . This feeling of impotence. All that work.

F: That's a very interesting observation because all killing is based upon impotence. . . So be the Ph.D. . .

D: There are three billion people in the world, and maybe ten thousand make decisions. And my job will help those who make decisions to make them wiser. I'm not gonna shake the world, but it's gonna do a hell of a lot more than the other two billion nine hundred and something million will do. It's gonna be a worthwhile contribution.

F: Do you see how you're getting more and more rational—the opposites coming together now? How do you feel now?

D: I feel I want to be rational.

F: Yah, yah. I think you did a very good job here.

Q: In this case we saw a lot of violence and aggression which turned out to be a result of a feeling of impotence. What part does aggression play in the healthy, integrated personality?

F: I believe aggression is a biological energy which normally is used to de-structure food or whatever we have to de-structure in order for it to be assimilated. We have to distinguish between aggression, violence, sadism, and so on. They are all thrown into the same pot in modern psychiatry. They are all quite different phenomena. For instance, violence, as you saw here, is the result of impotence. If you don't have any other way to cope, then you start to kill. The aggression is used for any kind of work, but you see that aggression is often not motivated by coping, but by hatred against a parent—not against a *real* parent—against a *fantasied* parent. In my work, I often ask, "What do you need a mother for?" You don't have to drag her around. Throw her in the garbage pail. Don't waste time hating her. And this is what I am talking about, emptying out the middle zone of fantasy. If you have forgiven her, you have assimilated whatever you have projected in her, then you can give her up. If you eat a steak today, what do you do with the steak? You make it your own, and this is the case with any unfinished situation, any incomplete gestalt, once you digest it and use it for nourishment. The role of aggression in the well-integrated personality is as a means of coping with a situation—certain situations require aggression. Other situations require, let's say, rational behavior; other situations require withdrawal. You notice here already how much I work with the contact-withdrawal, coping-withdrawal situation. If you can't cope with a situation as it is, you withdraw to a position where you feel more comfortable, or where the unfinished situations wait, and then you come out again. This rhythm is so essential for life. If you don't listen to this rhythm, are one-sided, then you are either a bumptious noisy person, extroverted, or you are completely withdrawn. This is not a heart. (makes fist) This is not a heart. (opens hand) This is a heart. (opens and closes hand) Contact-withdrawal. Remember, it's always the rhythm.

You notice how much I use this empty chair, and how by identifying with your own power, you re-own it and chew it up and assimilate it, and make it your own again. This is the growth process, the process with which we mobilize our potential. If you understand Nietsche correctly, he talks about the Superman, he doesn't talk about the comic strip Superman, the Nazi type, the one with the big muscles—he is the *Undermensch*. He talks about the person who is capable of using his potential up to any great possibility. Again I say, it only comes about if you allow the growth process to take place.

Any deliberate change does not work. Change takes place by itself if you take back, assimilate, whatever is available. The fact is that we are so much more than we believe that we are in our wildest dreams. I had an interesting experience about six months ago. I was bored, so I thought, "Well, why not use this time of boredom to start writing?" So I started writing about my life, and it is beginning to flow—mostly in words, partly poetry, but it flows. I have written in this short time over 300 pages and I think it will be a beautiful book; I call it *In and Out of the Garbage Pail.* I let the excitement take over. I am seventy-five. So think what you have in front of you.

BETH

Beth: (harsh, grating, strong voice) In my dream, there is a steel band, like part of a truck wheel, around my chest and I can't get out. I feel trapped in the steel ring and I keep trying to get out—

Fritz: Okeh. For this, I need a strong man, somebody to come up here. (man steps up) Beth, become this steel ring in your dream. Put your arms around his chest and try to keep him trapped. (she does this, and squeezes tightly) Okeh. (to man) Now *you* try to break out from this steel ring. (there is a brief, vigorous struggle and he breaks free)

B: (discovery) But I'm not made of steel!

F: Yah! Get the message?

B: I really thought I could hold him!

F: Okeh.

MARIAN

Marian: (quietly) I might just cross my legs if I want to, so I'm going to. I'm not sure, really, why I want to come, but ah, for one thing I've had a tumultuous week. I feel all disturbed as a result of a week up here and so I think ah, maybe if I talk to you I'll feel better, and I'm not really sure why. I think for the first time I've had some questions posed to me regarding my own self-worth, and my own self-concept is real mixed up now. And during your lectures I've been trying to sort myself out and, ah, I really don't know where I am now. And I felt, ah, I had felt rejected this week and I had felt rejected by you this noon. And I'm sure it must be in my imagination but may I tell you about it?. . . When I mentioned ah, having ah, spent an enjoyable marathon experience at your house, I felt like I got two messages—probably within me. But the messages I got from you were, one, when you turned away I thought—I said within myself—"You know, you don't matter, so what are you talking to me for?" And the other one was I felt. . .

Fritz: What was the sentence—"You don't matter"?

M: I felt that I didn't talk directly to you.

F: You said some words like, "You don't matter."

M: Yes. This is what I said to myself.

F: I know. Can you say it again, "You don't matter"?

M: Yes. You don't matter. /F: Say this again./

You don't matter, at all. /F: Say it again./

You don't matter at all. /F: Say it to a few more people./

You don't, you don't really matter. You're worthless—don't matter at all. I don't like it.

F: Well, elaborate on this. How don't we matter?

M: Well, you matter but I—this is what I was thinking to myself.

F: I know. I want you to tell it out again.

M: And you want me to say it to you?

F: Yes.

M: I can say it but, see, I don't believe it.

F: I still would like you to play this phony game.

M: O.K. You don't really matter. Who do you think you are that you're so much more important than I am?

F: Go on.

M: I don't think you're any better than I am. . . So why do you give me that feeling?

F: Say this to a few more people.

M: (giggles) Let's see. You don't really matter to me. You're not important. Betty? I know your name so I'm saying that to you and I don't really (laughs) believe it but I'll use your name. Ben? Why do you make me feel that—that you're so much more important. You don't matter. . . I'm not comfortable doing that.

F: What do you experience when you do this? What's your discomfort?

M: A real sense of betrayal. A—you know, a kind of a—"Well, why am I saying these horrible things?" Ah, it's a kind of a—a lonely feeling. I think there's nothing worse than rejection. I don't like it. I feel, I feel very badly when I feel rejected. . . and a sense of not being, you know, real and genuine inside. . .

F: So the sentence would be, "I reject you because you're not real."

M: Yes. This is what was told to me this week, you know, in—in words. I mean really. Not in what I felt but—well, no. I take that back. It wasn't really, that you're not—you're not real. It was "Why are you smiling? I don't feel that you really mean it." That's what was said to me... And ah, times when I felt other people were noticed and I wasn't, you know, over and over again... So my feeling of self-worth just took a real nose dive... And it's a—a new experience for me because I haven't felt it. But now it takes me back. I wonder, you know, for how long people—And I don't think they *have* felt this and now I'm—I'm beginning to ah—feel more and more that it's a figment of my imagination as I talk about it—as I'm talking about it to you.

F: Let's investigate this imagination a bit further. Talk to Marian. Say "Marian, you're worthless, you're unreal." Just depress her.

M: Marian, I think you're worthless, you have no value... I'm feeling very bad when I say that. It just b—brings on a feeling that I had, you know, a few times that ah, that I don't like...

F: You just made her cry... So let Marian talk back...

M: Well, I think I have, I'm sure I have value and I don't know why you tell me this. I feel I have been a very valuable person in my life, so why do you make me feel this way?

F: Change roles again.

M: Well, you—you're such a fake...

F: How? Tell her how she is a fake.

M: You smile when I don't really think you mean it. You're trying to act like you have goodwill toward people, when I don't really think you do. I think you're trying to make believe.

F: Now Marian? What does she answer?

M: But I *do* have goodwill for people. I think—I think well of people... You don't think I do... So I don't know why I got this horrible hang-up just this week...

F: Who gave you this hang-up?

M: It was an experience I had in a group. It was a...

F: Who gave you this hang-up?

M: Who? Several people in the group. There are none of them here right now.

F: Can you tell them what they did to you?

M: Threat—you threatened my personal integrity, saying that I didn't really mean what I said and that I was phony. I told you of times that I had ah, been instrumental in cheering people, helping them. And you questioned this. You said, you know, "Have you ever been successful in ever trying to make anyone else feel good?" My answer was "Certainly I have. I think of many times I've been helpful to people."

F: Come on, give them hell. . .

M: (stronger) I don't appreciate your questioning my integrity.

F: Now you're picking up voice. Now make *them* cry. . .

M: (strongly) You know I—I think—I think they're. . . I don't ah, believe they're worth my—expending my energy on you because I think you're so full of hops that I'm not even going to waste my breath on you further. I don't care what you think about me. I know what I think of myself.

F: See, now you took back what you had projected. . . How do you feel now?

M: I feel better. /F: Yah./ I feel kind of silly. (giggles)

F: Let's undo *this* projection. Tell me that I'm silly.

M: You, Fritz? That you're silly? /F: Yah./ Well I really think that ah—I can't tell you that you're silly because I've already sort of undone it from the other one. But—because I don't think you're silly. I think I'm silly, or I think I was. I don't think I'm silly now.

F: Can you forgive Marian for having been silly?

M: Yes, I can.

F: Tell her that.

M: Marian, I forgive you for being so silly as to take your projections out on other people or to, at low ebb, project on someone else. . . Thank you, Fritz.

F: You see, the trouble with the self-torture game is that when you torture yourself you act as a gloom-caster. You poison the whole atmosphere and depress everybody in your environment. Just try to absorb that.

GAIL

Gail: (nervous laughter) It's a lot scarier up here than I thought it was gonna be.

Fritz: Talk about this experience. "*It* is scary."

G: My heart is pounding. All the rest of you people got up here and worked, and—wow.

F: Okeh. Withdraw into your body, to your anxiety.

G: My—I can feel my heart pounding, and my pulse is—and my arms, and my legs, and my neck. . . Actually it's not a bad feeling.

F: Enjoy it.

G: It's a good strong heart. . . I feel the warmth of the fire on my back—that's nice, too.

F: Now come back to us.

G: I'm not so scared now—it works every time, Fritz.

F: So what do you experience now?

G: I'm looking at you. I see you. Last night I had a dream in which I was in a group—I am in a group.

F: Say this to the audience. Maybe somebody might be interested. Ask them whether anybody might be interested in the dream. I'm not your only audience.

G: I really don't care whether they're interested in my dream.

F: Yah. Develop this.

G: I'm *much* more interested in working with Fritz than I am—entertaining you. I'm not here for your entertainment.

F: Do you feel the truth, the real, in your voice now? /G: Mmm./ Can you develop this still further? "I'm not here for your entertainment—"

G: If you get something out of what happens when I'm working, that's fine, but if you don't, well—that's fine too. I'm not here to (laughs) live up to your expectations.

F: Then you touched *me*.

G: Yeah—I'm not here to live up to *your* expectations.

F: Good. Do you hear your voice? It suddenly came down. Beautiful.

G: Yeah. I'll try that one again. Fritz, I'm not here to live up to your expectations.

F: I don't believe you yet.

G: I'm here to live up to *my* expectations, unfortunately. That's where I get hooked.

F: Ahah. So talk to Gail. Tell her what you expect from her.

G: I expect you not to muck up and lose the chance you have

for growth. I expect you to stay in touch with Fritz, and not play your own silly games. And if you—you do screw up, I'll really punish you for that. I'll make you feel awful.

F: How? How do you punish?

G: I'll uh. . . I'll make you feel like a shit, but I don't know how to—how I do that, exactly.

F: Okeh. Let's try this with the group: "If you don't live up to my expectations, I'll make you feel like shit." Say this to the whole world.

G: (laughs). . . If you don't live up to my expectations, I'll make you feel like shit. And I'll do that by withdrawing from you, I think. I think that's the way I do it. . . Yes.

F: Let me work on a hunch. Can you say this to God too?

G: Uhuh. . . If you don't live up to my expectations, I'll withdraw from you. You won't exist for me. . . It works. (laughs) And if you don't live up to my expectations, I'll withdraw from *you*. (left hand pushes toward audience)

F: Say this to the audience again, and say this time, "If you don't live up to my expectations, I'll blot you out."

G: If you don't live up to my expectations, I'll blot you out.

F: Now blot them out with your right hand, too. Blot them out with both hands. . . Again. . . Can you *really* blot them out?

G: Ah. I get the fluttering again. /F: Yah./ (breathlessly) Wow!

F: There's some new strength coming.

G: I am—my breathing is shallow. And I feel a bit dizzy.

F: So withdraw again.

G: My dizziness increases. . . If I fight it, I get—I get a slight bit of nausea, so I guess I'll try to go with it. (sighs). . .

F: Did you ever faint? /G: No./ That's the best way of blotting out. /G: Yeah./ That's what they did in Victorian times. The ladies always fainted. Either they got headaches or they fainted. . .

G: I can take deeper breaths, now. . . when I go. . . I feel. . . and the fluttering is gone. . . My hands are still weak.

F: Come back, and say this, again, "With weak hands—" /G: Yeah./ "If you don't live up to my expectations, I blot you out with weak hands. . ."

G: If you don't live up to my expectations I blot you out with weak hands—and they really are. I blot you out with weak hands. . . I just don't have any strength in them. (sighs). . . Blot you out. . .

F: Can you make up a fantasy what would happen if you were to blot us out with *strong* hands?

G: (quickly) Nothing. . . I blot you out—uh—yeah—

F: What happened?

G: I blotted you out with strong—if I really used my hands, I'd hit you.

F: Ah! Finally. Say this again.

G: If I used my hands and they were strong, and I am blotting you out—if, in fact, I did that (laughs) I would hit you. . . But I don't. I blot you out with my—with my voice, and not my hands.

F: You blot out by withdrawing. "I'm weak."

G: Yeah. . . Yeah. . . Yeah.

F: Instead of using your strength.

G: The dizziness, too. Yeah. Right. . . Instead of making *them* go away, I go away.

F: Exactly. Now, go back to Gail. "If you don't live up to my expectations, I will blot you out with strong hands."

G: (rapidly) If you don't live up to my. . . (slower) If you *don't* live up to my expectations, I'll blot you out with strong hands. Yeah. . . Yeah, Yeah! (laughs)

F: Again.

G: Wow!. . . If *you* don't live up to my expectations. . . uh. . . I'll blot you out with strong hands.

F: Let's try a step further. "If you don't live up to my expectations, I blot you out with a strong voice."

G: (laughs) You're gonna get me, aren't you? (with stronger voice, quickly) If you don't live up to my—If—

F: You nearly got your voice.

G: Wow, I don't know where she is, either. It's fabulous. I'm not really with you here. I haven't separated you out, either. If *you* don't live up to my expectations, I'll blot you out with a strong voice.

F: Say this again.

G: (louder) I'll blot you out with a strong voice! /F: Louder./
I'll blot you out with a strong voice! /F: Louder./
I'LL BLOT YOU OUT WITH A STRONG VOICE!

F: Now say it with your whole body, and voice, and everything.

G: (takes breath) I'LL BLOT YOU OUT WITH A STRONG VOICE! I'LL BLOT YOU OUT!... Huh... yeah... I feel it in my back, too. Although I feel stronger, I still feel the fluttering, here. But I feel stronger. I feel that—I *really* do, too. I *really do* blot you out. Poor weak, insignificant thing... Why don't you fight back?

F: Say this again.

G: Why don't you fight back? /F: Say it in the imperative./
Fight back! /F: Again./
Fight back! /F: Again./
Fight back!...

F: Now change seats.

G: I don't even like to look at her, any more.

F: Say this to her.

G: I—I can't even look at you. I'm kind of looking around the corner. You're too strong.

F: That's a lie. You've got the strength.

G: It's *easier* if I don't fight back.

F: Ah. That's right.

G: (sighs) Then it'll make trouble. I don't—

F: Oy! You're collapsing again.

G: Ahhh... you can't squash me any more!

F: Say that again.

G: You can't squash me any more! *You can't*—(deeper) You can't squash—Wow! You can't squash me any more... You can't squash me any more.

F: Change seats.

G: How about that? I think she means it. Let's try her out. I squash you! Fight back! There's no fun in squashing you. You're too easy. That's not right either.

F: Talk more to this person sitting right there.

G: Fight back. I squash you. I give you asthma.

F: Now do this to me. Squash me. (she puts her hands on Fritz's chest and pushes gently) (laughter)

G: I'm not squashing you?... (she pushes strongly like very heavy artificial respiration)

F: How do you feel now?

G: Stronger.

F: Yah. Now do this to yourself. Give yourself asthma. (she exhales loudly and rapidly) Louder. More. (she continues heavy breathing, begins to cough, then wheeze) Much more.

G: (wheezes become more pronounced, louder coughs, then subsides to heavy breathing) My hands are hot. . .

F: Now make all kinds of noise, for instance, orgastic noises or something.

G: (wheezes, with some grunts) That wasn't right. (pants, grunts, louder) Ah. Uh. Uh.

F: You're squeezing.

G: HUH. HUH. HUH. /F: Louder./

    HUH. HUH. HUH. /F: Louder./

(she continues to make the same sound, like *huh* coming up from the guts, deep, with full breath behind it)

F: Louder. Do this to her. "*HUH!*" (laughter)

G: (laughs). . . Thank you.

MARY

Mary: Did you want a dream? (laughter)

Fritz: You see, the first step is—I always listen especially to the first sentence. In the first sentence she put responsibility onto me.

M: All right. I'm in a—there's sort of a war going on, and I'm in Ohio and I'm trying to get home to Michigan, to Grand Rapids. And ah—it's like the second world war—you know, you gotta show the ID and everything—or like movies I saw of the second world war. For some reason I haven't got the ID and I'm with another woman; I don't know who this woman is, I can't remember. But anyway we have an awful time and we're arranging to go across Lake Erie, and we snuck in like we were the French underground or something. And I'm trying to get—I'm trying to get home is the main thing, and I can't seem to get there. That's it.

F: Okeh. Can you play the *frustrator* here?

M: The frustrator?

F: Yah. You see, there are two kinds of dreams: wish-fulfill-ment, in the Freudian sense, and there are frustration dreams—nightmares. You can already see how full of frustration this dream is. You try to get home and something always prevents you. But at the same time, it's *your* dream—you are frustrating yourself. So play the frustrator, "Mary, I don't let you get home. I put obstacles in your way."

M: O.K. I'm not gonna let you get home. . . just keep talking?

F: Yah. It's your frustrating part of yourself. Get this out. See how well you can frustrate Mary to prevent her from getting home.

M: Gee, I don't know. Ah—well you gotta take this route or that route or—or some other way, and I'm going to keep you from getting there. I'm not gonna let you remember how to get there, I'm going to get you doing too many other things to get there—too many other activities. I'm not gonna let you cross the lake. . . I'm just gonna *keep* you all up tight—(puts up right hand as if pushing away)

F: Do this again.

M: I'm gonna keep you from doing it.

F: Do this to Mary.

M: Do it to me?

F: Yah, sure. You're the frustrator.

M: All right, stay back where you are. Don't go ahead.

F: Now change seats and be Mary.

M: But I wanna go ahead.

F: Say this again. . .

M: But I *want* to get there. . .

F: Change seats.

M: I'm not gonna let you. I'm too angry at you. I am *not* going to let you get there. . .

F: Go on writing the script. Go on with the dialogue.

M: Back and forth? /F: Yah./ I'm not sure where I'm going at the moment. Ah. . .

F: What's your right hand doing? I've noticed it a few times.

M: What's my what?

F: Right hand doing.

M: It's scratching my head because I—I. . . Well, I think where I wanna get is, I—I want to find, to get to myself. That's the home.

F: That's right. There's a beautiful poem by Hoelderlin, and Heidegger, one of the first existentialists, writes about it. Home-coming means to come into your own—into yourself. And you prevent yourself from home-coming. /M: Mmm./ And you've already said you prevent yourself from being angry at yourself.

M: Yeah, but I really am. The angry me is winning—I mean keeps fighting the maturity or something and keeps winning. It keeps preventing me from maturing I guess—from finding myself.

F: Say this to her. "I'm angry at you."

M: I'm angry at you—I'm angry at you because you won't look at me. . . I'm angry at my mother because she wouldn't listen to me, because she wouldn't love me for what I was.

F: Okeh. So we have to switch the encounter now, to one between you and your mother.

M: (softly) Mother, you called me selfish whenever I wanted to do what I wanted to do. and Mr. Psychiatrist, you're calling me selfish in the same way. I can't seem to get beyond it. So I—Mother, if I did what you did I became weak—if I did what you wanted me to do I became weak, but I—I stayed selfish.

But you *were* selfish. You always wanted to get ahead of the other guy. You wanted to eat, you wanted to get—you know, "me first" all the time. And you think only of yourself and if you're not happy then by God you're gonna get there somehow. . .

But I really don't know how to become unselfish. I ah—

F: You were looking at me. What do you want from me?

M: I need—I have trouble staying with it. I reached—I got stuck at—like an impasse.

F: Are you actually feeling the impasse?

M: I cop out. I feel it. Yeah.

F: How does it feel to be at the impasse? How do you cop out?

M: I don't like it, damn it. You know, I shouldn't do this. What the hell am I doing it for? Ah—this is what I do. I get in a group of people, I get in front of people and *bang*, I can't get in my feelings, because I feel self-conscious or something.

F: Tell this to the group.

M: I cop out to you and I don't mean to but I do. And this—I think this is the angry me in me saying "Mary, you know, you're not gonna get there."

F: All right, close your eyes and cop out. Go away. Go to any place you like to. Where would you go to?. . .

M: Want me to tell you where I am? /F: Yah./ Lake Michigan, watching a—walking along the beach.

F: By yourself?

M: Yeah.

F: Yah, and what—/M: I like it there—pardon?/ What do you experience there?

M: (softly) Well, I like the water washing my—banging against my feet and—I guess that's where home is—part of home. We have a cottage there. I guess I feel whole when I'm walking on the beach.

F: Now come back to us. How do you experience being here? Can you contrast the two experiences? Which one do you prefer?

M: I like being here.

F: What do you experience here?

M: A lot of nice people, a lot of interested people.

X: Mary, do you want to say *friends*?

M: Yeah. Friends, I guess.

F: All right, cop out again. Go away again. . .

M: I don't want to go away.

F: Okeh, you feel more comfortable here? /M: Yeah./ There's still something incomplete—Ahh. You just interrupted. What were you doing with your hands? No, now you are cheating.

M: That? (moves hands)

F: So let right and left talk to each other.

M: Right, you're going like that. Oh.
   I want to hide you.
   But I don't want to be hidden.
   But I want to hide you.
   No. No, don't hide me. I wanna go away.
   I've gotta grab you and hide you. . . Well, I'll just let you be.
   Then I don't need to hide.

F: Say this again, "I don't need to hide."

M: I don't need to hide. /F: Again./
   I don't need to hide. /F: Louder./
   I don't need to hide. /F: Say this to your mother./
   I don't need to hide.

F: Did you say this to her? Does she listen?

M: I don't know. What am I hiding from her?

F: That is the sixty-four dollar question. The main question, of course, is what do you need your mother for? Why do you still carry her around?

M: You mean why do I carry her around? /F: Yah./ I must want to. I must want to stay with her existence.

X: Mary, do you think you've lost your ID card or are you hiding it?. . .

M: I think I'm hiding it. . .

Y: Was the other woman with you your mother?

M: I don't know. I think my sister.

F: (to group) Please. There's one thing that's taboo in Gestalt Therapy—mind-fucking, interpretations. You just started to do this. I know in group therapy this is the main occupation. But we want experience. We want reality here.

What do you experience now, with all this interference?

M: I didn't like it too well.

F: But you didn't speak up.

M: (to group) I didn't like too much interference because I'm trying to concentrate.

F: You're *trying* to concentrate. What does it mean?

M: Get with my feelings towards my mother.

F: This is an effort?

M: Sometimes.

F: Now say this to your mother.

M: O.K. Mother, sometimes it's an effort to get with my feelings towards you—that I really don't want to hide myself. I don't want to be what you want me to be. I want to be myself. /F: Again./

I want to be my*self*, Mother, and if that means /F: Louder./ being selfish, it means being selfish, damn it! /F: Louder./

O.K. I wanna be myself. I wanna be *me*. I wanna let me come out and if that means being selfish, it means being selfish.

F: Now say this with your *whole body*.

M: O.K. I wanna be—I wanna be *me*. I've gotta be *me* somehow. I'm not gonna be what *you* want me to be.

F: Now you still say it mostly with your voice. The rest of yourself is still dead and not involved. Get up and say it with your whole self. (she gets up). . . What do you experience now?

M: A little bit of shyness, again.

F: Say this to your mother.

M: Mother, I'm shy. . . I love all these people but I'm still shy.

F: So go back to your cabin by Lake Michigan and say it there. . . Can you say it there?

M: Yeah, I can, but I can't get back to my cabin very easily.

F: Where would you be comfortable enough to say it?. . .

M: Maybe on that beach.

F: Okeh, can you go there?. . . Shout it across the lake.

M: (shouts) Hey Mother, I want to be *me*.

F: It's still false. Can you hear it?

M: Still harsh, yeah.

F: Now we have to pick up something else—shyness. Can you dance shyness?

M: Can I dance shyness?

F: Yah. I want you to dance it.

M: (gets up and dances) Like that? You mean like this? /F: Yah./ (chuckling) I don't want to see everybody out there.

F: How do you feel about this now?

M: Oh, good. I enjoy it.

F: Now try again to say it to your mother.

M: You mean yell it out. . .

F: I don't care whether you yell it, as long as I have some feeling that you actually *get the message across*. . .

M: It's hard for me to do because the love for her comes in.

F: Say this to *her*—

M: And that's a conflict.

F: Ahh. Now you're getting to your impasse. /M: Yeah./ Now say this to her.

M: And she's dead, too, so that, you know, it's done.

F: But you still carry her. She is not dead.

M: O.K. Hey Mother, I can't say it to you because I love you, too, and I want you to love me. And that's it, I want you to love me so I do what you want me to do. *Damn it.*

F: Play her.

M: That's right. I want you to do what I want you to do. But I do love you but it was just hard to get at you because you were selfish. And besides that, I wanted a boy. I didn't want a girl.

Well Ma, I wanted to *be* a boy.

F: Tell her that she's selfish.

M: You're selfish, damn it, because you didn't want me, you wanted a *boy*. And you got *me* and look what happened. You got a big tall me you didn't know what to do with. But I gotta be *me*.

F: Can you say "I got to be a girl."

M: I gotta be a girl.

F: Say this again.

M: It's hard to say.

F: Yah. Again you're stuck.

M: I still want to be a boy. Ah, I gotta be a *girl*, Mother, and I don't feel like a very pretty girl.

X: I think you're very pretty.

F: Somebody wants to be "helpful." (laughter)

M: I don't feel that I'm pretty. . . I can't at times, and other times I can. (sighs)

F: Now play coy again.

M: Shy?

F: Well you call it shy. I call it coy. (laughter)

M: You mean look around at these people? They don't see—

F: I see. So they can't see that you have no prick. Yah?

M: That I have no—Oh! (all laugh) I'm embarrassed.

F: This was my guess. It's your embarrassment. /M: What?/ This was my guess, that this was your existential embarrassment. You're supposed to be a boy, and a boy without a prick is not much of a boy. Okeh.

JOHN

John: When I find my mind going through this whole—

Fritz: Talk to your mind.

J: But I find my mind going through—

F: Talk to your mind.

J: I want to talk to you.

F: Okeh. Thank you. Who's next?

J: You aren't that hostile.

F: I'm not hostile. If you don't incorporate that—I am not interested in mind-fucking. If you want to work, you want to work.

J: O.K. I'll try. I still think you're a little bit hostile, but I'll try.

F: Say this to Fritz. Put Fritz on the chair. Say "Fritz, you seem to be a little bit hostile—"

J: Fritz, you seem to be a little bit hostile. Not just a little bit, a lot.

F: Play Fritz.

J: Play Fritz. Get off my platform—get off my platform, you goddamned intruder for trying to act like a human being. For trying to say what you're thinking yourself, for trying to act real, for trying to act like a real person. Get off my platform, you don't belong up here because you're nobody. I'm somebody. I'm God. You're nobody. You're a goddamned nothing, you don't—

F: Say the same sentence to the audience. "I'm God—"

J: They do exist, though.

F: Say the same sentence to the audience.

J: I am God. You don't exist.

F: That's not what you said.

J: I forgot what I said.

F: So please get off the platform.

J: That's the most hostile goddamn thing I've ever heard. Why won't you let me work this out?

F: Because you're sabotaging every step.

J: I've only—you've hardly given me a chance at all. I've said two things.

F: Yah.

J: And you immediately want to flush me down the toilet. Now, *why*? I don't think that's fair.

F: That's right. I'm not fair. I'm working.

You notice that anybody who brings even a *little* bit of good will along, how much then is happening. But with all the saboteurs and poisoners, and so on, I am not going to show *any* patience. If you want to control me, make a fool out of me—sabotage and destroy what we are trying to do here—I am not a part of that. If you want to play games, go to a psychoanalyst and lie there on his couch for years, decades, and centuries.

J: I dig what you're doing. I have up to now, that is.

F: Umhm.

J: And now, you know, I do something that—you know—in one sentence you don't approve of—and I've known other fellows, and gals, who came up here, and, you know, they want to—you know, you let them work it through. You instantly want to get me off your platform. Why? That doesn't seem fair to me.

F: Ask Fritz. He might answer you.

J: Play Fritz? Ask Fritz, you said.

F: Ah! For the first time, you listen.

J: Play Fritz... Play you... Huh. I can't play you. I think you're... I think you're so omnipotent that maybe you're insisting that I'm the one playing God, not you.

F: Ahah. You're getting it, now.

J: Well, I can get it intellectually, and I know I do this, some, but... I don't know that I was doing it then.

F: Will you please, each time—this is for the whole group—instead of saying "but," say "and." *But* is divisional. *And* is integrative.

J: I'm sorry. I don't understand what you're saying. I want to, but I don't. I missed it... Don't—I'm *not* that anxious, either. (short dry laugh) Would you repeat it—what you want me to do?

F: No. If you don't want to cooperate, you don't cooperate. If you sabotage every step, how can I work with you?

J: I *want* to cooperate. Will you give me a chance?

F: I gave you three chances so far. No, I gave you *six* chances. Go back to your chair.

J: (sarcastically) Thank you. I appreciate your cooperation, too... I really came up here to tell you a dream... but I feel somehow that would be just following the procedure right now, rather than talking about the exchange that you and I have had, and the feelings that I have about the exchange we've had.

F: Okeh, play Fritz. What would Fritz answer.

J: What would Fritz ask?

F: *Answer...*

J: What would Fritz answer... Fritz would answer (sigh)—I'm Fritz. I'm trying to be Fritz... I'm telling you to cooperate. I'm telling you to be open. I'm telling you to bend yourself to my will.

F: Say this to the audience.

J: I'm telling you to bend yourself to my will.

F: Again.

J: I'm telling you to bend yourself to my will.

F: Okeh, switch chairs. Answer this.

J: I don't want to bend myself to your will. I think you're a pompous old shitty crappy bastard.

F: Ah! Thank you. The first cooperation. (laughter)

J: You had cooperation the first time I sat down here, you goddamn bastard. You just didn't see it.

F: Can you do this again?

J: You're goddamn right, I can. . . I got through because of *me*, not just because of you. You wanted to kick me off this stand, you pompous old bastard. *I* got through because *I* persisted, not because *you* did anything. . .

F: So you win. (laughter)

J: That's a real put-down. . . I don't like the audience laughing at me.

F: Say this to them.

J: I don't like you laughing at me. I think you're laughing at me. I think you're joining in his hostility.

X: We're laughing *with* you.

J: I hope so. I don't believe it, but I hope so, because I wasn't laughing, (laughs) but you were laughing at me.

F: You were not aware that you were just laughing at this moment?

J: Was I laughing?

X: Yeah, you're enjoying it too, aren't you?

J: I guess so. I guess I am. Well, I know I'm competitive, I know the theory's right.

F: Could you go on a little bit with your mud-slinging. I like that.

J: You seem more human at this moment. It's harder to sling mud at you now that you seem human, than when you wouldn't let me stay up on your stand.

F: (sarcastically) How cooperative can you get? (laughter)

J: You want me to sling a little mud at you, huh? O.K., I think you're a goddamned—I think you're competitive, too! You want to be God, you want to show off your whole production to this group here. I'm not convinced that this is better than analysis, or individual private confidential psychotherapy. You know, maybe you're just a goddamned big pompous ass who is satisfying his own omnipotence by *being* up here. . .

F: So, now, can you play that role? Play a pompous ass, omnipotent. Play that Fritz that you just spoke to.

J: God! That's what I don't want to be! That's what I'm afraid I'll be. If I really—am me. A goddamn pompous ass like you are— O.K., I'll do that. Ahh. How'll I do it? Ahh. O.K., now you, you get up here to tell me your problems, and I'll help you, and I'll help all the people sitting here, because you know, I really know *everything*. All right. All right. I'm Fritz Perls, I know everything. I haven't written a whole string of books, but I've written a few things, and I'm seventy-five years old. You know, since I'm seventy-five, and I was born in the last century instead of this one, I really should know everything. You know, I really do know everything because *I*, after all, am *Doctor* Fritz Perls who all you people should come to hear.

F: Now, can you play the same role as yourself? The same spirit.

J: God! That's what I don't wanna be. O.K. You have come here to hear me, *me*—John. I am great, I'm something, you should all hear me because *I* have something to say. I'm important. I'm *very* important. In fact, I'm more important than *all* of you—you aren't *anything*. *I'm* important. I'm *extremely* important. You oughta learn from me. I shouldn't have to listen to *you*. Gee, I don't want to say that.

F: You feel more at home, now?

J: A little. A little more, yes.

F: Okeh, let's have the dream, now.

J: I—dreamt—shall I stay in the present tense? I dreamed? I am dreaming—of coming to Esalen, and in coming here I dreamt of several people—three men, three young men about my age, in their early thirties—ah, being on horses. I remember some names that I heard before I came here. One name was John Heider, and some other guy, and some other guy—there were these three guys on horses, and then there was Schutz or you who, you know, you weren't on horses, you were just somewhere back there. It was these three guys that I was feeling in competition with.

F: Yah. Were you aware that everybody whom I asked to work on a dream to tell it in the present tense, did it, but you are the only one who sabotaged it again and again—going back into the past, making stories. . .

J: I am, now that you've mentioned it—yes.

F: Yah, but you don't hear yourself.

J: I hear it, I didn't instantly feel how to do it, and I was so eager to please you, that I thought I would do it first in the past tense, and then later in the present tense. (laughter) That obviously doesn't please you.

F: I have assumed that any nincompoop could immediately understand it, but if you are not above that class, if you have to—

J: I'm not a nincompoop but you're so *goddamn* hostile. (laughter) I think you're a great fellow and you've got something to offer, but why do you be so damn hostile?

F: (laughing) Because you're a pompous ass! (laughter)

J: Don't you realize that I'm bright too, or something? What is it? (laughter) (John goes back to his dream) O.K. I am—I am—uh— I'm nothing, or I'm something very small, something very inconsequential. I don't even really *feel* my own existence, I don't even really feel my own body. I don't even really feel my own self. I'm not on a horse. I'm small. I'm smaller than I really am in physical appearance, and there are these three men on horses.

F: Fine, we've got a polarity now. Now, play again this insignificant John.

J: Play the significant John?

F: *In*significant John.

J: Play the insignificant John.

F: The one who appears in the dream.

J: Play the insignificant John.

F: And then, take the other role—the pompous ass John. And let the insignificant one and the pompous ass have an encounter.

J: (rapidly) I am—I'm nothing. I feel like nothing. I don't even feel like I exist. You pompous ass. I don't even feel my own self, I don't even feel my own body—because you, you pompous ass, won't let me (voice begins to break)—you goddamn bitch. You try to run everything, and I'm squelched. I don't feel my body, I don't feel my penis, I don't feel my head, I don't feel my toe, I don't feel my arms, because *you* want to squelch me. You won't let me exist, you won't let me feel that I'm *real*, (almost crying) you won't let me feel like I'm really functioning, here and now.

F: Play him.

J: (rapidly) You don't *deserve* to exist, you goddamn nincompoop. You're just a pisshead, you're just a piece of shit, you're *nothing*. You *shouldn't* exist. You don't dare to exist. You're too afraid to exist. You don't wanna get your head above the water. You don't wanna *put* yourself, so people can see you. You're *nothing*! You aren't even a speck of dust, you're not a speck of dirt. You aren't a parcel of water! You aren't a can of shit—you're nothing! You aren't here and (voice breaks) you never *were* here, you never *will be* here, and I *hate* you! (cries) I don't want to hate you.

F: Play him.

J: (heavy breathing and crying) I don't feel like I did. I don't feel like anything, because you won't let me exist. You try to step on me, you're nothing. You *are* nothing. Ohh. You won't let me. You won't let me exist, you try to step on me. You're—you bastard, you—you—*you're* the shithead.

F: Say this louder, "You are the bastard—"

J: *You* are the shithead, *you* are the bastard!

F: Louder.

J: *You* are the bastard! *You* are the shithead! You're the goddamn godly—the godly goddamn godly—God, I hate you, because you won't let me exist. You're stamping me out. But it's *me*. I *know* it is me.

F: This is your polarity. You are both.

J: Yeah. I know it.

F: And there's nothing in between. Omnipotence and impotence. All or nothing—nothing in between. You have no center.

J: I know it.

F: So, play him again.

J: I . . . ah—you're nothing. You have no right to exist. You shouldn't be here. You're—you're just a speck of piss, a speck of shit, you're a speck of dust, you aren't—you aren't even those things because you don't exist at all. You're nothing! You never *were* here. You never *will* be here; you never *could* be here. You're *not* here now. You never will be here, because you're *nothing*.

F: Take the other role again.

J: I did something when you interrupted, made an interpretation, I kind of lost it. I was feeling it up till then.

F: Well, I suggest—accept this being nothing. See how far you can go into the role of being nothing, "I'm a piece of shit," or whatever.

J: I am a piece of shit. I'm nothing. I don't exist. I'm not a person. I don't have toenails, I don't have feet, and I don't have a penis, I don't have balls, I don't have a finger, I don't have hands, I don't have a heart—

F: Every word is a lie. Say this again, but add each time, "—and this is a lie."

J: I don't have toes (crying) and this is a lie, because I *do*. I don't have feet, and this is a lie, because I do. I don't have legs, and this is a lie, because I do, goddamit, they're there. And I don't have a penis, but I *do*, because it's there, and my balls are there, and my rectum is there, and it's all there. My *stomach* is there. My *hands* are there. My head is there—I can think! I can think as well as you can think.

F: Now talk to the pompous ass again. . . from the new point of view.

J: From the new point of view?

F: Well, you have just discovered that you're *not* nothing, that you're something.

J: Well then, you're not such a pompous ass. I don't *want* you to be such a pompous ass. . . I'm afraid you still are. I'm afraid that it's really *me*—you'll be a pompous ass and so I'll be a pompous ass.

F: Now take the pompous ass position again. Pompous ass, how do you exist?

J: How do I *exist*? I exist just because of my nothingness—

F: Wait a moment. And each time, also say, "—and this is a lie." Give him the works and each time add, "—and this is a lie." "I am God, and this is a lie. I am a pompous ass, and this is a lie."

J: I hear you. I'm *God*, and this is a lie. I know *everything*, and everyone should listen to *me*. I have the truth to give, I have the truth to give to *you*, and you should listen to me, and this is a lie. (crying) Because then I won't—I'll still be so alone. (hard crying) I don't want to be alone. I don't know what else to say. I'm a—I know everything, and you know nothing, but that's a lie, because there are a lot of you are warm people, said nice things to me, and you're something too. I'm not everything. . . I don't know what else to say.

F: Okeh, let's play the whole thing all over, the underdog and the topdog. Let's have a new meeting. Maybe they can discover something.

J: (quietly) The underdog and the topdog—I always feel like I'm the underdog, I *am* the underdog. I always stay *quiet*, I don't *say* anything. I don't *express* myself. I just sit back *quietly* listening to mind-fucking talk. Everybody's talking too much mind-fucking talk. It seems like I could be real, but I'm not real, I don't *say* anything, I don't *exist*, I'm *nothing*, and I *want* to exist. And it seems like you, you goddamn bastard, it seems like you're the mind-fucker, and I'm the something—I'm something real, if I could just say it. But you won't let me. You're always talking, you—you're talking, you're always saying something, you're always—I never say anything. I just sit back and *listen* and *nod*, and I'm *compassionate* and *kindly* and I *help* you and I say the right things, and I make the right interpretations. I'm a *good* social worker, I'm a *good* therapist, I do the right things. I help people and they pay me, and I go out, but I don't really feel real. I don't very often feel real.

F: Okeh, now, be the topdog again. What are you? He just told you that you are a mind-fucker.

J: I'm getting confused—either—I can't switch it so easily.

F: This means integration is starting. They both learn from each other.

J: Ah. He just told me that I'm a mind-fucker. Yeah. Ah... (cries) But I'm not a mind-fucker, I don't wanna be—I don't want to be a mind-fucker. I don't want to be so pompous, I don't want to be so much better than everybody else. I just want to feel like I'm part of people. I just want to feel like I'm one of people. I don't want to be part of—I want to be myself but—I just want to feel like—I just wanna feel like I'm something too. I don't want to be a pompous ass.

F: What do you feel physically, now, and emotionally?

J: Oh, I'm tingling all over. Every—every part of my body's tingling. I should have an erection, too.

F: Now just follow up the transition from being *no*-body to be *some*-body.

J: Follow up—the transition—from being nobody to being somebody.

F: Write it in two words: *no body*, to *some body*.

J: Ohhh. You mean describe it, say what I'm feeling? Ahh. I don't know. I have to sit in the middle here somewhere.

F: Ahah.

J: There's no chair there. (laughs) What do you do then, hah? Does it *have* to be just a constant dialogue? Is that what life is? Is it just a *dialogue* between two *parts* of yourself? Can't you *be* someplace somewhere in between? Can't you feel *real*. Always have to be two parts, either feel like a nothing or a pompous ass?

F: Can't you have a center?

J: What?

F: Can't you have a center?

J: I *want* to have a center. I'd like to sit down here—that's what I'd like to do—but I want to be equal, I don't want to sit on the floor! (laughter) O.K. (sits on floor) That doesn't seem right. I want to be here (pulls chair to the middle) that's where I want to be, right in between. Hahhh. Ahhh. I don't want you to think I'm a pompous ass, and I don't want you to think I'm nothing. I don't know *where* I am.

F: You're coming closer. . . (long pause) So what do you experience now?

J: I feel somewhat more real. The tingling all over was something I didn't expect. I'm afraid that you would have lost me if I hadn't been as strong as I was, but I'm glad I was as strong as I was, and I wonder if somebody—this sounds like the pompous ass again—I wonder if somebody who was weaker would have left and been submissive and simply acted out one side of myself.

F: It's always the same, it's always a polarity—you have this polarity. We have other polarities—bully and cry baby and so on. And whatever you start with, there is always the opposite there to supplement. I knew right from the beginning. There is an old story about this: A rabbi is standing in front of his congregation and says, "I was such a good rabbi; now I am nothing. I'm really nothing. God, I was such a good rabbi and am nothing." And so the cantor, the singer, picks it up. He says, "God, I was such a good cantor and I am nothing. I'm really nothing." A little tailor in the congregation picks it up. "God, I was such a good tailor and I am nothing, really nothing." And the rabbi says to the singer, "Who does he think he is to think he's nothing?" (laughter)

Please note the *real* opposites are impotence vs. control madness. If you feel you have to control everything, immediately you feel impotent. For instance, the very moment I want to crawl up the wall, here, I am bound to feel impotent.

QUESTIONS II

Q: Seeing that I *did* sabotage earlier, and this is my pattern, how can I become more aware of it so I can stop?

F: By sabotaging *deliberately*. By making up, "I am a *great* saboteur." Now sabotage *this*. . . (laughter)

You never overcome *anything* by resisting it. You only can overcome anything by going deeper into it. If you are spiteful, be *more* spiteful. If you are performing, increase the performance. Whatever it is, if you go deeply enough into it, then it will disappear; it will be assimilated. Any resistance is no good. You have to go full into it—swing with it. Swing with your pain, your restlessness, whatever is there. Use your spite. Use your environment. Use all that you fight and disown. So, boast about it! Boast about what a great saboteur you are. If you were in the Resistance movement in the last war, you would be probably a hero.

Q: Well, this is. . . Do I have to, for example, sabotage with *you*? Or with everyone I meet? Or—

F: See, you sabotage already. I told you to *boast* what a great saboteur you are.

Q: I *am*—a terrific saboteur.

F: So go on.

Q: Terrific.

F: Come on. Tell us.

Q: Well, I wrote some songs that went to the top of the hit parade in Canada when I was 17, and a friend of mine—I co-wrote them, and a friend of mine stole them, and I let my mother discourage me from suing, and I was happily unhappy about that for a long time. And I started a nightclub in Toronto in partnership with my father and he stole it from me. And I ran to my mother and she said, "What do you need a club for? All the bums go there," and in the meantime, you know, very—well—good people went there, so I sort of went into a real depression and kept flunking in school. That was—you know—very good. I believed that I was stupid.

F: Sure, sure.

Q: I had the lead in *David and Lisa* and got myself canceled out of it by going back to Toronto, instead of staying there as my agent recommended. I know I have talent in art, and I have talent in music. I have talent. I'm a talented person. And I'm learning to love me, and this is—this is sort of screwing up my sabotaging, because—and I—I help people, I help people and I decided that now that I know *I'm* people, I want to start helping me, and—

F: How do you sabotage *that*?

Q: Well, I avoid—avoiding reading by—I'm accepted at UCLA, but I'm afraid to really follow through and write an exam.

F: Now, tell your parents, "All I want to do with my life is that I want to disappoint you."

Q: All I want to do with my life is that I want to disappoint you.

F: Now I would suggest that you reconsider your life. Maybe your life might have a different meaning, not just to disappoint your parents. Whether it's a worthwhile existence for you, is for you to decide. In other words, just throw your parents in the garbage pail. What do you need your parents for?

Q: Yes. Thank you. This was the hand that you earlier said was not—that you said was paralyzed. So I'd like to shake yours.

F: There is often this great need to disappoint—parents or others who are overambitious for the person.

Q: Is the experience of these two parts, which we are always seeing on the stage, in ourselves and others—If these two parts—if they're so far apart that they're like, you know, voices, or something "out there," can this technique still be used, to integrate?

F: Yah. If you get the right polarities, and you change from fighting into listening to each other, then the integration will take place. It's always the question of fighting vs. listening. This is rather difficult to understand because it's a difficult polarity. If you have ears, the road to integration is open. To understand means to listen.

Q: What about the possible dangers of assuming that we can do the same thing, either with ourselves or with others. I've seen a lot of amateur Fritz Perls'.

F: I have seen this, too. This is what I am trying to fight—the whole quack business, and turning-on business and anyone who has had a few encounter sessions going out and doing encounter work. Just as dangerous as doing psychoanalysis.

I might talk a bit here about the historical significance of Esalen

Institute. Esalen is a spiritual colony island. Esalen is an opportunity. Esalen has become a symbol, a symbol very similar to the German Bauhaus, in which a number of different dissident artists came together, and out of this Bauhaus came a re-catalyzation of art all over the world. Esalen and Gestalt are not identical. We are living in a symbiosis, a very practical symbiosis. I live and work here in a beautiful house, but I am not Esalen and Esalen is not me. There are many people, many different forms of therapy: soul therapy, spiritual, yoga bits, massage bits. All, whoever wish to be heard, can have seminars in Esalen. Esalen is an opportunity, and has become a symbol of the humanistic revolution that's going on.

The second thing I want to say is, there are quite a mixed number of programs here, and I like to distinguish two types of programs: one is a *growth* program, and the other is one that can be condensed into the *fallacy of instant cure*—instant joy, instant sensory awareness. In other words, the "turner-onners." I want to tell you, I do not belong to them. Last week we got another "instant"—instant violence—a Chinese guy who did karate and some people got very badly hurt, and I think we have enough education for violence in TV and comic strips. We don't need Esalen to reinforce that.

Q: I'd just like to ask one question. I tried reading your book, *Gestalt Therapy*, but I wish that somebody in this group of leading thinkers, and so on, would write a book in very simple language, if they could, explaining these same theories so that the average person without technical education, etc., could maybe really get something more out of it. Is that a—I know it's sometimes difficult to write about an involved subject without using technical language.

F: Did you find my language here too technical?

Q: No, but in that book, I did.

F: When did I write that book? In 1951. No, I am much more in favor now of making films and so on to bring this across, and I believe I have found a more simple language. As a matter of fact, I believe if I can't come across in some uncommon sense, then my message is no good. I am slowly learning.

Q: Dr. Perls, will you—as you've been formulating and experiencing what has come out as Gestalt Therapy, I want to be reassured, I want to hear you say it, it seems like it's a process of discovery. Yet I think that people can arrange themselves to fit the expectations of the therapist, like, I sit here and watch person after person have a polarity, a conflict of forces, and I think I can do it too. But I don't know how spontaneous it would be, although I think it would *feel* spontaneous. You've experienced people over a long time; are we fitting you, or have you discovered us?

F: I don't know. My whole definition of learning is that *learning is discovering that something is possible*, and if I have helped you to discover that it's possible to solve a number of inner conflicts, to get an armistice in the civil war in ourselves, then we have achieved something.

Q: Do you feel the workshop—do you feel the audience—is an essential part of the encounter that goes on? Can it be done with you alone with the person who is encountering himself?

F: Can you make a statement?

Q: Well, what I'm wondering is, how—

F: That's not a statement, it's still a question.

Q: Well, I personally think that what went on, on the stage there, can be done without the audience.

F: O.K., now we have got your statement.

Q: Dr. Perls, I have enjoyed very much watching you work. What about follow-up on those people who have come to a different point of realization or work-through. What would you suggest that they do?

F: I don't. You have to find your own way, as you found your way to me.

Q: Can one get the same benefit by a dialogue which one has with one's self? Can one have a kind of benefit out of that? Or are we always doomed to kind of wander around—associations, and so on—until I meet somebody like you outside to point out some facts and things like that?

F: I think I answered this question.

Q: I don't get you.

F: It depends whether the two parties listen or fight. Take any example in history, in yourself. If the U. S. and North Vietnam would listen to each other, if the different factions and cliques in the U. N. would listen to each other instead of walking out and fighting, if husbands and wives would listen to each other, the world would be different.

Q: But sometimes there are objective facts—I mean, there are two parts and one says this and one says that and you can define listening by saying, well, if the outcome is good it's a sign they listen, but this is kind of begging the question. How can you tell beforehand whether they are listening or not? /F: You can't./ Can't you imagine a situation where they would be listening to each other, and yet nothing will come out of that.

F: Yah. Then the war goes on.

Q: Excuse me. Can I re-phrase my question?

F: Oh, I'm sure you can.

Q: Let me do that, then. Can you tell whether they listen to each other or not? You're judging by the outcome, just by the process of viewing the process itself. Can you tell here that they are listening to each other—you don't know what will come out of it, but they *are* listening to each other?

F: Yah. I can tell *exactly* by the tone of voice, by the gestures.

Q: Another question. There were cases which you finished up very fast—there were persons which you finished up with very fast, and there were others which were very prolonged, and sometimes I got the impression that you don't want to get involved in certain directions.

F: You are perfectly right.

Q: Can you elaborate on the criteria of this division?

F: Yah. Whenever I see the chance that I couldn't finish a situation, and leave the people hanging, something I cannot handle in this context, then I refuse to go on. The only meaning of this seminar is to demonstrate that I believe that Gestalt Therapy works, that you don't need to lie on a couch for years, decades, and centuries. That's all I want to demonstrate.

Okeh. Thank you.

Intensive Workshop

The following transcripts are taken from audiotape recordings made at an intensive four-week Gestalt Therapy workshop involving 24 people at Esalen Institute during the summer of 1968. They illustrate, especially in sequential sessions with the same individual and in the group interaction, some aspects of Gestalt Therapy not brought out in the previous transcripts from weekend dreamwork seminars.

PLAYING THE ROLE OF THE DREAM

Fritz: Now, I want you all to talk to your dreams, and let the dreams talk back—not the content, but as if the dreams were a thing. "Dreams, you are frightening me," "I don't want to know about you," or something, and let the dreams answer back. (all talk to their dreams for several minutes). . .

So, now I would like each one of you to play the role of their dreams, such as, "I only seldom come to you, and then only in little bits and pieces," or however you experience your dreams. I want you to *be* that dream. Reverse the role, so that you are the dream, and talk to the whole group, as if you were the dream talking to yourself.

Neville: I fool you, don't I, because I'm full of important facts about you, and I won't allow you to remember me. That annoys the hell out of you, doesn't it? Confuses you, and I get a big kick out of it when I depress you, and watch you kind of sink deeper and deeper as the day goes along. You wouldn't have any difficulty remembering me if you just concentrated on me a little. So I play hide-and-seek with you, and I kind of enjoy your discomfort with it. I fool you all.

I play games with you and then elude you, so that I confuse you all. . . I make you see a different me, don't I?. . .

Glenn: I don't come on very clear, very often, because you don't seem to understand me very well. I would put on many spectaculars, if you paid more attention, but as it is, you pay little attention to me and I do kind of a shoddy job for you.

Raymond: I'm sneaky. You know I'm here but I won't let you know what's going on.

Blair: I'm going to mystify you. I'm going to be symbolic, impenetrable. . . keep you confused. . . unclear.

Bob: I'm all enclosed in mist, like that mountain over there. Even if the mist left, you'd have a hard time getting things out of me.

Frank: You shouldn't be ashamed of me. You should come out and meet me more. I feel that I can help you. I'd like to meet you more.

Lily: I can see, and hear, and feel and talk, and touch, and do everything you want to do.

Jane: I'm merry, exciting, interesting, I'm going to really turn you on, and then when we get to the end, I'm going to turn you off. And you're not going to get to see the end. And then you'll go around pouting all day, because you didn't get to the end.

Sally: It's not us that disturb your sleep. If we could find a chance when you would listen to us, and then after this, we'd be clear, like lightning, it's very shocking. We're going to shock you, but you'll shake it off in a little while, and when you wake up, going about the chores of the day you'll take us with you. But if we keep doing this, over and over again, finally, you'll find that nothing goes right. You'll try to hide from all your faults, all your fears, but we will be there to upset you.

Abe: Be good enough to yourself to remember that we've given you some very fine moments, often of meaning, sometimes power. Recently we've given you horror—frightening horror, and also recently you've turned away from us.

Jan: I don't think you really want to remember me, or know me. I don't feel you want to enjoy me. Every time I do let myself get close to you, you always say, "Well, I'm too tired to write you down or pay attention to you. Maybe in the morning I'll do it." I feel you're still trying to avoid me.

Fergus: I'm very weird. I'm the only honest, the only spontaneous part of you, the only free part of you.

Tony: I feel very sorry for you.

Nancy: I'm not going to give you the pleasure of knowing me, or the enjoyment of feeling grown up.

Daniel: You know that I'm made of all kinds of bits and pieces left unfinished during the day, and it's better that I have them, than just forget about them. Besides, sometimes I'm very beautiful and very meaningful, and you know that I'm doing much good for you, especially when you look at me carefully.

Steve: I am a multi-colored cloak that sweeps down and carries you off, gives you power.

Claire: You're just playing games, and I am really all. And you can wait for me forever.

Dick: You're very much aware of my existence, but most of the time you ignore me.

Teddy: I am a very creative, interesting situation. Plots, juxtapositions, that you'd never think of in your waking life. I'm much more creative, I'm much more frightening, and I appear to you not as pictures. You know what's going on when I'm there; afterwards you forget. But I'm not in movies; I'm a kind of knowing. You would like to see me in pictures but I don't appear.

June: I am going to make you *miserable*, I am going to *destroy* you, I am going to *encompass* you, and push you *under*, and make you feel as if you can't breathe. And I'm going to *stay* here and *sit* on you!. . .

Fritz: Well, possibly you noticed something very interesting for quite a few of you, how the dream as such symbolizes your hidden self. I would like you to work with that in the groups, to more and more act out *being* that thing that you just imagined was a dream. I don't know how much those who have played their dreams realize how much of themselves came through, but I'm pretty sure that most of you can easily recognize that this is the part of you that you don't like to bring forth. If you take *literally* what I asked you to do, to play your dream as if the dream was a person, these instructions would be complete nonsense. How can you be your dream? And then as you express it, finally it became so real. You really felt this is the person here. Sometimes there is a surprise, if this person had managed to wear his mask with grace and confidence. For instance, you noticed how much came out of June. I don't know how many of you have seen this tremendous destructive power of hers. It came out very clearly. Very beautiful.

JUNE

June: The dream starts in an automobile that is parked in a great cavelike underground parking lot, by a train station, and I'm a little girl. I'm only about seven years old. . . My father is sitting beside me in the car and he looks *very* big, *very* dark. There are no lights on—it's a blackout, and I know that he's taking me to the train station to put me on the train to go back to school, because I have my school uniform on, my blue middy and my blue skirt, and there's an air raid going on, so we have to sit in the car, and the bombs are falling and it's very noisy.

(thin, small voice) I'm very frightened. Daddy, I'm very frightened. I don't want to go on the train and I don't want to go back to school. (very faintly) I just want to stay home with you and mother.

(sternly) Are you frightened of the bombs, June? Or are you frightened to go back to school? Don't be frightened of the bombs, because this is a dream, and the car will protect us.

(faintly) I just don't want to go back to school. I don't like it there.

Well, I'd like to have you stay home from school. I'd like to have you come back to the hotel and enroll you in a school in the neighborhood, but your mother doesn't want you back there. . .

(whining) But you make the rules.

I don't make the rules. I have to live with your mother.

But bombs are dropping.

Fritz: You be the pilot. . .

J: There's a great feeling of power, to fly an airplane and find someone to drop bombs on and then just—press down the button. (confidently) I'm in control of this airplane and I can fly it anywhere I want to fly it, and I can drop 'em. Plop. Drop 'em. Plop. I have pedals all over the floor and every time I hit a pedal, a bomb drops. (fainter) I sure as hell frighten *some* people.

F: Okeh. Be still the bomber, go to Vietnam.

J: I can—I can (breathless and trembly voice) I can fly the plane there, but I can't drop the bombs! They're real people there. The people in my dreams aren't real people. . . There aren't any—there aren't any knobs, or any pedals on the floor, so I can't bomb. I can drive the plane. I can drive it and I can go around in circles, and I can dive low and be shot at, but I can't shoot back. . . I don't wanna shoot back.

F: So go back and throw the bombs once more on that car.

J: (almost crying, helpless voice) There's a little girl in that car. I can't do that. . . Yes, I can. . . I did. They fell all around the car.

(rocking) And I'm the car, and I'm rocked, and I'm shattered, but the inside is intact, and the people in the car are safe. They're very frightened.

F: Much ado about nothing. You just can't do anything to you. . . You're safe. . .

J: *You* can't do anything to me, but *I* can do things to me.

F: Okeh. Let's try once more.

J: Yes, sir.

F: Be a bomber and drop napalm bombs on the Vietnamese.

J: All right. . . I'm coming now over the edge of the land, and I have a whole cargo full of deadly napalm. Jelly stuff. Now I go lower, and lower, because this time I'm really gonna hit it, and I want to see what I hit. . . (cries, chokes) Oh, *nooo*!. . . I hit a lady, who was running with a child in her arms, and a dog behind her. . . (cries) and they *writhed in pain*!. . . and I didn't kill them. . . but they burned.

F: So find somebody else to kill.

J: Here?

F: Doesn't matter, as long as you get the killing out of your system.

J: (cries) My mother. . . how can I kill her. (softly and intensely) I want it to hurt. . . Boy, do I want it to hurt. . . Oh! I killed her. (still crying) Into the swimming pool, all filled with acid, and she dove in. There's just nothing left. (laughs). . . (quietly) You deserved it. I should have done it a long time ago. There aren't even any bones left. She just disappeared.

F: I didn't get what you mumbled, there. Are you willing to tell it to us? You don't have to, only if you want to.

J: (calmly) I filled the pool, filled it—I filled their swimming pool all full with acid, and she didn't know it. It was all clear.

F: Whose swimming pool?

J: My mother's and father's swimming pool. And she came down to swim, she dove in. . . and she—she *burned*. And she fell to the bottom, and the flesh came away and dissolved, and the bones started to go down, and they dissolved. And then it was all clear and blue again. . . And then I sorta felt *good*. I should have done it a long time ago.

F: Say this to the group.

J: It felt good! I should have done it a *long* time ago. Muriel, it felt *really* good, and I should have done it a long time ago. It felt good, Glenn. Her agony felt good. Her death felt good. I should have done it a *long* time ago.

F: Okeh. Now close you eyes. Withdraw to your seventh year of life. Become seven years old.

J: (faintly) All right. . . Seven?. . . Oh boy, am I ugly. *Very* fat. I have crooked bangs. They slope from here to here, because I have to cut them myself because nobody cuts them. My hair is. . . frizzy and unkempt. My nails—they're all chewed down. From my neck to my knees I'm like black—dirty!—because all I have to do is button my middy buttons to say I washed, and I brushed my teeth, and I didn't disturb last night, and they never undid the middy buttons to see if you washed any further than your wrists. And my middy had jam on it, and ink on it. . . They make us bathe under a sheet, in little cubicles, and when I was seven—I am seven—I don't wanna bathe under that sheet. (cries) And a bell rings, and that means we have to go out in the hall, and we line up. (cries words) And who can I talk to? and I don't even know—ugrh—that no one wants that child. (wails) I always get five demerits. I never get candy or ice cream. I eat potatoes and stuff. My grandmother sends me a box of candy, and I'm not allowed to keep it. I have to put it in a big chest, in the dining room, to share it with everybody. . . and I don't even get *any*. (burst of crying) Please can I have one to eat?—and then I won't have any next week. (sobs)

F: Okeh, June. How old are you now?

J: About nine.

F: And your real age? What is your age?

J: I'm just thirty-five.

F: Thirty-five. Play a thirty-five-year-old woman talking to this girl. Let the *now* girl talk to the *then* girl. . . Put her in that chair, and you sit here. You are thirty-five, now.

J: (gently) You're not a *bad* girl. Little nine-year-old girls aren't *bad*. You're just pretty dumb, and not even that's your fault. . . I don't care if you write backhand. . . I don't care if you've got holes in your teeth from eating chocolate. And, June, I don't care if you're fat. I don't care if you're dirty, because all those things are really very superficial.

F: Now I want you to come back to us. I'd like to just have a bit of bullshit about this. Any idea what makes you hug this memory to your bosom so much?

J: It went on for such a *long* time.

F: Okeh, look around, what's going on here.

J: I don't know. It doesn't have the *faintest* relationship with anything that I'm doing here and now.

F: So, I'm interested that you have to drag this girl with you, that you can't let her go.

J: Yeah. . . Sometimes. . . I don't ever feel like I'm *dragging* her. I feel like she's—she sits there, and she like waits for an opportunity when somebody puts me down, and—boy, then she just takes over, and I'm a child.

F: *Exactly*, exactly. Now say, "I am waiting for an opportunity to play the tragedy queen," or something, and so on.

J: Uh, I can; I'm not sure it's gonna fit.

F: "I play you for a soft touch."

J: I wait for an opportunity to play on your sympathy, and warmth, and understanding. . . and then if I get it, I'm very grateful, and I feel better, and I feel thirty-five years old again. So that I can cope. But the minute I feel that I *can't* cope, then I shrink, and I'm little, and I let somebody else cope with me.

F: Then you pull her out of the garbage bin?

J: (strongly) Yes, then I pull her out, I present her to myself, I accept her, and I act her, until I find somebody who is sympathetic, gets sucked in, and then they're kindly, and then I feel reassured, then I can put her away.

F: Now go back to her. Talk to her. Tell her about the con game you are both playing. . .

J: Baby, we've got a game going. I didn't even know it until just now. (laughter) I'm thirty-five years old. I'm not fat. I don't have dirty wrists. (laughter) I can buy a box of candy and eat it whenever I want to. I have *many* people who love me dearly. I have many people that will give me support when I need support, so what do I need *you* for? (laughter)

F: What does she answer?

J: Ahhh, she says, You're not altogether *su-re*. You know? Ah— I'm—a *very* handy little girl to have around. (laughter)

(laughs) *An acid bath for you, too*! (much laughter)

F: And for the professionals—this is to show you—this is one of the famous traumata the Freudian analysts peddle around. They live on it for years. They think this is the *cause* of the neurosis, instead of seeing it's just a gimmick. Psychoanalysis is an illness that pretends to be a cure.

You understand, it is very difficult to bring home that all that happens here takes place in fantasy. Neurosis is a compromise between psychosis and reality. June sits on a comfortable chair. Nothing can happen to her. Yet all these things in her dream are taken for real. This is why we are far from realizing the fact that we are playing roles. There are no bombs here, there is no killing, there is no little girl, *these are only images*. Most of our whole striving in life is pure fantasy. We don't want to become what we *are*. We want to become a *concept*, a fantasy, what we *should* be like. Sometimes we have what people always call the ideal, what I call the curse, to be perfect, and then nothing that we do gives us satisfaction. There is always something we have to criticize in order to maintain the self-torture game, and you see in this dream the self-torture game taking place to quite an extent.

GLENN I

Glenn: I kind of feel quivery, and there's sort of—excitement is in my chest, kind of shaking. I don't like my voice. . . Conscious of my knee burning, and calves. My pants pulling on my legs. As I sat down, I caught my pants.

Fritz: What has this to do with your not liking your voice?

G: Nothing. It doesn't.

F: You jumped from your voice to your legs. . . In other words, with your not liking your voice, you were in the intermediate zone. . . And instead of experiencing your voice, you judged it, /G: I judged it./ you *did* something. . .

G: Yes. Rather than hearing it as hollow, and kind of shaky, I hear it as being *bad*.

F: Yah. I noticed you changed from a writer to a judge. (laughter). . . You see, once you judge, you can't experience any more, because you are now much too busy finding reasons and explanation, defenses, and all that crap. . .

G: I find it hard even to sit here. I'm judging that I'm impatient, that I should do something.

F: Okeh. Stay in the intermediate zone. Get a bit more acquainted with what is going on there. . .

G: I'm not even sure how to do that. I feel (laughs) like I'm invoicing. I judge, and then that's O.K. It's where I am, in the intermediate zone. (laughter) The laughter—makes me feel better. I feel that I'm holding my neck stiff and with that goes, "That's not what I should do," I should be relaxed. . . My throat's tight. . . I feel that I have blinders on, that I can't move my head. (moves head) But I can. I feel that I'm digging a hole somehow, that I'm backing myself into a corner. . . I don't want to do that. . . I'm beginning to feel that everybody's judging me, that you're judging me, that, by yawning, you judge me, by being restless, you judge me.

F: You see how the intermediate zone expands more and more. You lose more and more touch with yourself and the world. You have a very nice, juicy paranoia. (laughter)

G: I'd rather narrow it. I'm really beginning to feel silly. (laughter) It's as though it's exactly backwards. Now I'm doing what I've been trying *not* to do for days—staying in this fucking intermediate zone. (continuing laughter)

F: Now what happened with this laughter? Did you put this laughter into your framework of reference? Was it interpreted as a hostile attitude toward you or. . .? I had the impression you jumped out of your paranoia, and you just enjoyed the laughter.

G: Yeah, it was just funny. Toward the end, I started in readjusting, judging. (screams of laughter) Yeah. (humorous) It's as though I just can't let it *be*. I've got to decide whether it's plus or minus.

F: I think we can safely say that in your intermediate zone there is what we call the topdog, the superego. . . judging you, telling you what to do.

The unpleasantness has to be got through, whether it's frustration, or the extreme other case, the situation where you have to face the experience of being dead—the real impasse, the real implosive layer. It's not pleasant to get in touch with one's death, but there is no other way out than go through that hellgate of mire, that extreme suffering. I don't preach suffering. You know that. You know me better than that. But I'm willing to invest myself whenever a suffering, an unpleasantness comes up.

And as for myself, I can tell you one of the most important solutions of the unpleasantness. You know how unpleasant boredom is. I tackle the boredom, finally, and decide whenever I get bored, I start writing, and the boredom has changed into tremendous excitement of writing. Now this is true in every case. If your bladder's full, it becomes unpleasant. If you hold back further, it becomes more and more painful. And then the pissing comes, and the pissing is pleasant. You feel relief, after. So each time, facing and working through, and really staying in touch with the unpleasantness is the only means of growing and consolidating one's position. So what we have to do is, to understand more and more where you become phobic, at what moment you want to avoid your pain, and more and more learn to work through the situation.

Now, for instance, *right now*, enter the heaviness. . . Look upon this heaviness as a song, piece of poetry, enter it, wallow in it if you want to. . . Let's start with Glenn. You find it unpleasant to be in touch with people—rather, get in touch with yourself. Look around and tell each one how unpleasant it is to be in touch with each one of us. . . Let's try some extreme. Say to each one of us, "I won't suffer you. You are too dirty, too joyous—"

GLENN II

G: Be in the middle zone. I won't—I won't suffer you.

F: You may include me.

G: I won't suffer you, Fritz. I can't stand the feeling of—longing, for your approval, so I avoid you.

F: Stay a bit longer with me. You are not willing to suffer me because I don't give you enough approval.

G: (chuckling) I actually feel that you give me a *lot* of approval. I'm not sure—/F: Enough?/ Yes, it's enough—

F: I don't believe you.

G: O.K. O.K. I don't believe that either. Oh, I always turn it back on myself. I can't stand the feeling of wanting something, because if I really get in touch with that, I won't get it. My catastrophic expectation is that you won't come across. You sit and puff your cigarette and. . .

F: So say this to me.

G: You sit and puff your cigarette and. . .

F: And you won't suffer it.

G: Yes. . . Uh—It's very difficult for me to look at you, (voice begins to break) for you look at me with kindness, and I—

F: Can't suffer that.

G: (voice breaks) I can't suffer that. Yes.

F: Let go a bit more, and become human. (Glenn cries). . . Breathe.

G: I'll not suffer how that feels. I will withdraw from it.

F: So withdraw. That's all right. For a moment, if you come back. You go away, withdraw in order to jump better. . . Where are you going?

G: I keep coming back to you. Ah—as soon as it quiets, then I. . . (cries) I can't suffer—the feelings of—(cries) of loving you. (goes on crying) Of wanting to please you and. . . I find myself blocking your face now, just blocking. . . (through tears) One of the things which is so painful is you look at me without expectations. You make no demand. And I find that beautiful. I don't suffer myself to look at you. . . I'm so happy. . .

F: Now take two more. . .

G: I can't suffer to get in touch with myself. It's so much easier to be angry, or hurting, or pushy.

F: Be a tough guy.

G: Whoooh. I get you in the position so that you don't—smile at me.

F: I would like you to make up a dialogue. Two guys are having an encounter. One is called the Toughy, the other the Softy. Let them meet each other, get in touch with each other. Softy sits here; Toughy sits there. Or would you like the other way around? Let's put Toughy in there.

G: Yeah. He's the one you look down at. Sitting here now, I have no respect for you, particularly.

F: I guess they both are not willing to suffer each other.

G: Yeah... You can't stand it... when I get all gooey. You think that it's better not to show anything. I'm not so sure you're tough at all. I think you're just kind of wooden. (sighs)

Yeah, but it's a lot better. I'm—I'm—I don't hurt nearly as much as you do. I push people around, and I kind of smile about it, now and then. Yeah. And you don't listen to what I say, 'cause when you're soft and feeling close to somebody, it's not going to come across. I keep telling you, you gotta play it cool, because if you start in really feeling in touch, people will go away. They'll withdraw. They won't have anything to do with you. Nobody wants somebody around holding onto them...

(sighs) You, you are so lonely! I at least know I'm lonely. You think you're just alone. If I don't feel—if you don't let me feel *with* people, if you don't feel—let me feel so that I could reach out and touch—

F: "Reach out and touch." What is your right hand doing?

G: It's reaching out.

F: It's reaching out, yah. /G: (softly) Wow./ Now change, change hands. /G: Yeah./ Say this again and reverse it.

G: Because I could feel my fingers quiver when I reach out with this hand.

F: Now develop this.

G: No. I want to reach out, but I feel no one wants me to touch them, and I feel—that I'm not—touchable, at the same time.

F: Now do it again with your right hand.

G: Do it again. I'm—(right hand is a fist)

F: Fine. Start with this.

G: This is a pretty good way to be.

F: Now touch him with your fist.

G: That works too. 'Cause Toughy doesn't do that. Or, rather—that's odd. Toughy doesn't—the cry-baby is also the only one who will touch someone with a fist. *He* won't do a thing.

F: Now open your right hand, and reach with both hands...

G: (heavy breathing)... Yeah. I don't want to suffer that... (crying) I reach with both hands. I feel them longing.

F: Now touch with both fists.

G: I guess. . . I don't mind my fists.

F: Okeh. Then be Toughy again. Be fist again.

G: I feel that I'm not so much Toughy. I just won't—I won't. /F: Say this again./ I just won't. That's—I won't!

F: Say it more with your legs.

G: I won't. I won't. *I won't*.

F: What are your hands doing?

G: They're holding on.

F: They're holding on.

G: Yeah.

F: So talk to your seat.

G: Seat, I'm holding onto you—you—I'll make damn sure you'll stay right here, underneath me. I'm holding onto you, too, 'cause it hurts. . . I don't know *why* I'm holding on so hard to you. I hold on so that—I hold on till it hurts. You let me go where I am. I sit on you.

F: Now hurt the seat. (Glenn scrunches and mashes chair) Hold onto mama and hurt her.

G: Yeah. . . I hurt.

F: Huh?

G: I hurt. I hurt you, Mom, though by just not doing anything.

F: What do you feel in your anus?

G: I'm tight.

F: Hold onto your shit.

G: Yeah.

F: Now have an encounter between your sphincter and the shit.

G: (laughs) Sphincter, huh? That's this guy. No. I said hold on. I won't let go. Be damned if you're going to push it past me. Yeah. I get a satisfaction in sitting there holding it.

F: You understand your emotional constipation now?

G: Yeah. . .

F: Okeh. What do you feel in your anus now?

G: It's still very tight, but I feel it. It's not just a—

F: Close your eyes and stay with the tightness. Let develop whatever wants to develop. . .

G: I want to blow up. And I feel pretty sick.

F: Yeah. . .

G: I don't fit. (laughs) My stomach kinda says, "Wouldn't it be nice if you could relax."

F: Let's do some phony sentences. Just repeat this sentence, "I won't be born. . ."

G: I hope not. . . wow. . . I won't be born. (laughs) I won't be born! Hahh! I've got you now. I. . . I WON'T. . . I wonder if it's a breech birth? I don't wanna come out. I want to spite you. I feel like I wanna smile. I wanna sit here and say, Now I've got you (heavy breathing). . . and now I'm in touch with you. (laughs defiantly) You were going to push me through, and you're not gonna do that any more. You were gonna teach me to be tough. That's what *you* think.

F: Okeh. Come back to us.

G: Ginny's got air all around her. You're so clear to me. I see you as a separate, beautiful person.

F: Are you more in the world, now?

G: (tremulous) I'm happy to stay. . . with this part. It's very clear.

F: I don't think we have yet emptied that symptom. But I think we got it back into focus now.

HELENA

Helena: I feel very heavy, heavy in the chair. I feel the floor, the soles of my—soles and heels of my feet on the floor, and it feels very hard. My foot is moving up and down—cracks in the ankle. I see Fritz's eyes close. I hear his breathing. . . Daniel's face looks concerned. . . I feel my cheeks flush—warm hand underneath my cool hand. . . I can hear the machine; it's very quiet. The room seems very quiet. Stillness. Frank looks puzzled, impatient—that's judging. I see your foot moving. I feel cheeks very hot again. I saw you turn your head to the side. I see your eyes. . . (long pause)

Teddy: (softly) Do you feel all right, Fritz?

Fritz: Mmm. *Wonderful!*. . . (low, deep, with a sense of excitement) I am going through a very intense experience. I don't know whether—if I remember having had this experience—so completely *there*, without *any* role-playing, or *any* attempt to relate, or so on. Complete unity of—there was a struggle to be physically all there—and integration. *Enormous* experience of the colors. I can't relate it.

It was *so* intense that for awhile I thought I couldn't bear it. I had a *little* bit of this once when I heard for the first time the Bartok violin concerto, and I thought either I go crazy or I understand music.

H: I just thought that anything that I would say was meaningless because something very strong was happening here.

F: You felt it.

H: *Yes.* That's why I couldn't talk. I just couldn't talk.

F: It was really the experience—as if the outer and inner zones just came completely together, with *nothing* in between. Just one world. . . (long pause)

H: (resuming) I'm aware that I'm censoring a lot of things, and I'm not seeing individual faces but a group—colors and figures, but nothing specific. . . I feel very disjointed. That's not true. That's a lie. I don't feel disjointed. Ah! Ah. I feel very comfortable in the chair—quiet inside. I tasted my lips and they were salty. . . I'm tasting my lips and they are salty. I notice June's eyes and they are like two black marbles, and her dress is like a tapestry. And Dick looks like he's coming out of a cowboy picture—he just needs a gun. . . Now my heart is beating faster, I'm getting more excited. . .

F: What's the relationship of this excitement to the previous situation—that he looks like a cowboy.

H: He became alive for me—a character—not just blending with the wall. He suddenly came out of the wall with a cocked head, and June and then Dick—and I felt my heart starting to beat. I felt pleasure.

F: Did he become alive?

H: For me. Yeh. For me.

F: You also became alive?

H: Yeh. I started to feel more excited about looking—as if a veil lifted. And it wasn't just Dick there, smoking a cigarette, but he became a whole character. And June's eyes and dress—she became a character.

F: So withdraw into yourself.

H: I feel my hands and my arms and my legs all tingling, and my head feels very light—not my whole head, just the back of my head feels light, but the front—here—there's a pressure across the front. My heart's beating more regularly, but I still have the very light feeling here—the top and the back—very light. . . Jane looks like she comes from Brooklyn—from that book, the book about the gangs. . .

F: Basically, I like what you experience. I am very much disturbed by the feeling of. . . you are doing a *reportage*.

H: Umhm. . . I'm reporting.

F: I feel more than reporting—*making* a reportage.

H: Which reportage?

F: Doing the whole thing for the next issue of next week's so-and-so—Journal of Gestalt Therapy or something. Let's introduce a little bit different factor. Whenever you go out, use the word *you*, then go back and use the word *I*. Shuttle between *you* and *I*.

H: When I talk about the others—*you*. The out. . . I feel stuck and I'm aware of judging myself, that I'm a schmuck up here, wondering what to say next. I'm aware of bringing my hands together, being impatient. . . Huh!. . . I discover that I'm very hot. . . and that Ginny's dress is *very* bright—your dress is very bright. I'm still doing the same thing. . . (sarcastic) So your dress is bright!

F: So let's change from a reporter to a clown.

H: At least, more lively.

F: Clowning is always a good way out. Where other people get a paranoia, you become a clown. The difference is not so great. You see, the paranoiac uses any kind of material which he wants, which he needs for *his* aggressive purposes. The paranoiac is looking for a fight, so he looks for injuries and all kinds of things. Likewise, the clown uses anything he can get hold of for his entertainment purposes. Okeh.

BLAIR

Blair: I have an unfinished situation with you, Fritz.

Fritz: Yah.

B: (quietly angry) I don't know what kind of Gestalt bullshit you were trying to pull last night, when I asked you for a match, but all I want is a simple yes or no when I ask you for a match, and not a bunch of verbal messin' around until I come up with the right combination of words and you come across with the match. And another thing, if I—if I want a damned sermon on social etiquette, I'll ask you for it. As far as I am concerned, you enter my life space when I get up there on that damn chair and no other time. I'm not interested.

F: (gently) So what should I do?

B: Just don't mess up my mind when I ask you for a match. You can say a yes or no and that's enough. And I'll let you know when I want you, and that's up there on the hot seat.

F: You made one mistake. You didn't ask me for a match.

B: (loudly) Oh, yes, I did. Ninety-nine percent of the people in America, when you say, "Have you a match?"—those people who are over ten years old, that is—don't come up and say, "Yeah, I got a match," or some cute little fucking thing like that. You knew what I meant. Why did you fuck around?

Dale: Those are all dishonest people.

B: Ohh, don't give me that crap, Dale.

F: Are you coming to my defense?

Dale: Oh, nononono, I'm just telling him. (laughter) No, you do fine for yourself.

B: (still mad) That's bullshit. That's the Gestalt game, that's what that is. And you can't look at me honestly and say you didn't know that I wanted a match.

F: (coyly) Oh, I knew that you wanted a match.

B: Then why did you pull all that crap?

F: Because I pull all that crap. Because I am the *one per cent*! (laughter)

B: Ohh, brother. I want to get out of here.

F: That's a good resentment.

B: You know, I'm gettin' so I don't even resent you any more. (laughter) (Blair waves an admonishing finger at Fritz) You earn your money when you sit in that chair, and—(Fritz mimics Blair's pointing finger) Yeah. *"Bad boy."* (laughter) You are a—O.K., you play your rules; I'll play mine. Just don't—My rules are, when I ask for a match, you know—just give it to me. (laughter) Give me a straight answer.

F: So can you also appreciate what I did?

B: Of course. Let me tell you, (laughter) I'm not alone on *that* jazz, Fritz. But that doesn't keep me from bein' damn pissed. The fact that—

F: The fact is that the blah, anemic guy you were two weeks ago is now coming out with the real anger.

B: Shh! I wasn't blah and anemic before. (laughter) No, that's a fact. . . I had something else I wanted to say. . . This is what I wanted to say. The fact is, I love you, but that doesn't keep me from hating your guts sometimes, too.

F: Of course not. I hope so. . . But you set out as if hating is bad. You "shouldn't" hate.

B: I've had a couple of feelings this morning, Fritz, that I'm kind of enjoying. (laughter)

F: Okeh. Thank you.

I see as a major difficulty in the awareness, the now process which we like to reach, an unawareness of one's activity. Let's try to get this very clear. It's very simple for most people, with a little bit of training, to discover what's going on in the world, to discover colors, people, and so on. It's also relatively easy—except if you're really desensitized—to discover your own sensations, or emotions. But where many people slip up is they're not aware of their activities. There's so much activity going on in the intermediate zone, like "I'm rehearsing," "I am playing the fitting game," "I am out to fool you." This awareness of the activity of what one is doing, is something I would like you to pay special attention to. This might be the key reason why people who are otherwise very sensitive and often capable of seeing lots of things in other people, are incapable of getting to the *now* awareness, to reality, to themselves. . . Okeh.

MURIEL I

Muriel: (soft, rich voice) Now I'm aware of sitting very deeply into the chair. The chair is supporting me under my thighs, and behind my back. . . Uh—

F: You see an activity projected. The chair is supporting you, as if the chair is doing something for you.

M: Mmhm, I feel that it is. Ah, I'm glad it's there supporting my thighs. . . I feel it behind my back, also pushing. I'm leaning back on it and it's. . . equal. I feel that I'm way back in the back of my head. I'm aware that my eyes are way up looking at those three bolts or something, and beams, and I see the semicircle cut by the large beam. . . and how the beam—oh!

F: Are you discovering something?

M: Yes, the beam and the vertical thing in that painting. . . are the same and I wonder if. . . uh, if the painting was painted that way or if when it was put up there, something happened (laughs) in the interaction between the beam and the painting.

Steve: It's the sunlight.

M: (interested surprise) It's the sunlight. Now I notice that there are other human beings in the room. I see Sally in her deep blue and white Japanese thing and you look *very* rested, and refreshed.

F: Can you describe the blueishness a little bit more in detail? What kind of blue is it?

M: It's almost black across your chest as it goes down and when you—when it comes down on the arm part, it gets lighter, and uh, I see the white rectangles following the contours of the fabric. And now I notice the pink and blue at the bottom of it, and the gold of your wedding band.

F: Yes, do me a favor. Use the word *discover* as much as possible, because this wasn't there before. It's very often difficult to understand the idea of the phenomenon. . . The world exists, but it *doesn't* exist until you *discover* the world. It's only a theory until you *see* it. So now you *discover*, now you have enriched your world by something new. Now close your eyes and also see if you can do the same within yourself; go on a discovery voyage.

M: I discover that both elbows are pressing down. . . I discover that my fingers are very heavy, and are falling, uh, hanging, is what I mean, hanging heavily. Uh, I discover a red trembly something in front of both my eyes and my eyelids are trembling, and I see red vibrations.

F: Again, let me emphasize the difference between a person who is on the discovery thing, always discovering something new, for whom the world gets richer and richer. More and more new things and experiences come in, in contrast to the person who maintains the status quo—the cliché person.

M: Close my eyes again? /F: Yah./ I discover a swirling motion on top of my head. Uh, and as I breathe, I catch my breath on top and tighten my shoulders. It's unpleasant. Uh, I'm still doing it, and that's a surprise. I feel, uh, caught in the swirling in the top of my head; I'm not going on. It feels like it's rising. (sighs) And when I breathe like that, it stops. . . (opens eyes)

F: Ah, you came back to us. What do you discover in *this* world?

M: I discover that Helena looks like a statue (laughs). . . I discover that Dick has a crooked smile. I discover Bob writing as busily as ever.

F: Now the essence of the real discovery is the "Ahah!" experience. Whenever something clicks, falls into place; each time a gestalt closes, there is this "Ahah!" click, the shock of recognition. So you had a very successful journey to the outer world, so return to the inner world.

M: Uh, I don't want to. I will because you told me to. . . Um, I have like a small cramp over here and my massaging of it feels good, feels *very* good. . . Once again, I'm in the top of my head. . . and I experience not wanting to go on.

F: How do you experience this, "I don't want to go on"?

M: Well, I made like a down movement in my chest and that did something up here and stopped it. . . I opened my eyes, Fritz, I. . .

F: Are you aware of your smile?

M: No—now I am. . . Um, I want to smile and open my eyes, and—

F: You see, there's something going on in the intermediate zone. A conflict between, "Fritz told me to," and "I don't want to do it." Become a bit more aware of the process in the intermediate zone.

M: I feel safer with my eyes open, right now. . . As soon as I close them, I get that swirl in my head.

F: Can you do this in intervals of five seconds? Keep your eyes open for five seconds, close them for five seconds and go back to the swirl, then go back to the world, go back to the swirl—see what happens then.

M: Uh, you look interested, Teddy, and that pleases me. Bob is holding his finger over his mouth as if to keep it closed. (closes eyes) The swirl is pushing my head back, that's what I was resisting before. . . Uh, I found it difficult to talk back there, but it's extremely comfortable—oh!

F: So come back to us. . .

M: I see interest in Fergus' face, and that pleases me. . . Sally, you're holding your mouth—I wonder about that.

F: So, go back to your inner world. . .

M: My head wants to be held. (rests head on hand). . . The more I rest it—oh, yes! This is good. . . If I leave it free, the swirl pushes it somewhere and as I rest it on my hand, my hand is holding it and I don't feel the swirl.

F: So come back. . .

M: Jane looks like a cat woman, peering from behind her hair.

F: Close your eyes. . . Your experience?. . .

M: Trembling, hoarseness, clearing my throat, trembling behind my eyelids. /F: Open your eyes./

I don't want to look at the people. /F: Close your eyes./

Stronger swirl. /F: Open your eyes./

I *really* don't want to look at the people. /F: Close your eyes./

Even stronger swirl. /F: Open your eyes./

I don't want to look at *any*body. /F: Close your eyes./

My eyes are really trembling now, and I'm holding my hands, holding my head.

F: Can you try now to integrate this. Look at us and at the same time, pay attention to the swirl, bring your swirl with you. It might be very difficult, but try. . .

M: Uh, oh! /F: Yah?/ I just, saw like—like a light of a halo behind—um, Sally's head and as I look at Teddy's face, I see the contours under your flesh—the bone structure. (softly) Wow, uh—

F: A little discovery, a little step forward, a new way of looking. Close your eyes again.

M: I want to keep them open. (closes eyes) Now I see the—sort of the phosphorescent shapes of—it's Teddy, and, I don't know—oh, it's Frank.

F: Yah, you take them back with you. Okeh, this is as far as I want to go. So, can I have some feedback.

Jane: I was interested the whole time.

Frank: It was beautiful, beautiful. This is obviously an interpretation: You hold back on giving yourself beauty and richness.

Dale: That swirling in the back—you kept on not wanting to do it. When you finally let yourself do it, it was beautiful.

F: The main thing is, not a single sentence was phony.

M: That pleases me very much.

F: This is a very good example of the integration of the inner world and outer world. When they came together, *WOW*! Then there's no interference from the intermediate zone—no explanations, no interpretations, no judgments and all that. This is the decisive moment—the difference between the old stale routine, always the same, in contrast to the discovery, which always means something new, adding something to your life, adding something to your knowledge, adding something to your growth. There is something in this world that wasn't there before. This happens only by being in touch with the now.

MURIEL II

Muriel: As I'm looking around the group, I find myself doing some kind of tragic goodbye scene. It's time to get to it, whatever *it* is.

My dream is right over here. When I got up this morning it just appeared, and it's been there the whole day standing right there. /F: On your right side./ Yeah, right over there. . . And it's sorta being very nice about the whole thing. It's telling me it's there and it's gonna stay there, and I don't have any choice. . . "It's time," and "Get down to business." And then right in front of me, over there, is that person that I saw in the mirror last night, whom I don't know and have never seen before. I don't know who she is. . .

F: So where are you now?

M: (as if awakening) Ohh! I'm in never-never land. I meet this stranger, and it's traveling backwards, backwards—

F: Where are you now?. . .

M: Well, it's very white.

F: You haven't taken any drugs?

M: No!. . .

F: Do you see me?

M: Yes. Sure.

F: Do you see the others?

M: Yeah. When I look. I see everybody very clearly. . . And now I'm puzzled, as if something's the matter. And I think that when I did the now thing, just the little exercise, and I had the swirl in my head, and did a little bit of integration—I thought afterwards, yeah, that's the sort of thing that I do when I'm stoned on pot. . .

F: So shuttle between your experiences and your experience of the group.

M: Umm. You look like The Great Stone Face now. . . And inside I can—I hear my heart beating—boom, boom, boom. . . The room seems very bright. The lights seem very bright. And you *staring* at me, Fergus. You look to me like you're dead, with your eye-lashes moving.

F: Yah. Like an Alfred Hitchcock picture.

M: (laughs a little) You look like an elf or a goblin, with your hair all messed up. . . (closes eyes) My feet just said, "This ain't it." That's it. . . My hands are cold, and I can feel the air around them when they move, to that massage stuff. I can see them with my eyes closed, all tan. (opens eyes) Oh boy! (still speaking softly) There's lots of light in here, lots of light, and I immediately go to the dream, where I couldn't get enough light to see. . .

Dale: I feel like this whole room's just "up"—at another level. I mean like nobody's real, or. . . like I don't even feel like you're there, Fritz. (laughs) Let's all fly to the moon or something. I dunno.

Jane: Yeah, I feel the same way.

M: Now I'm afraid to tell you what I just saw, because it's like being stoned. . . Sally, your cheeks are pink like a porcelain doll, and your eyes are *deep* and *dark* and staring out from *'way behind*. . .

F: You know something? You're right.

M: Yeah. (laughter) Oh, thanks, Daddy.

F: But that's all?

M: Right!

Dale: Aw, gee. Shucks. I want more.

M: More what? Oh, I love to look at your face, Sally.

F: So. Go back to yourself.

M: Ohh. Just impatient feet, mainly. And now I've got a heavy head. Lots of heaviness around there—moving all around. . . Now I feel a great calmness and stillness has settled over everybody. I'm busy. . . It's *scary*, Fritz!

F: Yah. Depersonalized. It's scary. Sure it's scary. . . It's a world without a soul. Something like a glorified Madame Tussaud.

M: (murmurs) Oh, wow. . . That's just what I feel like.

F: Yah.

M: I feel scared.

F: Stay still more within yourself. . .

M: Now I feel a sign of—just a very faint trembling of my eyelids—just *very* faint. I usually have so much *stuff* going on inside. I don't see anything, though.

F: Okeh, come back to us. . . and say goodbye to us.

M: I don't wanna say goodbye.

F: Hm?

M: I don't want to.

F: I would like you to. You brought it up at the beginning.

M: Yeah, I know, that's what it feels like. (faint voice) 'Bye, Abe, I'll see you sometime—maybe. . . 'Bye, Dick, have fun making pictures. . . 'Bye June, I don't know if we'll see each other again. (a little stronger) I said goodbye to you before. . . 'Bye. . . I did it a'ready: goodbye. . . Hm. . . (almost inaudible) 'Bye, Teddy. . . (to Fritz) You, too, huh?

F: Umhm. . .

M: (sighs). . . I don't wanna say goodbye to you.

F: What do you want?. . .

M: (sighs) I *really* don't know. . . O.K. 'Bye. (sighs) That evidently means "Don't look. . ."

F: When you said goodbye, you crossed your legs.

M: Right. Closing up, too. (quickly) Goodbye!

Dale: I don't think you really said goodbye to Fritz. You made a sound, and you—

M: Well, I did it as much as I did to anyone else.

Dale: Oh, no. You stayed with Teddy for a long time.

M: I think I'm afraid it would be so horrible if I really did it.

F: Exactly.

M: Well, saying a *real* goodbye is the same thing as death.

F: Yah.

M: So—

F: So, you don't want me to die.

M: Nnn.

F: What's your objection?

M: Oh, I want to have you around, so I can be with you and sit in the hot seat when I get nervy enough, and so you can cure everybody. . . I just feel numb.

F: Okeh. Close your eyes and enter your numbness. (she sighs) Yah. This fits.

M: Hm?

F: This fits, yah. Enter your numbness.

M: I made a face right away. It's just very *very* heavy, especially on my face. . . and. . . well, it's like some thick stuff was attached to me, on my face, and now it's widening out. . . uh. . . I'm not. . .

F: The following is merely an experiment. I have no idea if it will work, if we are on the right track or not. Would you say good-bye to your mirror.

M: I feel like I'm in it, now. . . I immediately see myself as about eight years old.

F: Okeh. Say goodbye to the eight-year-old girl.

M: Are you really gonna go away? Yeah. She says Yes. Now she's turning around and walking away—just fading out, right into nothing.

F: Go back to the mirror. Can you say goodbye to that person?

M: I don't know that person.

F: Talk—is it a he or she?

M: She—it's me.

F: Well, first you have to make her acquaintance.

M: Now I *really* get it.

F: Yah. . .

M: (sighs) Well, she's just there in the mirror.

F: Talk to her.

M: Who are you? I've never seen you before. I don't recognize you. I don't feel like. . . I don't feel like I know you. I've never seen you before. Your eyes don't look like that, usually.

F: What *do* her eyes look like now?

M: Well, they're brown—they're my eyes—they're brown and they're open, and—and—there's a little sparkle in each one of them which is about one-twentieth the size that I usually see in the mirror, and then there's like a dead spot in each one. Like that.

F: Now change seats. . .

M: She doesn't say anything. She just looks and her expression doesn't change.

F: Give her a voice. "I don't say a word—"

M: I don't say anything. I just—I'm here, looking out at you. Looking out at you. And I don't feel *any* life in me, and those two little spots that you see in my eyes, that's just the light from outside, that doesn't come from me.

Well, where did you *come* from? You know, I'm not like that, and you're my reflection in the mirror, so—

F: Say this once more, "I'm not like that."

M: I'm not like that. /F: Again./

I'm *not* like that. /F: Again./

(louder) I'm *not* like that! /F: Again./

You're not me! /F: Again./

(very loud) I'm *not* like that! /F: Again./

(with quivering laugh) I am *not.*

F: Your voice becomes real. So be her again.

M: So who's making the reflection in the mirror? Hahaha. . .

You got me. . . I have no answer for you. That's gotta be so. You're my reflection.

F: Say this to the group.

M: It's gotta be so, you're my reflection?

F: Uhuh.

M: (very low) It's gotta be so, you're my reflection. . . (continues, with various intonations) It's gotta be so, you're my reflection. It's gotta be so, you're my reflection. It's gotta be so, you're my reflection.

F: So what do you actually experience?. . .

M: Well, I feel like the top half is wanting to move, and like there's blood in there.

F: Move it. (Fritz reaches for her hand) Let me. . . It's—it's not warm yet.

M: A little bit warm. It's sweaty. Wow, this air in here. *Oh, wow!* Where have I *been?*

F: Where *have* you been?

M: I don't know.

F: When you came to this seat, you were in a trance, you weren't here.

M: *Crazy.*

F: Yah. Out of this world, that's where you were.

M: Just crazy.

F: See me?

M: Sure. I just remembered that Abe did a hypnotizing thing at the massage class yesterday. . . O.K. Now I feel it coming back again.

F: Going back into your trance? /M: Yeah./ Okeh. Go back. /M: Go back?/ Go back into your trance.

M: Well, now I feel all this *motion* in my hand, and down my neck, all this *motion*.

F: It is more difficult now to die, to be dead.

M: Umhm. . . Oh. . . Huh—and my hands are doing the massage thing, like we did today when I did Dale's leg, and really got excited and got with the rhythm.

F: Close your eyes, and go back to that now.

M: To where?

F: To Dale's leg.

M: I'm doing this stroke, and I watch Molly do it, and she uses her whole self, and does the whole thing, and so I imitate how she stands and what she's doing and I really get into that leg, and I *feel* all the insides of the muscles and I *really groove with it*. I just did a whole leg and I really got into the rhythm of it, just loving every minute of it. I don't feel that way now. Time gets in the way of doing this but—

F: Okeh, say goodbye to that leg and come back to us.

M: It's pretty good. It's—it's *very* still. . . There are two eyes like a ghoul looking at me. . .

F: Can you be those eyes, look at us?

M: They feel *really* big, and they're *not* seeing. I mean, they're seeing all the things that I said before, but like—there's more to see.

F: Now go back to the leg, to the massage.

M: Dale's leg? Well, I'm on a calf of the leg, that's where it was really groovy.

F: So what do you discover?

M: Well, all this stuff underneath!

F: What else?. . . I thought I heard you discovered grooviness or joy or so.

M: Well, it's like the thing went by itself.

F: Yah.

M: And, I don't know—it wasn't such a deal—was it such a big thing? You know, I got a boot out of it.

F: Okeh. Can you say this to the group now.

M: Well, I sorta see everyone doing their own thing, now. Tony's 'way behind, somewhere, like that, and Dale's being therapist, and June's being friend and hostess.

F: Your voice is still not in reality, still in a trance.

M: O.K.. . .

F: Let's compromise. Right now, you are not dead, you are only half dead.

M: O.K. . .

F: Try the following: Let your upper carriage talk to your lower carriage.

M: Oh, yeah, O.K. Hey, what are you doing down there?

Let's get going; what's holding you up?

I don't know. The chair.

F: You get your support from the chair, not from your legs.

M: Right. Right. Well, can't you get up and stand on your own two feet?

F: I doubt it.

M: I'll consider it. I'll think about it.

F: You are much more comfortable up there.

M: Yeeeah. Right. Right. Right. Don't have to walk around. Don't have to go up to anybody. . .

F: I would like you to discover the ground, the floor.

M: O.K.

F: Get up. See how much support you can get from your legs.

M: (faintly) Well, like my feet are there. I feel the rug. . . Oh, boy. Everybody looks so far *away*. . . I feel so *tall*, standing up.

F: Ah! Can you feel how much space you occupy in this room?

M: Wow! Yeah.

F: You feel ten-foot tall?

M: Naw. Naw. But I'm taller than I am. Well, it's not quite fresh. (sighs) No, it's not connected—not connected.

F: You know something? You sound as if you don't quite believe that you exist.

M: Huh. . .

F: And consequently, we don't exist. . . You know the story of the Zen monk and the butterfly. Chuang-Tze dreamt he was a butterfly, and then he was pondering, now what is it? Am I a Zen monk who just dreamt I was a butterfly, or am I a butterfly who dreams he is waking up as a Zen monk.

M: O.K.! So, back to the leg!

F: You discover *his* leg, but not *yours*.

M: No, well, it was like I couldn't tell the difference between my hands and the body that was moving and the leg that was in there, and the muscles I was feeling, /F: Yah, yah./ and everything like that.

F: I don't want to talk about confluence. That is a too difficult thing, but this is what you experience—no ego boundaries.

Dale: This is the first time I've been trapped in fantasy-land. I was completely trapped.

Jane: It was fascinating. I had the fantasy that you were a witch, and that you were hypnotizing all of us. But I enjoyed it. I enjoyed being in the trance and all that.

Daniel: We have had many hypnotizers here, but none as powerful as you.

F: Yah. No. It's different. She is not the hypnotizer. She is the somnambulant. She is the sleep-walker. She is hypnotized, in a trance, and everybody walks with her in the trance. It's *beautiful* for an artist.

Jane: It was fascinating. You just turned me on. I just had a very good trip.

M: I don't even know what you're talking about.

Dale: It was so very real. I wasn't sure I could walk out of this building and find ground out there. In fact I'm still not sure.

F: Anyhow, you took us all on a trip. Let's have re-entry now.

CLAIRE

Claire: I want to get—

Fritz: "I want;" get out of this seat. You want. I don't want any wanters. There are two great lies: "I want" and "I try."

C: I am fat. . . This is my existence. (whimpering) I don't like it and yet I like it. And I constantly bug me with this fact. And that is always with me. . . And I'm tired of crying about it. . . Do you want me to get off this seat?

F: No.

C: Don't you want me to get off?

F: No.

C: Yes?

F: No. . . I neither want you to get off nor do I don't want you to get off.

C: Are you going to sit here, Claire, or are you going to try and do something about what you're doing. (sigh) You just want to sit here and stay fat. . .

(in a section which is omitted here, she relates a long dream of being fat and rejected and does some largely unproductive dreamwork with this)

F: Okeh, now. I think I told you previously my diagnosis.

C: That I'm empty.

F: No. This I find very often in fat women, that they have no ego boundaries. They don't have a self. They always live through other people and other people become themselves. You can't distinguish what is me and what is you. "If you cry, then I cry. If you enjoy yourself, then I enjoy myself." This is your problem.

C: And so how should I confront my problem? I've been—After you told me that, I stayed aware of it and—and—I do that, a lot of times. So now what?

F: I don't know. You see, all the time, all the time you speak, you talk about your image, your concept of yourself. When for a moment (in the omitted dreamwork) you became yourself, got in touch with yourself, then you felt good and sexy. . . until again you had to—

C: Well, yeah. I can keep feeling good and sexy and having sex all the time and all that, and—and—and—but you can only, you know, make love twelve hours or something. (laughing) You can't have it all the time—

F: You see, again a fantasy. . . Again a concept. You have to eat occasionally, and things like that.

C: Yeah, you do. And then you stay fat.

F: Now work on this idea that you have no contact boundaries. What you touch, what you taste, what you see, whatever the contact boundary is, is fuzzy, or maybe nonexistent, so you are boundless, so you have to get fatter and fatter until you occupy the whole universe.

C: I feel that. That's what I'm afraid of. Um. Well. All right. So—with Abe—I don't know how to—My first tendency is just to *be* Abe.

F: Yah. Exactly. Can you feel like Abe? (Claire copies Abe's posture) Now, feel like yourself. Close your eyes and get the awareness of yourself.

C: Umhm.

F: What do you feel?

C: I feel uncomfortable in this position.

F: Ahah. And what else?

C: I feel separate from Abe. I still feel with you, like I'm an image of Abe, right in here. But I feel my own vagina—

F: That's all? Do you exist of anything else except the vagina?

C: Oh, sure. I feel my arms and my hands and the chair underneath me and the way it hurts, here, sitting in this position.

F: Good. Now go back to Abe. How do you experience Abe?

C: I'm separate, and then I can bring him here, too.

F: Can you allow him to stay out there, and be in touch with him instead of consuming him? Without swallowing him up and contributing to your fatness?. . .

C: (hesitantly) Sure.

F: So, what do you experience?

C: He's just there, and he's rubbing his leg—

F: Yah.

C: And looking. . . and I'm over here.

F: I don't quite believe you. I think you are trying to please me.

C: I feel myself here, and I feel him there.

F: And what do you see there? What do you experience?

C: Oh, Bob is playing with his leg and looking. I see your beard and your eyes are looking and your mouth is closed tight—

F: Are you still here?. . . Do you have any reactions to him?

C: (more animated) Yes! I feel like a woman over here and he's sexually appealing to me. I feel like flirting with him, now. I don't feel this thing that you're talking about. I don't feel this—if there are extremes, I don't feel them. I don't feel that—that—he is *really* me or I'm really him, nor do I feel that he is *totally* separate from me, over there. I feel a connection between us, but the connection is not—ah—a real connection, it's just sort of there.

F: Take Sally. . .

C: Well, I see Sally there, and I see her feet are moving and—and—

F: And how do you experience yourself? Close your eyes.

C: More like Sally than like Abe. Now I feel more like Sally. I don't think that's unusual, though.

F: But you don't *react* to her.

C: I don't react on my own.

F: You don't *react* to her. You destroy her. You don't react to her, you destroy her by taking her in.

C: I don't—I *take* her in, you say.

F: Rather than reacting to her. There is no contact. *Contact is the appreciation of differences.*

C: In other words, how do I feel about Sally?

F: Yah.

C: Well I *feel* that you're just kind of interested, and—uh—I—

Frank: You're still describing.

Dale: You're still her.

C: Well, one of you says I'm still her, and the other says I'm describing her.

Dale: It's the same thing.

Frank: It's close.

F: It's the same thing. In both cases you don't have a reaction *to* her. Your own self is blotted out.

C: I—I—I don't particularly care whether you're interested in me, right now.

F: You're still not reacting to her. You're reacting to a mirror. . . Can you imagine a glass of water. Now, how does one drop of water in this glass of water react to the others?

C: It stays separate.

F: (friendly chiding) Ahnh-ah. There is a confluence. There is no reaction. There is a sameness. There is no contact, no boundary. Take ice cubes—yes, they can have contact with each other. They touch each other; there is some difference there.

C: I'm having so much trouble really connecting what you're saying.

F: Sure, sure. I know. You have—

C: Ice cubes—have contact with each other, and they stay as separate ice cubes.

F: Yah. And water?. . . When the ice cubes melt, are they still in contact?

C: They are blending in.

F: They are then in confluence. Any feeling of contact goes.

C: Well, the thing that screwed me up about the water was that I—somebody told me that a drop of water *does* stay separate, and I didn't know that.

F: You're lying. Nobody told you that.

C: Well, I'm not /F: You are lying./ willing to use my authority.

F: You're inventing it. Ad hoc.

C: I don't want to deal with that. I want to deal with the ice cubes and something else that's blended together. . . With the air. . . a particle of air—just keeps changing, and moving into other parts. I can't even imagine what a particle of air is like.

F: Okeh. I show you something. Watch my cigarette smoke. . . Do you see the smoke? /C: Yes./ Now watch it. It has contact with the air, right? /C: Yes./ Can you see the contact diminishing, becoming more and more confluence?

C: Yes. Until it's all enmeshed, together.

F: Can you tell me now, what is smoke and what is air?

C: No.

F: Well that is your situation. You don't know what is smoke and what is air. *Contact is the appreciation of differences.* You don't know what is self and what is other. I would say *probably* with the exception of your sex relations. Your genitals still have contact functions, from how you describe it. Even there, I am not quite sure. When you screw, do you feel the difference between your vagina and the prick?

C: Of course.

F: Good, then *there* is contact. So apparently your intensity of sex—

C: I feel that when I'm touching someone, too. They're separate from me. You're separate from me, now. That's why I don't understand. I'm not you. I don't feel that I'm you, at all.

F: Yah.

C: Well, I. . .

Dale: You project something onto a person, and then the only way to get it back is to take him in.

C: The—I'd like to try and take that, and see what I can do with it. It sounds foreign to me. If I project onto Steve what I think he feels, then I'm investing something in him, and then I need to get it back. Is that what you're saying?

Fergus: Well I think the thing for you to do is to get fatter and fatter.

C: (sarcastically) Oh, thank you.

F: Right now, for instance, you are all willing to be swallowed by her. She plays hungry, stupid, "You have to nourish me." And everybody comes in and wants to be sucked in by her. That's one thing please don't do—whenever someone gets stuck, *don't* come to the rescue. . .

C: Yeah. I feel that would be a very easy way to—to stop this particular session for me. You know, for me to say I'm trying to suck people in, you know, so then I've got to say to myself which I've said many times, there is absolutely no reason if you want to lose weight, why you shouldn't lose weight. It's just that you want to suck people in and feel sorry for yourself and all that. Well I've lived with that for years.

F: Now, you try to suck *me* in.

C: Yes. Exactly. I *know* that. So one of my—so where does that leave me? It still leaves me with my stupid problem and—/F: Still leaves you hungry./ I'm playing stupid.

F: So you're still hungry.

C: Yeah. . . Which feeds the other problem.

F: Which feeds the other problem. . .

C: And so now I say, well, how can I deal with this? I'm still stuck with this.

F: "Give me answers. How can I deal with this. Come on, come on, give me, give me, give me."

C: I—you know—really, I don't even *want* the answers any more, because *nobody* is really, you know—everybody's got an answer and it isn't doing me any good.

F: "Come on, give me the right answer, the one that's really nourishing, get me out of my impasse."

C: So I'm back to the same thing. *I'm* the one that has to give *me* the answer how to get out of the impasse.

F: No. Answers don't help.

C: Well what the fuck does?. . . What does help?

F: Another question. "Come on, come on."

C: The answer is, you just stop eating if you don't want to eat.

F: Here are all the typical symptoms of the impasse. The merry-go-round—everybody sees the obvious except the patient. She drives you crazy. She is stuck. She is in despair. Mobilizes whatever gimmicks and tricks she has, to get out of the impasse. I feel that you started out with some kind of feeling inside, that you are dead. Or you call it bored. Bored and empty. You have to fill yourself. . .

C: Yes. I do eat when I am bored and empty. I eat sometimes when—when I'm full and not bored, too.

Jane: How are you dead, Claire?. . .

C: (clears throat). . . I don't feel dead. . . Oh, shit.

F: "I feel dead. I feel dead when I'm bored. No, I don't feel dead." So you're on the merry-go-round again.

C: No, I'm just bored and empty, not dead.

F: So be bored and empty.

C: Bored and empty and I—when I refuse to be in touch with myself. When I am *not* in touch with myself. It's a little trick I play on myself.

F: Exactly. Instead of getting in touch with your boredom and emptiness, you want to fill it again with some other—

C: Yes! And it doesn't work, either.

F: Of course it doesn't.

C: It never works.

F: You can put a million dollars worth of artificial flowers into the desert. It still doesn't bloom.

C: Yeah. That's right.

F: If you avoid your emptiness and fill it up with phony roles and dummy activities, you get nowhere. But if you really get in contact with the emptiness, something begins to happen—the desert begins to bloom. That's the difference between the sterile void and the fertile void. Okeh.

JANE I

Jane: Ah, in my dream I'm going home to visit my mother and my family. . . and I'm dr—I'm driving from Big Sur to—to my mother's house. . .

Fritz: What's going on right now?

J: It's really scary up here. I didn't know it would be half as scary. (this workshop session was held in a large room, with another seminar group of 30 people observing)

F: Close your eyes. . . and stay with your scariness. . . How do you experience scariness?

J: Shakiness in my upper chest, (sighs) fluttering in my breathing. Ah, my—my right leg is shaking. My left leg—now my left leg's shaking. If I keep my eyes closed long enough my arms are going to start shaking.

F: At what moment did this scariness come up?

J: I looked out there. (laughter)

F: So look again. Talk to those people there. "You make me scared" or whatever.

J: Well it's not so bad now. I'm picking and choosing.

F: So whom do you pick and choose?

J: Oh Mary Ellen, and Alison. John. I skipped over a whole bunch of faces.

F: Now let's call your father and mother into the audience.

J: I wouldn't look at them.

F: Say this to them.

J: Ah, wherever you're sitting I'm not going to look at you. . . because I don't—You want me to explain it? Oh, no. (laughter) O.K., I'm not going to look at you, Mom and Dad.

F: What do you experience when you *don't* look at them?

J: More anxiety. When I tell you the dream it's like—it's just the same.

F: Okeh, tell me the dream.

J: O.K. I'm going home to see my mother and father, and I'm anxious the whole time when I'm driving home. And I—there's a long flight of steps up to the house—there's about sixty steps. And in the dream I get m—more and more afraid each step I take. So I open the door and the house is very dark. And I call to my mother—Oh, I notice that all the cars are there, so they're home. I call to my mother and there's no answer. I call to my father and there's no answer. I call the children and there's no answer. So I—it's a very, very big house and so I go from room to room to look for them and I—I get into the bedroom and my mother and father are in bed but they're, they're just, they're not my m—they're skeletons. They don't have any skin. They're not, they don't talk. . . they don't say anything. And I shake—This dream happens over and over and lately I've gotten brave enough to shake them. But. . .

F: In the dream you can play the part. . . What happens when you shake them?

J: Ah, nothing. I mean I—I just feel a skeleton—a skeleton. And I yell really loud in the dream to them both. I tell them to wake up. And they don't wake up. They're just skeletons.

F: Good. Let's start all over again. You're entering the house, yah?

J: O.K. I'm entering the house and I first—I first walk into the kitchen and it's very dark, and it doesn't smell like I remember it. It smells musty like it hadn't been cleaned in a long time. And I don't hear any noises. It's usually very noisy—a lot of children noises. And I don't hear any noises. Then I go to what used to be my bedroom, and there's nobody there, and everything is clean. Everything is neat and everything is untouched.

F: Let's have an encounter between the kitchen of your dream and your bedroom.

J: The kitchen and the bedroom. O.K. I'm the kitchen, and—I don't smell the way I usually smell. I usually smell of food. I usually smell of people. And now I smell of dust and cobwebs. I'm usually not very neat but now I'm very, very neat. Everything is put away. Nobody's inside of me.

F: Now play the bedroom.

J: Bedroom. . . I'm very—I'm neat. . . I don't know how to encounter the kitchen.

F: Just boast about what you are.

J: Well, I'm as neat as you are. I'm very neat, too. But I smell bad like you do, and I don't smell like perfume, and I don't smell like people. I just smell like dust. Only there's no dust on my floor. I'm very neat and I'm very clean. But I don't smell good and I don't feel good like I usually feel. And I know when Jane comes inside of me she feels bad when I'm so neat and there's no one inside of me. And she comes inside of me like she comes inside of you in the dream. And she's very scared. And we're very—I'm very hollow. I'm very hollow. When you make a sound inside of me it echoes. That's how it feels in the dream.

F: Now be the kitchen again. . .

J: I'm very hollow, too—I, ooh. . .

F: Yah? What happened?

J: I feel empty.

F: You feel the emptiness now. /J: Yeah./ Stay with the emptiness.

J: O.K., I. . . don't feel it there now. Wait. I lost it. I'm very, you know, I—

F: Stay with what you experience now.

J: I have the anxious feeling again.

F: When you become the kitchen. Yah?

J: Yeah. I'm the kitchen. . . And there's no fresh air inside of me. There's no good—I'm supposed to be encountering the bedroom. Hmm. Ohhh. . .

F: Just tell all this to the bedroom.

J: I'm as musty as you are. And it's very incongruous because I'm very clean and spotless. And Jane's mother usually doesn't keep me so neat. She's usually too busy to keep me so neat. Something's wrong with me. I'm not getting the kind of attention that I usually get. I'm dead. I'm a dead kitchen.

F: Say this again.

J: I'm dead. /F: Again./ I'm dead.

F: How do you experience being dead?. . .

J: Well, it doesn't feel bad. . .

F: Now stay as you are and be aware of your right and left hand. What are they doing?

J: My right hand is shaking and it's stretched out. And the left hand is clenched very tight and my fingernails are pushing into the palm of my hand.

F: What does your right hand want to do?

J: It's O.K. the way it is. I think it wants not to shake.

F: Besides this, anything else? Does it want to stop? To reach? I can't read your right hand. Continue the movement. (Jane makes reaching movements with right hand) You want to reach out. Good. And what does your left hand want to do?. . .

J: My left hand wants to hold back. It's holding tight. My right hand feels good.

F: So change. Let the left hand do now what the right hand does, and vice versa. Reach out with your left hand.

J: No. . . My left hand doesn't want to reach out.

F: What's the difficulty in reaching out with your left hand?

J: It feels much different, and my right hand isn't clenched: it's limp. I can *do* it. I can *do* it, yet—

F: This would be artificial. /J: Yeah./ Now reach out with your left hand again. . . (softly) Reach out to me. . . (Jane reaches out. . . sighs). . . Now what happened?

J: It started to shake. . . and I stopped it.

F: Now have an encounter between your right hand and left hand as it was originally, "I am holding back and you are reaching out."

J: I'm the right hand and I'm reaching out. I'm free. I'm very relaxed, and even when I shake, it doesn't feel bad. I'm shaking now and I don't feel bad. . .

Ah, I'm the left hand and I don't reach out. I make a fist. And now my fingernails are long so when I do it I hurt myself when I make a fist. . . Ohh. . .

F: Yah, what happened?

J: I hurt myself.

F: I want to tell you something that is usually the case. I don't know whether it will be the case with you. The right hand is usually the male part of a person and the left side is the female part. The right side is the aggressive, active, outgoing part and the left side is the sensitive, receptive, open part. Now try this on for size to see if it might fit with you.

J: O.K. The loudmouth can come out, you know. /F: Yah./ But the soft part is. . . not so easy. . .

F: Okeh. Enter the house once more and have an encounter with what you encounter—namely, silence.

J: Encounter with silence. /F: Silence, yah./ Be the silence?

F: No, no. You enter the house and all that you meet is silence. Right?

J: Yes. You annoy me. The silence annoys me. I don't like it.

F: Say this to silence.

J: I am. He's sitting right there. You annoy me. I don't like you. I don't hear much in you and when I do, I don't like it.

F: What does silence answer?

J: Well, I have never had a chance to come around much because when you were young there were many children around you all the time and your parents are both loud, and you're loud, and you really don't know much about me. And I think maybe you're afraid of me. Could you be afraid of me?

Now let's try that one. Yeah. I don't feel afraid now, but I could be afraid of you.

F: So enter the house once more and again meet silence. Go back to the dream.

J: O.K. I'm in the house and it's very silent and I don't like it. I don't like that it's quiet. I want to hear noises, I want to hear noises in the kitchen and noises in the bedroom and I want to hear children, (voice begins to break) I want to hear my mother and father laughing and talking, I—

F: Say this to them.

J: I want to hear you, laughing and talking. I want to hear the children. I miss you. (begins to cry) I can't let go of you. . . I want to hear you. I want to hear you. . . and I want to hear you.

F: Okeh, let's now reverse the dream. Let them talk. Resurrect them.

J: Resurrect them. /F: Yah./ I have them there.

F: You say you try to shake them. They are only skeletons. /J: (fearfully) Ohhh./ I want you to be successful.

J: You want me to encounter—I'm confused. (has stopped crying)

F: You are in the bedroom. Right? /J: Yeah./ Your parents are skeletons. /J: Uhuh./ Skeletons usually don't talk. At best they shake and rattle. /J: Yeah./ I want you to resurrect them.

J: To make them alive.

F: Make them alive. So far you say you would blot them out. That's what you're doing in the dream.

J: I shake them in the dream. I take them and I shake them.

F: Talk to them.

J: Wake up! /F: Again./

(loudly) Wake up! /F: Again./

(loudly) *Wake up!* /F: Again./

(loudly) *Wake up!*. . . And. . . (loudly, almost crying) You can't hear me! Why can't you hear me?. . . (sighs) And they don't answer. They don't say anything.

F: Come. Be phony. Invent them. Resurrect them. Let's have a phony game.

J: O.K. We don't know why we can't hear you. We don't know. We don't know that we even don't want to hear you. We're just skeletons. Or are we still? No. . . We don't know why we can't hear you. We don't know why we're like this. We don't know why you found us like this. (crying) Maybe if you never went away, maybe if you never went away, this wouldn't have happened. It feels right. That's what they would say. That's what they would say.

F: Okeh. Take your seat again. . .

J: I feel like I want to tell you that I went away too soon and I really can't go all the way away. (almost crying)

F: Tell them that you still need them.

J: I still need you.

F: Tell them in more detail what you need.

J: I still need my mother to hold me.

F: Tell this to her.

J: I still need you to hold me. (crying) I want to be a little girl, sometimes—forget the "sometimes."

F: You're not talking to her yet.

J: (sobbing) O.K. Mother, Mother, you think I'm very grown up. . . and I think I'm very grown up. But there's a part of me that isn't away from you and I can't, I can't let go of.

F: You see how this is a continuation of our last session? You started out as the toughy, the brazen girl, and then the softness came out? Now you begin to accept that you have soft needs. . . So be your mother.

J: (diffidently) Well you know you can come back any time you want, Jane. But it's not going to be quite the same because I have other little girls to take care of. I have your sisters to take care of and they're little girls, and you're a big girl and you can take care of yourself now. And I'm glad you're so grown up. I'm glad you're so smart. . . Anyway, I don't know how to talk to you any more. I mean I know—I respect you but I don't understand you half the time. . . (sobbing) and, and. . .

F: What happened right now? What happened when you stopped?

J: I felt a pain in my stomach. I felt frustrated.

F: Tell Jane that.

J: Jane, I—(crying) I have a pain in my stomach. I feel frustrated; because I don't understand you because you do such funny things; because you went away when you were so young and you never really came back. And you ran away from me and I loved you and I wanted you to come back and you wouldn't come back. And now you want to come back and it's too late.

F: Play Jane again.

J: (not crying) But I still need you. I want to sit on your lap. Nobody else can give me what you have. I still need a mother. (crying)... I can't believe it. I just can't believe what I'm saying. I mean I can agree with what I'm saying but—

F: Okeh, let's interrupt. You woke up anyhow. Go back to the group. How do you experience us? Can you tell the group that you need a mother?

J: Hmm. (laughter) (Jane laughs) I can tell you, Fritz. Ah, no, there's too many.

F: All right, now let's see whether we can't get these things together. Now have an encounter between your baby dependence and brazenness. /J: O.K./ Those are your two poles.

J: (as brazenness) You really are a punk. You sound just like a punk. You've been around. You've been around for a long time. You've learned a lot of things. You know how to be on your own. What the fuck's the matter with you? What are you crying about?

Well, I like to be helpless sometimes, Jane, and I know you don't like it. I know you don't put up with it very often. But sometimes it just comes out. Like I can't work with Fritz without it coming out. I can hide it... for a long time, but... if you don't own up to me I'm gonna really, I'm gonna keep coming out and maybe you'll never grow up.

F: Say this again.

J: I'm gonna keep coming out and maybe you'll never grow up.

F: Say it very spitefully.

J: I'm gonna *keep* coming out and maybe you'll *never* grow up...

F: Okeh, be the brazenness again.

J: (sighs) Well I've tried stomping on you and hiding you and shoving you in corners and making everybody believe that you don't exist. What more do you want me to do with you? What do you want from me?...

I want you to listen to me. . .

F: Is brazen Jane willing to listen?

J: I just started to listen. . . O.K., I'm gonna give you a chance. I feel like if I give you a chance. . . (right hand makes a threatening fist)

F: Yah? Yah?—No no no, don't—don't hide it. Come out. You don't give her a chance, you give her a threat.

J: Yeah, I know. That's what I do.

F: Yah, yah. . . Give her both. Give her a threat and give her a chance.

J: O.K. I'll give you a chance. (right hand beckons)

F: Ahah, this means, "Come to me."

J: Yeah. Let's get together. Let's try to get together and see what we can do. . . But I'm warning you, (laughter) if you keep making a fool of me the way you do, Jane, with your crying and your dependency. . . you're never gonna let me grow up. (thoughtfully) I'm never gonna let you—Hm. (laughter) Well.

F: Be the other Jane again.

J: Well, I don't want to grow up—this part of—I don't want to grow up. I want to stay the way I am.

F: Say this again.

J: I want to stay the way I am.

F: "I don't want to grow up."

J: I don't wanna grow up. /F: Again./
I don't wanna grow up. /F: Louder./
I don't wanna grow up. /F: Louder./
I don't wanna grow up. (voice begins to break) /F: Louder./
I don't wanna grow up!

F: Say it with your whole body.

J: (crying) I don't *wanna* grow up! I don't wanna grow up. I'm tired of growing up. (crying) It's too *fucking hard!*. . . (sighs)

F: Now be brazen Jane again.

J: Sure it's hard. I know it's hard. I can do it. I can do anything. I go around proving it all the time. What's the matter with *you*? You're always behind me. You have to catch up with me. . . Come and catch up with me. . .

O.K., I'll catch up with you, Jane, but you have to help me.

F: Tell her how she can help you.

J: You have to allow me to exist without threatening me, without punishing me.

F: Say this again.

J: (almost crying) You have to allow me to exist without threatening me and punishing me.

F: Can you say this without tears?

J: (calmly) You have to allow me to exist without threatening me, and without punishing me.

F: Say this also to the group—the same sentence. . .

J: You have to allow me to exist without threatening me and without punishing me.

F: Say this also to Raymond. (fiancé)

J: (crying) You have to allow me to exist without threatening me. . . you know that. . .

F: Got it?

J: Yes. . .

F: Okeh.

JANE II

Jane: I had a dream last night that I'd like to work on. I'm at this carnival, and it's very noisy and it's very hectic. . . And I'm going through the crowd and I'm bumping into people and they're bumping into me and I'm not having a good time. And I'm holding onto my little brother's hand, so he won't get lost. And we're going through the crowd, and he says he wants to go into a—uh—this carnival ride where people get in these little seats and go through a tunnel. And—uh—

Fritz: Back to the "and" bit. You use "and, and, and," as if you are afraid to let events stand for themselves.

J: Yeah. So, we don't have any money—we don't have any money to get into the ride. I take a watch off my wrist, I give it to my brother, and I ask him to ask the ticket man if he'll take the watch for both of us. He comes back and tells me the ticket man won't take the watch, so we're gonna sneak in.

F: Okeh. Let's start the whole dream all over. This time you're not dreaming it; your brother is dreaming it.

J: (more boisterous) Well, we're at this carnival and it's real fun except my sister's got ahold of my hand. She's constricting me at the wrist so she won't lose me. She's got me—she's holding me very tightly on my wrist, and I wanna—I want her to let go of me. I don't really care if I get lost. But she does, so I let her hold onto my wrist. There's a ride I wanna go on. I don't care if she goes with me or not, but I know she won't let me go unless she can go too, unless she can be with me. She doesn't. . . she doesn't wanna be by herself. . . We don't have any money to get on—to get on the ride, and she gives me her watch. I'm really happy that—that we have a way of getting in. I go up to the ticket man and it doesn't work, but I really wanna go on the ride.

F: Say this again.

J: I really wanna go on the ride. /F: Again./
   I really wanna go on the ride. /F: Again./
   (louder) I really wanna go on the ride!

F: I don't believe you.

J: Ohh. . . *I* don't; my brother does. (laughs) Umm. I really want to go on that ride, Jane. I really want to go. . . Whether you go with me or not, I wanna go. It's *fun*. So gimme your watch. . . So she gives me her watch. The ticket man says no. Jane! We're gonna sneak in. She doesn't want to. Well, then *I'm* going to sneak in. Ohh. You don't want to go without me, so you'll sneak in, too. O.K. So we'll sneak in. Now, instead of *you* taking *my* hand, I'm gonna take your hand, 'cause I'm gonna help you sneak in. So hold on, and go under the gate, I'm very small, I'm very young—

F: Interrupt it, now. Close your eyes, experience your hands.

J: Hm. My right hand's stiff, very stiff. It's pointing. My left hand is shaking and it's—it's open. It's—um—both my hands are shaking. Both hands are shaking. And my knees and my ankles feel stiff. And I don't feel a heaviness in my chest like I usually do. But I feel heavy in the chair, and my right hand is pointing. And now—

F: I noticed that when you pulled, the right hand is the brother, the left hand is Jane.

J: Hm. . . I forgot where I was. I'm Jane. Oh, we're gonna— yeah—I'm gonna sneak in. So I'm very scared, but I'm more afraid of losing him than of sneaking in and getting caught, so I take his hand and—I take his hand—

F: Wait a moment. What's your brother's name?

J: Paul.

F: *Paul* is still dreaming the dream.

J: Oh. O.K. So take my hand. I know how afraid you are of doing things like this, but I also know that you're *so* afraid that I'll get lost, so I can get you to sneak in with me, 'cause I want to sneak in to this ride. And I love to have fun, and I'm gonna have fun whether you're afraid of it or not. So we go—we go under the railing, and we go between people's legs, in and out, past the ticket man—

F: I don't believe you. You are not in the dream. Your voice goes Ahhhhhhrrrrr. . .

J: My legs are aching and my upper leg's kind of. . . I have Jane by the hand. We're going—we're going (voice becomes more expressive) we're going between the legs of all the people and we're—we're crawling, and (bright, happy) I like it, I like doing this, and she's afraid. (sigh) And we're gonna—we're gonna go up to the door, and we're gonna go through the door, and she's *pulling* me, and I'm *pulling* her. I'm trying to pull her through, and she won't come with me. So I grab her wrist like she had my wrist and I pull her and I'm littler than her, but I can pull her through, and she's on her hands and knees and I'm pulling her along. And we go through—we go through the door, and I hop on the ride, and I leave her standing there, and the little clod goes in the door—she doesn't—she loses me. Once I got in there, I could go on the ride. . .

F: Now say goodbye to Jane.

J: Goodbye, Jane!. . . I'm—I didn't want to say goodbye to her. I'd rather have fun. . . Jane's standing back there looking like a jerk. She's standing there with her legs shaking, and I don't give a shit. I really don't give a shit. It's easy to say goodbye to her. (laughs) She's standing there like some fool, and she's calling me, she's calling my name. She looks frantic, she looks like she's in a panic. (disinterested) But I'd rather have fun. She'll be all right.

F: Okeh. Now change roles again. Be Jane again.

J: The dream is very long.

F: There is so much already there.

J: Be Jane again. O.K. I'm at the carnival with my brother and we're going through—I really *don't* think I want to be here, and—

F: Tell us. Tell *us* your position. . .

J: What I just said?

F: Your whole position. The situation is open, right? Very clear. There is your brother, and there is you. You want to hold onto him; he wants to be free.

J: Well I think—I think he's younger than me, and he *is* younger than me and I don't want him—to do what—what I did. I wanna (quietly and hesitantly) protect him or something. I hold onto him. I think I—I think I keep trying to do what my mother can't do. . . It's insane. It's really insane. . . I talk to him. I tell him. Paul, stop taking drugs, and stop roaming around. (cries) Stop trying to be so free, because you're gonna regret it. When you're twenty, you'll regret it.

Now I want to take his side. He'd say, how can you tell me not to do exactly what you do?—what you did when you were sixteen and seventeen. How can you say that? That's not fair. I *like* what I'm doing. Leave me alone! You're—you're really a bitch. You're just like my mother, you're such a bitch. How can *you* be such a bitch when you already did this?. . . (sighs)

I. . . I'm trying to take care of you. I'm trying to take care of you, and I know I can't—(cries) I know I have to let go of you, but I keep trying in my dreams, to hold onto you, and to keep you safe, because it's so dangerous what you're doing!. . . You're gonna get all fucked up. (cries)

But you're not all fucked up! So look at you! You've changed, you've really changed. You don't lie any more. Much. (laughter) You don't take much drugs any more, like you used to. I'll change like that. I just have to do what I have to do. You don't trust me, do you? You're like my mother, you don't trust me. You don't think I'm strong.

F: Okeh, Jane. I think you can work this out on your own. I want to do something else right now. I want to start with the beginning. Always look at the beginning of the dream. Notice where a dream is taking place, whether you are in a car, whether the dream is taking place in a motel, or nature, or in an apartment building. This always gives you immediately the impression of the existential background. Now you start your dream out, "Life is a carnival." Now give us a speech about life as a carnival.

J: Life—life is a carnival. You go on this trip, and you get off. You go on that trip, and you get off. And then you bump into all kinds of people, you bump into *all kinds* of people, and some of them you look at, and some of them you don't look at, and some of them irritate you, and really bump you, and others don't, others are kind to you. And you win things at the carnival. You win presents. . . And some rides—most all the rides, the trips, are scary. But they're fun. They're fun and they're scary. It's very crowded, and there are lots of people—lots and lots of faces. . . And in the dream, I'm—I'm holding onto somebody in the carnival, and he wants to go on all the trips.

JANE III

Jane: The dream I started on, the last time I worked, I never finished it, and I think the last part is as important as the first part. Where I left off, I was in the Tunnel of Love—

Fritz: What are you picking on? (Jane has been scratching her leg)

J: Hmm. (clears throat). . . I'm just sitting here, for a minute, so I can really be here. It's hard to stay with this feeling, and talk at the same time. . . Now I'm in the intermediate zone, and I'm—I'm thinking about two things: Should I work on the dream, or should I work on the picking thing, because that's something that I do a lot. I pick my face, and. . . I'll go back to the dream. I'm in the Tunnel of Love, and my brother's gone in the—somewhere—and to the left of me, there's a big room and it's painted the color of—the color that my schoolrooms used to be painted, kind of a drab green, and to the left of me there are bleachers. I look over and there are all people sitting there. It looks as though they are waiting to get on the ride. There's a big crowd around one person, Raymond. (fiancé) He's talking to them and he's explaining something to them and they're all listening to him. And he's moving his finger like this, and making gestures. I'm surprised to see him. I go up to him, and it's very obvious that he doesn't want to talk to me. He's interested in being with all these people, entertaining all these people. So I tell him that I'll wait for him. I sit three—three bleachers up and look down, and watch this going on. I get irritated and I'm—pissed off, so I say, "Raymond, I'm leaving. I'm not gonna wait for you any more." I walk outside the door—I stand outside the door for awhile—I get anxious. I can feel anxious in my dream. I feel anxious now, because I don't really want to be out here. I want to be inside, with Raymond. So I'm going inside. I go back through the door—

F: Are you telling us a dream, or are you doing a job?

J: Am I telling a dream—

F: Or are you doing a job?

J: I'm telling a dream, but it's still—I'm not telling a dream.

F: Hm. Definitely not.

J: I'm doing a job.

F: I gave you only the two alternatives.

J: I can't say that I'm really aware of what I'm doing. Except physically. I'm aware of what's happening physically to me but—I don't really know what I'm doing. I'm not asking you to tell me what I'm doing. . . Just saying I don't know.

F: I noticed one thing: When you come up to the hot seat, you stop playing the silly goose.

J: Hm. I get frightened, when I'm up here.

F: You get dead.

J: Whew. . . If I close my eyes and go into my body, I know I'm not dead. If I open my eyes and "do that job," then I'm dead. . . I'm in the intermediate zone now, I'm wondering whether or not I'm dead. I notice that my legs are cold and my feet are cold. My hands are cold. I feel—I feel strange. . . I'm in the middle, now. I'm—I'm neither with my body nor with the group. I notice that my attention is concentrated on that little matchbook on the floor.

F: Okeh. Have an encounter with the matchbox.

J: Right now, I'm taking a break from looking at you, 'cause it's—it's a—'cause I don't know what's going on, and I don't know what I'm doing. I don't even know if I'm telling the truth.

F: What does the matchbook answer?

J: I don't care if you tell the truth or not. It doesn't matter to me. I'm just a matchbox.

F: Let's try this for size. Tell us, "I'm just a matchbox."

J: I'm just a matchbox. And I feel silly saying that. I feel, kind of dumb, being a matchbox.

F: Uhhm.

J: A little bit useful, but not very useful. There's a million like me. And you can look at me, and you can like me, and then when I'm all used up, you can throw me away. I never liked being a matchbox. . . I don't—I don't know if that's the truth, when I say I don't know what I'm doing. I know there's one part of me that knows what I'm doing. And I feel suspended, I feel—steady. I don't feel relaxed. Now I'm trying to understand why in the two seconds it takes me to move from the group to the hot seat, my whole—my whole *persona* changes. . . Maybe because of—I want to talk to the Jane in *that* chair.

She would be saying, (with authority) well, *you* know where you're at. You're playing dumb. You're playing stupid. You're doing this, and you're doing that, and you're sucking people in, and you're—(louder) not telling the truth! and you're stuck, and you're dead. . .

And when I'm *here*, I immediately—the Jane here would say, (small, quavery voice) well, that's—I feel on the defensive in this chair right now. I feel defensive. I feel like for some reason I have to defend myself. And I know it's not true. . . So who's picking on you? It's *that* Jane over there that's picking on me.

F: Yah.

J: She's saying. . . She's saying, (briskly) now when you get in the chair, you have to be in the here and now, you have to do it *right*, you have to be turned on, you have to know everything—

F: "You have to do your job."

J: You have to do your job, and you have to do it *right*. And you have to—On top of all that, you have to become totally self-actualized, and you have to get rid of all your hangups, and along with that—it's not—it's not mandatory that you do this, but it's nice if you can be entertaining along the way, while you're doing all that. Try to spice it up a little bit, so that people won't get bored and go to sleep, because that makes you anxious. And you have to *know* why you're in the chair. You can't just go here and not know why you're there. You have to know *everything*, Jane.

You really make it hard for me. You really make it hard. You're really putting a lot of demands on me. . . I don't know everything. And that's hard to say. I don't know everything, and on top of that, I don't know what I'm doing half the time. . . I don't know—I don't know if that's the truth or not. I don't even know if that's a lie.

F: So be your topdog again.

J: Is that—

F: Your topdog. That's the famous topdog. The righteous topdog. This is where your power is.

J: Yeah. Well—uh—I'm your topdog. You can't live without me.
I'm the one that—I keep you noticed, Jane. I keep you noticed. If it
weren't for me, nobody would notice you. So you'd better be a little
more grateful that I exist.

Well, I don't want to be noticed, *you* do. You want to be
noticed. I don't want to be noticed. I don't want. . . I don't really
want to be noticed, as much as you do.

F: I would like you to attack the righteous side of that topdog.

J: Attack—the righteous side.

F: The topdog is always righteous. Topdog *knows* what you've
got to do, has all the right to criticize, and so on. The topdog nags,
picks, puts you on the defensive.

J: Yeah. . . You're a bitch! You're like my mother. You know
what's good for me. You—you make life *hard* for me. You tell me to
do things. You tell me to be—*real*. You tell me to be self-actualized.
You tell me to—uh, tell the truth.

F: Now please don't change what your hands are doing, but tell
us what's going on in your hands.

J: My left hand. . .

F: Let them talk to each other.

J: My left hand. I'm shaking, and I'm in a fist, straining forward, and (voice begins to break) that's kind of—the fist is very tight,
pushing—pushing my fingernails into my hand. It doesn't feel good,
but I do it all the time. I feel tight.

F: And the right hand?

J: I'm holding you back around the wrist.

F: Tell it why you hold it back.

J: If I let you go you're—then you're gonna hit something. I
don't know what you're gonna hit, but I have to—I have to hold you
back 'cause you can't do that. Can't go around hitting things.

F: Now hit your topdog.

J: (short harsh yell) Aaaarkh! Aarkkh!

F: Now talk to your topdog. "Stop nagging—"

J: (loud, pained) Leave me alone! /F: Yah, again./
Leave me alone! /F: Again./

(screaming it and crying) *Leave me alone!* /F: Again./

(she screams it, a real blast) LEAVE ME ALONE! I DON'T HAVE TO DO WHAT YOU SAY! (still crying) I don't have to be that good!. . . I don't have to be in this chair! I don't *have* to. *You* make me. You make me come here! (screams) Aarkkh! You make me pick my face, (crying) that's what *you* do. (screams and cries) Aaarkkh! I'd like to kill you.

F: Say this again.

J: I'd like to kill you. /F: Again./

I'd like to *kill* you.

F: Can you squash it in your left hand?

J: It's as big as me. . . I'm strangling it.

F: Okeh. Say this, "I'm strangling—"

J: (quietly) I'm gonna strangle you. . . take your neck. Grrrummn. (Fritz gives her a pillow which she strangles while making noises) Arrghh. Unghhh. How do you like *that*! (sounds of choked-off cries and screams)

F: Make more noises.

J: Hrugghhh! Aachh! Arrgrughhh! (she continues to pound pillow, cry and scream)

F: Okeh. Relax, close your eyes. . . (long silence) (softly) Okeh. Come back to us. Are you ready?. . . Now be that topdog again. . .

J: (faintly) You shouldn't have done that. I'm gonna punish you for that. . . I'm gonna punish you for that, Jane. You'll be sorry you did that. Better watch out.

F: Now talk like this to each one of us. . . Be vindictive with each one of us. Pick out something we have done. . . Start with me. As this topdog, for what are you going to punish me?

J: I'm gonna punish you for making me feel so stupid.

F: How are you going to punish me?

J: (promptly) By being stupid. . . Even stupider than I am.

F: Okeh. Do this some more.

J: Raymond, I'm gonna punish you for being so dumb. I'll make you feel like an ass. . . I'll make you think I'm smarter than you are, and you'll feel dumber and I'll feel smart. . . I'm really scared. I shouldn't be doing this. (cries) It isn't nice.

F: Say this to him. Turn it around, "You should not—"

J: You sh—you shouldn't—you shouldn't—you shouldn't be

doing—hooo—you shouldn't be doing—you shouldn't be so dumb. You shouldn't play so dumb. Because it isn't nice.

F: You're doing a job again.

J: Yeah, I know. I don't wanna do it. (crying) I—I know how I punish you. (sigh) I'll punish you by being helpless.

Raymond: What are you punishing me for?

J: I'll punish you for loving me. That's what I'll punish you for. I'll make it *hard* for you to love me. I won't let you know if I'm coming or going.

F: "How can you be so low as to love somebody like me?" Yah?

J: *I* do that.

F: I know. How can you love a matchbox?...

J: Fergus, I'm gonna punish you for being so slow—in your body, but so quick in your mind. The way I'm gonna do that—I'm gonna excite you, try to excite you, and it's the truth. I'll punish you for being sexually inhibited. I'll make you think I'm very sexy. I'll make you feel bad around me... And I'll punish you for pretending to know more than you do.

F: What do you experience when you are meting out the punishment?

J: (more alert, alive) It's a very strange experience. I don't know that I've ever had it before, for such a long time. It's kind of—it's a feeling I used to get when I—when I got back at my brothers for being mean to me. I'd just grit my teeth and think of the *worst* thing I could do—and kind of enjoy it.

F: Yah. This is my impression; you didn't enjoy this here.

J: Mm.

F: Okeh. Go back and be the topdog again, and *enjoy* punishing Jane—pick on her, torture her.

J: You're the only one I enjoy punishing... When you're too loud—when you're too loud, I'll punish you for being too loud. (no sound of enjoyment) When you're not loud enough, I'll tell you that you're too inhibited. When you dance too much—when you dance too much, I'll tell you that you're trying to sexually arouse people. When you don't dance enough, I'll tell you that you're dead.

F: Can you tell Jane, "I'm driving you crazy"?

J: (cries) I'm driving you crazy. /F: Again./
I'm driving you crazy. /F: Again./

I'm driving you *crazy*. . . I used to drive everybody else crazy, and now I'm driving *you* crazy. . . (voice drops, becomes very faint) But it's for your own good. That's what my mother would say. "For your own good." I'll make you feel *guilty* when you've done bad things, so you won't do it again. And I'll—I'll pat you on the back when you do something good, so you'll remember to do it again. And I'll keep you out of the moment. I'll—I'll keep you planning—and I'll keep you programmed, and I won't let you live—in the moment. I won't let you enjoy your life.

F: I would like you to use this: "I am relentless."

J: I—I *am* relentless. /F: Again./

I am relentless. I'll do anything—especially if somebody dares me to do something. Then I've gotta tell you to do it, Jane, so you can prove it, so you can prove yourself. You've *gotta* prove yourself—in this world.

F: Let's try this. "You've got a job to do."

J: (laughs) You've gotta job to do. You're gonna quit fuckin' around, and—you've been doin' nothin' for a long time—

F: Yah. Now, don't change your posture. The right arm goes to the left and the left arm goes to the right. Say the same thing again and stay aware of this.

J: You've been doing nothing for a long time. You gotta do something, Jane. You've gotta *be* something. . . You've gotta make people proud of you. You've got to grow up, you have to be a woman, and you gotta keep everything that's bad about you hidden away so nobody can see it, so they'll think you're perfect, just perfect. . . You have to lie. I make you lie.

F: Now take Jane's place again.

J: You're—you're (cries) you are driving me crazy. You're picking on me. I'd really like to strangle you—uh—then you'll punish me more. You'll come back—and give me hell for that. So, why don't you just go away? I won't—I won't cross you up any more. Just go away and leave me alone—and I'm not begging you!! Just go away! /F: Again./

Just go away! /F: Again./

Go away! /F: Change seats./

You'll be just a half if I go away! You'll be half a person if I leave. Then you'll really be fucked up. You can't send me away, you'll have to figure out something to *do* with me, you'll have to *use* me.

Well then—then I—I would change your mind about a lot of things if I had to.

F: Ah!

J: And tell you that there's nothing I could do that's bad. . . I mean, if you'd leave me alone, I wouldn't do anything bad. . .

F: Okeh. Take another rest.

J: (closes eyes). . . I can't rest.

F: So come back to us. Tell us about your restlessness.

J: I keep wondering what to do with that. When I had my eyes closed, I was saying, "Tell her to just relax."

F: Okeh. Play *her* topdog, now.

J: Just relax.

F: Make her the underdog and you're the topdog.

J: And you don't have to do anything, you don't have to prove anything. (cries) You're only twenty years old! You don't have to be the queen. . .

She says, O.K. I understand that. I know that. I'm just in a *hurry*. I'm in a *big* hurry. We've got so many things to do—and now, I know, when I'm in a hurry you can't be now, you can't—when I'm in a hurry, you can't stay in the minute you're in. You have to keep—you have to keep hurrying, and the days slip by and you think you're losing time, or something. I'm *much* too hard on you. I have to—I have to leave you alone.

F: Well, I would like to interfere. Let your topdog say, "I'll be a bit more patient with you."

J: Uh. I'll be—I'll be a bit more patient with you.

F: Say this again.

J: (softly) It's very hard for me to be patient. You know that. You know how impatient I am. But I'll—I'll try to be a bit more patient with you. "I'll try"—I'll *be* a bit more patient with you. As I say that, I'm stomping my foot, and shaking my head.

F: Okeh. Say, "I *won't* be patient with you—"

J: (easily) I *won't* be patient with you, Jane! I won't be patient with you. /F: Again./

I won't be patient with you. /F: Again./

I won't be patient with you.

F: Now say this to us. . . Pick a few.

J: Jan, I won't be patient with you. Claire, I won't be patient with you. . . Dick, I won't be patient with you. Muriel, I won't be patient with you. Ginny, I won't be patient with you. . . And June, I won't be patient with you, either.

F: Okeh. How do you feel, now?

J: O.K.

F: You understand, topdog and underdog are not yet together. But at least the conflict is clear, in the open, maybe a *little* bit less violent.

J: I felt, when I worked before, on the dream, and the dream thing, that I worked this out. I felt *good*. I keep—I keep—it keeps—I keep going back to it.

F: Yah. This is the famous self-torture game.

J: I do it so *well*.

F: Everybody does it. You don't do it better than the rest of us. Everybody thinks, "I am the worst."

STEVE I

Steve: I want to work on a dream fragment. I'm standing in a field. It's nighttime, and the air is very cool. It's a really nice evening. I think there's some moonlight. I can see a little. And there's a cultivated field full of tomato vines.

Fritz: What do you experience?

S: My heart is beating fairly fast, my voice is high, some tension, stage fright.

F: How do you experience us?

S: I block you out. I was going into the dream.

F: Would you come back to us?

S: Sure. I'm quivering more, now. I feel quivering in my legs, in my hands. My left hand is holding myself. . . to keep it from moving. I quiver a lot, out here.

F: Are you aware of us?

S: No, not as a—no. I went back to myself. I look out at you, and my quivering decreases. . . I feel sweat on my forehead. I keep coming back to myself. . . I see people, I don't see anything special. I see you all. I'm not particularly interested in you. . . (short laugh) I want to go into my dream. . . I'm asking you for permission.

F: I don't give you permission.

S: Yeah. . .

F: I would like to work with how much you are *in*, or *out* of touch with us, with what's going on.

S: I don't feel in touch with any of you now. I look around and I see people doing things with each other—you—with—uh, Teddy and Helena, and with Sally. I see people looking at each other and not paying any attention to me, and—I don't feel like I'm a part of anything, I—

Teddy: That's what you saw just then?

S: No, no. I was back. I was back. No, right now you were looking at me. (laughs) Right *then*, you were. Right *now* you're looking at me, with some interest. I see Helena still sad—with her sadness.

Helena: I'm still in my thing. (she has just worked)

S: Yes. Yeah. Blair looks very much back—away, uninterested. Sally, you see me, but I don't get any feeling of anything that you do see.

F: Now you begin to *pay* attention.

S: Yeah.

F: Instead of *wanting* attention.

S: Yeah.

F: So, give us *more* of your attention.

S: Dick looks concerned, he is rubbing his face—*you're* rubbing your face. . . looking expectant. I don't know where Bob is. Bob, I don't know where you are. Jane, you're looking at Bob. . .

F: Okeh. I am willing to pay attention to your dream.

S: O.K. I'm in this field, it's night, it's a field of tomato vines. The ground is all moist and fertile, and there are no weeds.

F: Be this field.

S: Be this field. (lies down) I'm cultivated in rows, the dirt might—I am soft, moist earth, I am in rows—uh—with little valleys in between where the water can run down me, I'm nourishing these plants, there are a lot of stakes driven into me. The stakes are holding up the tomato plants. The tomato plants are living in me, the roots are in me, and they're growing up tall, and I'm cool, and moist, and nourishing. /F: Say this again./

I'm cool and moist and nourishing. /F: Again./

I'm cool and moist and nourishing. And there's also something else in me. There's a fence down the middle of this field and this fence is driven into me, too—big 4 x 4 redwood posts.

F: What do you divide with the fence?

S: I should be the fence, for that. (stands up and stretches out arms to sides) I'm the fence in the *middle* of the field. I am really senseless. The plants are the same on both sides of the field. The dirt is the same, the light is the same. The fence has two sides. *I* have two sides. I have two sides. I have a good side and a bad side. The good side faces this way. (behind) The bad side faces that way. (forward) My bad side faces that way. But I'm in the middle of this field, and it's—I'm senseless. I have no purpose. The field is on both sides. If I were to protect this field, or the plants in it, I'd have to be on the edge, or around the outside. I'm in the middle, and there are plants on both sides. . . I haven't described the—I want to be the tomato plants, and the posts, on the. . .

I'm a post holding up tomato vines, and there are strings around me, and around the vines, and I'm holding onto the vines like this. (makes circle with arms) If I didn't hold onto you, vines, you'd—you'd run along the ground, and then you wouldn't get any sunlight, because all these other tomatoes around here have posts and they're standing up straight and tall, and I hold you up.

F: I have difficulty in following you, so I suggest: be your voice.

S: Be my voice. My voice sounds kind of hollow.

F: "I am—"

S: I am hollow. I'm—I echo back and forth along a long tube. I am my voice. I am my voice. I—I'm edged with sadness. I have—around the outside there's—I feel like something is obstructing me around the outside. I'm—I come through, but there's something dragging, there's something holding me back, there's something dragging on me. As I come out, something holding back around the outside. . .

F: I am getting heavier and heavier.

S: Yeah. . . I'm casting a pall. . . I'm covering up. I'm blanketing. I am my voice. I am heavy on the bottom. . . I want to deaden you all—I think that's computing. I am my voice. Voice. . .

F: So what do you experience right now?

S: A heaviness, dry mouth. . . like hanging, like. . . everything. . . I feel like I'm hanging, I'm—everything is *dragging* down, just—I'm a drag. My tension in my shoulders—which I just relaxed. I had my shoulders up. Perspiration, warmth.

F: Okeh. Are there any human beings in your dream?

S: No. No. There's only one other part. I'm in the field, I'm looking at it, I'm just standing there, and the fence catches fire on the other side, all along one side.

F: Ahah. It's not completely implosive, not completely dead.

S: The tomato plants are alive. . . Yeah, the fire is the only moving thing. And as I see the fire, it's just like a flash and the whole outside of the fence is in flames. A gentle wind is blowing this way and the flames are going out like this—just on the one side. (the bad side of the fence, facing forward)

F: Dance it. Dance the flames.

S: (gestures like leaping flames) I'm attached to the fence. I'm attached to the fence, but I—

F: Talk to the fence.

S: I'm consuming you. I'm attached to you. I can't get away from you. I need you—you're my fuel—but I'm leaping out—away. I'm gonna sear all these tomato plants over here. I'm—when I'm in the dream, as me, I see that the fence is stupid and I'd like to get rid of the fence, but fire is the wrong way to do it because fire would burn all the plants near it, and I don't want that. In the—

F: Play fire. Talk to us as fire. "If I were fire I would consume all of you and that's bad," and so on.

S: Yeah. If I were fire, I would wilt you, I would kill you, you'd turn brown, you'd curl up, you—you'd die, your fruit would be aborted, the green fruit would never turn ripe. . . Even the posts you are attached to would burn. Everything would crumple in and shrivel and crisp and brown—

F: Can you use the word *I* instead of *it*. "*I* would do this. *I* would—"

S: I would cause you to shrivel and brown—

F: "I would shrivel you."

S: I would shrivel you. I would abort your fruit. I would kill you. . . You'd die. I'd kill you. I'd kill you. You'd just—if I flamed. As fire, I would kill you. Not the ones far away, but anybody close.

Anybody close, I would kill you. . . (slowly sinks to squatting position and cries deeply for some time). . .

I think of a poem my father wrote. I don't know if I can remember it all. He talks about loving the sea and—

". . . I make no demands upon the sea. . .
But when my hands reach out to other hands,
My touch is venom, and the gifts I bring—
Importunate demands, mistrust and questioning.
I am weary of the strife and pain.
I shall go back and love the sea again."

So. (softly) Thank you, Fritz.

STEVE II

Steve: I have some cord-cutting to do.

Fritz: Hnh?

S: (makes a snipping motion with right hand at navel) I have some cord-cutting to do.

F: Hnh? What has this to do with me?

S: O.K. That's an announcement. To everyone. I have another dull, drab, boring dream in which I am standing in the middle of a field again, only it's a different field. This one is—it's at the end of the season, and there are a lot of—of plants and weeds all together. Left-over plants. It's already been harvested. In the middle of this field there is a great huge oak tree, but I suspect that that's all fairly irrelevant. The important thing is that there's a figure, the very dim figure of an old woman and she gives me permission to stay to pick the flowers, and so on—do whatever I want. And at the time, in the dream, it seemed O.K., but later on, thinking about it, I didn't like it.

(challenging) Old lady, who are you to give me permission in my head, in my own dream, to walk around in my dream?. . .

(appeasing) I just want to give you permission, I just—I thought you'd like it here. I'm hurt by what you said. . . I'm in the intermediate zone. I'm thinking—uhh.

F: So work on the projection. Tell each one of us, "I give you permission. I allow you—" Be patronizing.

S: O.K. Daniel, I give you permission to be a little boy. Raymond, I give you permission to have the *biggest* shotgun fantasy you want. Jane, be as—as tough as you want—two guns on each hip. Sally, be as sweet as you want—be very kind and gentle and sweet and appealing. Dale, stay in your trap! Go back to your trap! It's a beautiful place to be. I give you permission to be trapped. Uhhh. . . Ginny, be as *confused* as you want. Go as far out in any direction as you want. Really complex. The more complex you can be, the better, and so—Frank, you're a marvelous clown—*I give you permission* to be a clown. Never come down. Lily, I give you permission to be a rubber band and go back and forth. Snap. Snap. Snap. Snap.

F: So go into the opposite, now. "I *don't* give you permission—"

S: O.K. I don't give you permission. Uhh. Bob, I don't give you permission to be a Zen master, to hide behind the impassive face and—I *don't* give you permission to—You must participate. You must dive in. Muriel, I *don't* give you permission to go on your head trips. I *don't* give you permission to go sailing around in the sky. Dick, I *don't* give you permission to—uh—

F: Are you aware that you are pecking? (Steve has been making short pointing movements with right hand)

S: Pecking? Yeah.

F: Short excursions.

S: Uh. Yeah. I don't know what to *do* with that.

F: (drily) I give you permission not to know what to do with that. (laughter)

S: Ohh, dear. (laughs) I didn't think you'd ever give me permission to do anything! O.K. Dick (more slowly) I don't give you permission to—stay stuck.

F: Tell him what he should do.

S: He should do the same damned thing I should do. (sighs) Melt, blow up, come alive, shit, be angry, I don't know what. Just— you know, cut loose. . . It's so easy to tell somebody *else* what to do.

F: Talk with your left hand.

S: Talk with my left hand. O.K. Yeah. Abe, I don't give you permission to be the authority, the autocrat, the dictator, the captain of the ship. I *don't* give you permission to do that.

Abe: What should I do?

S: Be part of the crew. Be part of the crew. Neither the captain nor the doomed man, the man who is about to be slit from his gullet to his ass. Jan, I *don't* permit you to be tragedy queen. I *don't* permit you to—uh, be sad all the time. I don't permit you to—

F: Now combine the two. "I neither permit you nor forbid you to—"

S: Ahhhhhh. O.K. Claire, I neither forbid you nor permit you—is that right? Yeah—I neither forbid you nor permit you—

F: Left hand, please.

S: I'm sorry. I neither forbid you nor permit you—to play the abused starlet, the great—ahh—emoter—

Claire: Give it to me good.

S: Ask for as much as you want, that's O.K. I neither forbid you nor permit you. Helena, I neither forbid you nor permit you to be you. You're great the way you are. You don't have a "thing" for me, now. For awhile, it was the Chinese madonna, you know—but that's disappeared, for me. Glenn, I neither forbid you nor permit you to be the jokester when you get scared... (murmurs) Blair, I neither forbid you nor permit you to vascillate between the little boy who is sad and unhappy and done in, and the angry authoritative son-of-a-bitch.

F: "You do your thing, and I do my thing." Take it from there.

S: Yeah. O.K. You do your thing, I'll do my thing. Nancy, uh—you do your thing, you stay behind the transparent glass, it's O.K.: I'll do my thing.

F: What's your thing?

S: My thing? Ohh! (laughter) Ahhh. (chagrined) Much the same as your thing, Nancy. (laughter) Much the same as your thing. God! I really feel alive!

Dale: You are.

S: Fergus, you do your thing, I do my thing—go staggering across the desert with your kidney stones. (laughter) I'll stay behind my (laughs) transparent glass. Oh, God. Neville, you do your thing, I'll do my thing. You can stay like one of those golf balls with all the rubber tight around so it's all scrunched in and I'll just stay behind my glass and kind of look out, now and then, and (chuckles) see what's going on—get a little air, too. June, you do your thing, I'll do my thing. You just continue with your big scenes and bouncing from one scene to another, and your voice that—(mimics breathlessly) "Ohh! I had such a *marvelous experience!*" (laughter) I'll do my thing, which is stay behind the glass and watch you, and sort of dart out now and then. Ahh. O.K.

Frank: You left out Fritz.

S: Oh, Fritz. Yeah. (laughter) Unhh. You do your thing and I'll do my thing. You sit up here and puff on your lettuce cigarettes, play King of the Mountain, and—Who do *you* go to for therapy? (laughter)

S: (lets out breath) This is a great experience. The chair isn't hot at all. How do they do it?

F: Simply by really going into *one* projection.

S: Yeah. Yeah.

F: It doesn't matter which projection you take, as long as you work it through.

S: Yeah. Really live it. Really do it.

F: This is what we want to achieve with this work on projection. Once it clicks, you are through the projection and it's all over. First you look through a window, and suddenly you recognize that you are just looking in a mirror.